I Have
Something to
Tell You

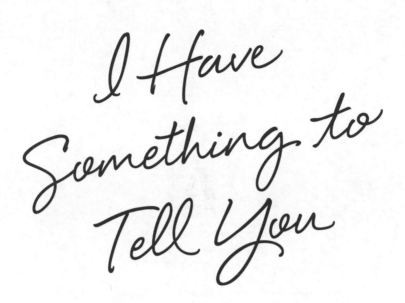

I Have Something to Tell You

A MEMOIR

Chasten Buttigieg

ATRIA BOOKS

NEW YORK LONDON TORONTO SYDNEY NEW DELHI

ATRIA
BOOKS

An Imprint of Simon & Schuster, Inc.
1230 Avenue of the Americas
New York, NY 10020

First Atria Books hardcover edition September 2020

ATRIA BOOKS and colophon are trademarks of Simon & Schuster, Inc.

For information about special discounts for bulk purchases, please contact Simon & Schuster
Special Sales at 1-866-506-1949 or business@simonandschuster.com.

The Simon & Schuster Speakers Bureau can bring authors to your live event.
For more information or to book an event, contact the Simon & Schuster Speakers
Bureau at 1-866-248-3049 or visit our website at www.simonspeakers.com.

Interior design by Silverglass

Manufactured in the United States of America

3 5 7 9 10 8 6 4 2

Library of Congress Cataloging-in-Publication Data is available.

ISBN 978-1-9821-3812-7
ISBN 978-1-9821-3814-1 (ebook)

For Wanda

Three

Contents

Introduction: Everything and Nothing

A couple of weeks before my husband officially announced he was running for president of the United States, he and I were eating dinner at an unassuming Thai restaurant in DC, enjoying an increasingly rare evening alone after a grassroots event for his exploratory committee. That night was the first time I'd introduced Peter, who was speaking to a crowd of hundreds of people, and afterward, security ushered us quickly out the door and into a car. On our way out, flashes of sneak-attack selfies and hands grabbing at my shirt were surprising; the energy in the room had been electrifying and wonderfully supportive, but also intense. We hadn't even launched yet, and here we were, filling large rooms to capacity and getting mobbed at the doorway. The fact that we needed crowd control at all still felt surreal.

We were disappointed that we hadn't been allowed to stay and mingle with the audience, but we soon realized we could use this as an opportunity for some much-needed alone time. Once we were in the car, the team finally agreed we could have a "date night," meaning we could grab dinner and go to bed when we wanted. Though the committee had only been up and running for a couple of months at that point, my understanding of luxury had already been completely transformed: getting Thai food and falling asleep at 10:30 p.m. felt like a weeklong vacation in a Tuscan villa.

Our dinner was mostly uneventful, but on our walk back to the hotel, we started to attract attention. Maybe it was the spring weather, but folks were excited to see a political couple out and about, and we were happy to oblige requests for photos and signatures. As we walked down 14th Street, I saw that a small group standing to our left were pretty much staring, and an older woman in the group looked particularly starstruck. We smiled and continued walking, but when I peered over my shoulder, I saw that the woman was following us, and I could see she was already getting emotional. I stopped Peter just as she touched his shoulder to turn him around, and she immediately began to tear up. "I'm so sorry to bug you guys," she said. "It's just—I'm the mother of two gay children and what you're doing for this country and for them . . . I am just so proud of you and so happy you're getting out there." Her children had caught up with her—they were a little embarrassed, but excited to meet us, too. "Hi, we're the gay children," the daughter joked as an introduction.

We all shared a laugh, hugged, and took a family photo together, and Peter and I walked away, hand in hand, overcome with joy. People were watching us and responding to our message! But at the same time, that brief encounter made it clear we had a huge responsibility. We knew we had to get this moment right.

Until that evening, I'd never considered that I could make someone's mother cry just by being myself. In 2019, almost overnight, I went from being a middle-school teacher from Traverse City, Michigan, to becoming a person strangers looked to for guidance, reassurance, and the perfect reaction GIF on Twitter. I'd always understood my work as an educator to be about making a small difference in the lives of my students—I never thought I'd be making waves on big issues as one part of the first openly gay couple with a real chance at the White House. The pressure was enormous. I probably wasn't as ready as I could have been, but that didn't matter—I learned the hard way that a presidential campaign is a matter of building the plane as it's taking off.

....

How did I get here? First, some background: in 2018, after three years of dating, I married Pete Buttigieg, the mayor of South Bend, Indiana. (Though you'll notice I call him Peter, because that's what he goes by with friends and family.) At the time I had no idea we'd be celebrating our one-year anniversary on the campaign trail, but just a couple of months after our wedding, Peter and I discussed him running, and I supported it wholeheartedly. As my partner, he had helped me feel safe and believe in myself—I thought he could do something similar for the rest of the country.

I'd never thought about what a spouse does on a political campaign, and that's by design. Political spouses are supposed to be everything and nothing at the same time, serving as the perfect supporter for the candidate by working nonstop without ever stealing the spotlight, messing things up, or getting in the way. "There's only one star," as many political operatives will tell you when you work as a surrogate, and it's not you. At the same time, the spouse plays a crucial role both in front of the cameras and behind the scenes. You know the candidate the best. You know what picks them up, especially when they're on two hours of sleep and have to go into their sixth interview of the day—you're on call for when the candidate needs to get into the right headspace. Actually, you're on call for everything. You show up when the candidate can't be there. You fill in all the gaps. By virtue of your marriage, you're required to be known to the public as "the candidate's spouse" at the very minimum, and you're expected to do a lot more than that.

Of course, I always wanted to help in whatever way I could. I love the guy—that's why I married him. But campaigning is . . . a lot.

Beyond the relentless schedule and the high stakes, I wasn't prepared for what having to exist in public on the national stage would do to me, my self-image, and my self-worth. Most people have gotten to know me over the last two years through the stories that have run about me in the media, or they've made assumptions about me based on my marriage (or even my social media). While my new platform has afforded me incredible opportunities that I wouldn't trade for anything, the way my life seemed to be getting away from me was frustrating. Although I never thought I'd want to write a book, I started to feel like I needed to tell my own story, as cheesy as that might sound. The more time I spent out on the campaign trail reflecting on my own life and seeing myself in other people's stories, the more I realized that the experiences and memories I was scared of, embarrassed of, or keeping hidden weren't as weird, mockable, or inappropriate to discuss in the context of national politics as I'd assumed they were. They were just real, the truth. Even more remarkable, people seemed to appreciate hearing about them.

Because the fact is, my story isn't rare. In fact, it's pretty common. I grew up in a conservative small town, with loving parents who worked so hard to support me but didn't know many gay people before I came out to them, terrified, at age eighteen. I lived my entire adolescence in shame, feeling like I'd never fit in in my high school or my community, and even after I came out, I couldn't shake the feeling that this essential fact about me meant I'd never find love or have a family. Despite being a goody-two-shoes high school student and working multiple jobs since I was legally allowed to do so, I struggled to finish college, and by my midtwenties I was sitting on about $100,000 of student loans and medical debt. I lived paycheck to paycheck for years after college, desperately looking for some sign of a happy, stable future, and I often didn't know if I was going to make it.

I certainly never thought I'd find myself living with a politician, but the experience has shown me that this story of mine isn't apolitical. Politics is in all our living rooms. It's around our kitchen tables and in our mailboxes. Whether I was hearing the stories of young queer people who'd been kicked out of their homes and didn't know what to do next, or talking to factory workers who were afraid of what was going to happen to their jobs, or hosting a roundtable with fellow teachers who felt they weren't getting the support they needed, I was constantly reminded that Americans should be able to see themselves in the people tasked with representing them at the highest levels of government.

So that's why I'm here now. We're currently living through a rapid shift in politics. (As this book goes to print, our country is grappling with the COVID-19 pandemic, as well as a long-overdue upheaval in the way we discuss and act on racial injustice and police brutality.) I think Peter and I are part of a group of young politicians and activists who have a unique opportunity to reimagine the world that's emerging. I don't want to waste the chance I've been given to do my part just because I came by it swiping through a dating app while I was wasting time at work. (Yup, that's how I met Pete Buttigieg.) I have by no means figured it all out yet, but I definitely learned a lesson or two on the way, and you can bet I'm ready to share.

One

1

Not That Kind of Camp

As the husband of a former mayor and presidential candidate, I realize that I'm the sort of public figure who, in Hollywood, might be described as D-list, if I made it onto any list at all. The problem is not just my awkward positioning in the middle of the Venn diagram connecting "figures the kids know about" and "figures people who watch cable news know about." The last name *Buttigieg* obviously stands out, but my unusual first name can sometimes throw the whole name-recognition project off track before you get there. Buttigieg's husband? What's his name? It's not uncommon for me to have to repeat it over and over again at the coffee counter until it is ultimately shouted back as "Chastain," "Justin," or "Charles." I used to take great offense when my name was mispronounced—I always liked that it was unique, so why didn't anyone else? With age, there came the realization that this would be my normal, that baristas are overworked and underpaid, and that if I wanted to streamline the coffee-ordering process I would have to assume an alternate identity. If it's prudent, I tell people my name is *James* and move on with my life.

Unfortunately, when it comes to understanding just how I got this unique name, the story is dissatisfying and inconclusive; there is an answer, but an incomplete one. My mom used to take on shifts as a nursing assistant in addition to doing the books for our family's landscaping business, and she swears that a woman she worked with at the hospital was putting on a Christmas play that featured a character named King Chasten. As soon as she heard it, she loved it. Of course, I've done extensive research, and I can't find a King Chasten anywhere. There *is* an Arthurian ballad that contains a command "... king, chasten thy wife ...," but based on the way that text continues, I really don't think my mom's friend would be in a play based on it. Regardless, it's not pronounced like the verb, which means "to have a restraining effect on" and which is the opposite of my personality (I hope). It's pronounced with a short *a* and a hard *t*: CHAS-ten.

If anything, my name is an expression of my parents' creativity. My parents, Terry and Sherri Glezman, are loving, dedicated people who live for their friends and family; they always made sure their children's lives were full of little adventures (and some bigger ones). Their parenting philosophy was neither hands-off nor helicopter, which allowed me to develop my independence in a genuine way without feeling totally unmoored. Though we've had our hard times, certain clichés ring true: they always wanted the best for me, and they absolutely "made me who I am today." Since understanding that is part of the point of writing a memoir, this is where I have to begin.

My grandfather moved between Traverse City, Michigan, and coastal cities for years before ultimately planting permanent roots in 1959, when he was relocated for the National Coast Guard. Since then, the extended family nearby has grown so large that we can't fit into a single house for our holiday gatherings—we now squeeze close to forty people at a time into my father's finished barn. (We'll talk about barns a bit later.) The woods and waters of Northern Michigan provided a lot of necessary set elements for my "rub some dirt in it, you'll be fine" childhood. Some of the best illustration I can think of happened at Fish Camp. What's Fish Camp, you ask? Well: Fish Camp was *the* annual father-son tradition in our family. The name refers to what we did (fish) and the vibe (camp, and not in the Susan Sontag sense). My mother's uncle, Uncle Gene, has a cabin in the middle of nowhere, just outside Baraga, in the Upper Peninsula of Michigan, and every summer my dad, two older brothers, and I would make the multipart journey together. The four of us would pile into Dad's truck and make the seven-hour drive north with a truckload of coolers, gear, and a bag full of beef jerky. Along the way, Dad would stop at the Mackinac Bridge so we could take in the view and buy a pop from the convenience store. We'd play car games across the UP, listening to talk radio or the local country music station, which was probably called The Moose, until the only signs of civilization were the occasional pasty stand, bait shop, or gas station (which most likely sold pasties and bait). Once we made it to Baraga, we'd stop and say hi to Uncle Gene and "Aunty Mares" (that's Aunt Marilyn in "Yooper" speak). Gene would probably tell us something like "The skeeters are bitin' real hard—make sure ya lather on da bug dope." (That's, uh, mosquitos are biting and be sure to wear bug spray . . . dontcha know.) A few more miles into the forest and the real adventure began—not only do you have to drive into camp on a dirt road, you used to have to take an ATV part of the way, and in the winter, the men who went to the cabin to hunt deer would have to snowmobile into camp. Ultimately, Gene was able to dig a road out to the cabin, which, honestly, is kind of a bummer. The act of parking the truck, throwing on your backpack, and trudging through the rich copper mud was thrilling. There was no electricity or running water. In the daytime, in addition to fishing, Dad would bring rifles for us to practice shooting clay pigeons or targets; I became a really good marksman, even though I never lost my unease around guns. Just seeing the guns on the picnic table made me nervous, and although my dad has gifted me a few guns for birthdays over the years, they remain in his safe back home in Michigan. Dad was also very adamant about gun safety, and took pride in teaching the three of us boys responsibility in every sense. This became something I could share with voters on the trail who, for better or worse, had a lot to say about guns. I learned a lot, and my dad always made sure I wasn't too far outside my comfort zone—but my unease never went away.

My favorite part of Fish Camp wasn't shooting combustibles; it was the fish. Evenings were spent cooking what we'd caught that day. We'd pump water from the well, filet the fish, toss them in some batter, and fry them over the fire in a skillet. The simplicity was remarkable. The sun would set, we'd build a bonfire, and Uncle Gene would tell scary stories about man-eating wolves, close encounters with bears, and the occasional camper-abducting alien. Once the fire died down, we'd be left with the bright northern stars. We slept in sleeping bags on bunk beds, with Dad closest to the door, a gun propped up near his bed just in case a bear or wolf came too close to camp. One part safety, the other, I'm convinced, just to scare the shit out of Chasten. Right when I'd start to doze off, my dad would say something like "Shh. Did you hear that?" Of course, there was nothing outside, and Dad couldn't keep himself from snickering.

I always prided myself on my performance at Fish Camp—throughout my childhood and adolescence, I was driven by a desire to be out in front. We were a competitive family, and sticking my neck out, both to win and to impress my parents, was always the name of the game. At home, my older brothers were Dad's boys, while one of my favorite pastimes was singing Celine Dion songs to my mom while she folded laundry. But I was secretly very good at a lot of things involving the Great Outdoors. I knew it drove my brothers nuts that I excelled at school and, occasionally, at being an outdoorsman. (To give them credit, while I preferred to sleep in and watch cartoons, they often found the energy to wake up at the crack of dawn and hunt and skin a deer.) They were always messing around and getting in trouble, in fairly elaborate ways. There was the time they almost started a forest fire because one of them had stepped on a bee's ground nest, gotten stung, and needed to seek revenge on "those fucking bees." They returned to the scene of the crime and proceeded to pour gasoline all over the nest. This came to my attention when Rhyan, the oldest, zoomed into camp on a four-wheeler and jumped off so fast that the ATV kept rolling a few more yards. Just as a small plume of smoke became visible on the horizon, Dad came rushing out of the cabin with my brother, grabbed a jug of water and a shovel, jumped on another ATV, and zipped off into the woods. It was a small fire, easily extinguishable, and the forest was saved. Rhyan and Dustin had a good laugh, but Dad was furious. The entire time, I remained in my folding chair reading Harry Potter.

Fishing was where I excelled. I was great at tying hooks—one of my brothers hated touching worms and putting them on the hook, but I never minded getting my hands dirty, a quality that has helped me excel equally at raising cows and, eventually, working as a barista at Starbucks. As a result, I always caught the biggest fish. Everyone at Fish Camp probably says this, but for me it was true. I swear. (Upon publication of this book, I'm sure all the reviews will come with headlines like "PETE BUTTIGIEG'S FATHER-IN-LAW DISPUTES CLAIMS MADE IN HUSBAND'S EXPLOSIVE NEW MEMOIR: 'Chasten didn't catch the biggest fish.'") One summer my dad lost his favorite lure after his line snapped while he was reeling in a fish; about an hour later, I caught a largemouth bass, and when we finally got home and began gutting it for dinner, there, lodged deep in the fish's throat, was Dad's favorite lure. I was really pleased with what this said about my fishing skills, though of course I never would have said that out loud.

Just kidding. Everyone hears this story . . . annually.

My dad is a no-bullshit kind of guy, reserved but very funny in his own way. He had very high, unspoken expectations that he put a lot of stock in, but most people know him for his generosity and love of surprises. (He once bought my mom a Persian kitten that we named *Sheetah*, as in "sheet of ice," which was an appropriate description of the weather when we brought her home. Sheetah seemed to hate all of us, but that was part of her charm.) It's always a pleasure to hear my dad laugh, because it happens so rarely. It happens especially when he is playing a practical joke, which, in a very dad-like way, he absolutely loves. When I was young I thought I was his easiest target, but now I wonder if he played those tricks on me so much because he thought the opposite—because he saw pranks as tests and learning opportunities, peculiar gifts that I could be trusted to handle without setting anything ablaze.

Some examples: In the summers, Dad would take us out on our small pontoon boat (which he named "the Pleasure Patrol"), and after I watched *Jaws*—at way too young an age—he would swim under the boat and pull my legs from below so that I thought I was being attacked by a shark. At Fish Camp, our usual fishing hole was a big, muddy, tree-lined riverbank; if you navigated the mud well, you could walk out into the slow river all the way up to your chest. One year a sturgeon jumped out of the river about ten or twenty yards down from where I was standing; I'd never seen a fish that big before (they can grow up to eight feet long), and my dad shouted from downstream, "Get out of the water! They'll eat your legs!" You'd think that, as a teenager, I'd have been able to recognize when he was teasing me, but when it came to monsters in the water, I never took my chances. I waded as fast as I could out of the river, and my dad couldn't stop laughing. My scream was most definitely heard from miles away.

Unfortunately, autumn offered little respite. Every year around Halloween, WTCM, the local country radio station in Northern Michigan, would play a spoken-word Halloween song/story called "The Legend of the Dogman," which had it that every seven years a creature that was half man, half vicious, man-eating dog (but not a werewolf?) roamed Northern Michigan terrorizing farm animals and tearing apart its victims. (Every year, the song would say, "The seventh year is here.") Every time the song came on, even though he knew I hated it, my dad would crank it up, rolling down the windows and howling as I pleaded with him to cut it out. When we went camping, he'd ask me as we walked through the woods: "Chasten, do you think the Dogman is out?" or whisper, "The seventh year is here," and I'd grip my flashlight tighter as Dad cackled. This particular torment culminated when he put a ladder up to my bedroom window and scratched at the screen, so that when I woke up I saw the Dogman glaring at me from outside. My bedroom was right next to the back porch, so by the time I'd jumped out of bed and sprinted to the living room, the Dogman had also shifted positions and was visible outside the porch door. That the Dogman was wearing my dad's clothes didn't register at the time. He very well may have eaten my dad already, then put on his clothes. That's a thing that *absolutely* could've happened. Hearing her son screaming bloody murder, my mom came rushing in, at which point my dad opened the door and took off his wolf mask. Mom was livid, but Dad, of course, could barely contain himself. He still calls me, every Halloween, to play the song through the phone. I still hate the Dogman, and I'm still wary around open water.

The most instructive of Dad's pranks took place at Fish Camp when I was about thirteen. From the cabin, we'd take our four-wheelers through the woods, following two-tracks or trails my uncle had cleared or mapped for us, until we emerged at the river. From there, we'd walk along the steep, coppery riverbank until we found a spot that spoke to us, miles from another human being. The silence was peaceful, but it was also a reminder of how remote we truly were.

One day, my brothers wanted to go to a different fishing hole than the one we were at, so my dad agreed to find a new spot with them. Dad made sure I was fine to stay where I was alone and said he'd come back to pick me up in a little bit. Then they all rode off on their four-wheelers and I settled in. The sun was shining, the birds were chirping, and I was more than happy to be alone. As I believe I mentioned, I was a skilled fisherman—I didn't need a chaperone.

Some time passed, longer than necessary to drop my brothers off and come back, but it was still daylight, so I didn't worry too much. I just kept fishing. But then the sun began to set, and I started getting worried. I pride myself on having inherited my father's pinpoint-accurate sense of direction, but I wasn't sure walking miles alone through the woods in the dark was the wisest choice. (Also, I was thirteen.)

Dad had never told us what to do if we found ourselves alone in the middle of the forest at night. What I did know was that I had waterproof matches in my tackle box, and how to start a fire, so that's what I did. I continued fishing to keep busy, but as the sun started to disappear behind the tree line, and the sky was getting darker and darker, the fear really started to set in. A few hours had passed. Eventually, I packed up my tackle box and turned my back to the river, figuring the monsters would come from the woods. Across the river was a steep bank, and the woods ascended above me by about a hundred feet. Surely the wolves were perched there, watching.

Finally, I heard the four-wheeler in the distance. The moment Dad came into the clearing I was running to him asking why he had left me for so long. I must have sounded like a parent myself: How could he do such a thing? Leaving his own child to fend for himself in the middle of the woods at night? There were wolves out here! I could have been eaten! BY THE DOGMAN! (Maybe this one was a little less than parental.) It turned out that Dad had been on the other side of the river the entire time, watching to see what I'd do. He was so trusting, and he truly believed in pushing us out of the nest to see if we could fly. Like it or not, I'd flown.

Mom still gives Dad a lot of grief for the cruel tricks he played on me when I was younger, but when I tell that story she seems more proud than protective. I think she knew he had done right by her and me, making sure I could take care of myself. I was going to be all right. I always felt closer to him on those trips—he gave me more than enough room to explore and be myself, without ever actually causing me harm.

....

If my dad had taken it upon himself to teach us how to trust our instincts and fend for ourselves (safely and responsibly!), my mom, Sherri, taught us the value of routine and reward. She is joyfully loud—in the best way— and wonderfully eccentric. Her smile is almost always on, even when, as you'll learn, she's dealing with immense pain. She has jet-black hair that's often expertly held in place with a whole lot of hair spray. (While waiting on Mom to get ready to leave, you knew it was almost time to go when you heard the sound of aerosol.) She wears a necklace and bracelet with individual charms that correspond to each of her children and grandchildren. Often when she yelled our names, you'd think there was a serious emergency: a heavy object about to fall and crush us, a pet-related tragedy. Usually she just wanted help carrying groceries into the house. She's never afraid to dance or sing in front of strangers, even if she doesn't know the words, and she loves to host family and friends, which means she always wants the house in impeccable shape. In a very Midwestern mom way, she decorated our kitchen with those wall decals that stated things like "It is around this table we understand best the warmth of being together," and there is always a Yankee Candle burning in the house. When we were kids, and my brothers were a bit older and often busy with extracurricular activities, many of the household chores fell to me. Every day, when I came home from school, I would do the dishes, sweep, vacuum, and tidy my room—it all had to be finished before I could do my homework. (I wonder if this wasn't a sneaky strategy to get me to look forward to my homework by comparison.) Now, when Peter and I come home to visit for the holidays, the house still looks like a professional cleaning service came through, and even when I've shown up as a surprise, the house has still been remarkably clean. We never had an allowance when we were younger, but we could earn our keep. "Why would I buy a dishwasher when I gave birth to three?" Mom always joked. Occasionally, she would pay me to do extra chores on top of my usual responsibilities—deep-cleaning the bathroom, shampooing the carpets, vacuuming the staircase, cleaning the garages, or washing the windows would earn me a few extra bucks, which I usually saved in a small wooden box under my bed with my arcade tokens and other beloved trinkets. I was always happy to vacuum, but the dusting was stressful, because it was always subject to the white-cloth test. Sherri ran a tight ship.

Mom was great at stretching our dollar and making sure we always had plenty of food on the table, and it always felt special, even if a lot of it was canned or from a box. At home, pigs-in-a-blanket (hot dogs wrapped in Pillsbury crescent rolls) were staples, as were canned tomato soup and canned peaches and pears. (After Peter and I started dating, I learned that pigs-in-a-blanket were a treat reserved for Christmas mornings in his family. For us, they were a "Mom just got home from work and is tired" staple.) We had mashed potatoes or mac and cheese with most dinners. In the years after I finished college, when I had to pay for something I didn't quite have the money for, I sometimes thought about my mom, in a bathrobe, her hair still wet from the shower, getting her purse and writing us a check for school lunches in the mornings, saying that it might not be enough. It always just went over my head when she did that; it never occurred to me that it not being enough could have some kind of consequence for me, and that's why she was mentioning it. Today I realize how hard it must have been to have to express that kind of worry to your kids—if it wasn't enough, she didn't want us to be caught off guard—but she never stressed us out about it.

And it's not like we didn't have nights out on the town. For special occasions, my family loved celebrating at Outback Steakhouse; I'm still a sucker for a Bloomin' Onion. Other times it just seemed like Mom and Dad had had about enough of us, and when that happened they'd take us up to the Burger King so we could eat a Kids Meal and play on the indoor playground—always an adventure. In retrospect, we seemed to eat a lot of fast food, but Mom always made it seem like a special treat, just as her cooking was. I still pine for her signature dishes when I'm away from home: she made terrific spaghetti, beef stroganoff, meatloaf, and hearty winter stews. On Christmas mornings, she'd serve her famous homemade cinnamon rolls, a tradition that continues to this day. When I was very young, in the fall and winter, Dad typically brought home meat from the buffalo packing slaughterhouse where he sometimes picked up extra hours. It was always a really special night when he brought home ribs; even though he'd work late on these nights, we'd always stay up waiting for him to get home and grill immediately. In the summer we would line up along the side of the road to buy sweet corn from a well-known local farmer. You had to watch the news to see when he was available.

My parents still live in the same house I grew up in, a cozy three-bedroom split-level in a subdivision just outside Traverse City. They bought it when my mom was nineteen and my dad was twenty, right after they got married. I think my father prides himself on having the nicest lawn in the subdivision—as a landscaper he has meticulously trimmed, pruned, mowed, and planted everything to his liking. Not a blade of grass untouched, no tree ignored, every hanging basket expertly placed. My two older brothers shared a room until my dad was able to build a separate bedroom in the basement for my oldest brother. I always had the same bedroom, across the hall from my middle brother, facing the backyard and our aboveground swimming pool, which Dad also took great pleasure in cleaning and maintaining. In the winter, we would fill up milk jugs and throw them out into the pool as the water slowly turned greener, to prevent the Northern Michigan ice from ripping the lining. From the back porch the deck separated the area into two small backyards. One yard was for the dogs, the first of which (in my time) was a Pekingese named Brittany. Brittany was succeeded by a black lab named Brisco, whom Dad trained extensively. Open the front door, and Brisco would run outside, grab the newspaper from the mailbox, and bring it back into the house. He followed Dad everywhere.

The other yard was for us kids to play in, and Dad has since turned it into a large garden, where he grows his own vegetables, which find their way every year into Mom's signature salsa. This is in keeping with his encroachment approach to the house in general. We have two garages. Though one is called "Mom's garage," it's also full of Dad's junk, with just enough space for her car. The other garage, "Dad's garage," is more like a workshop, where Dad now practices making his own maple syrup, smoking his own beef jerky and sausages, and making garland with fresh greens from the Upper Peninsula as he watches TV and periodically checks on the smoke shack.

My parents run their own small landscaping business, and from the time I was about ten or so I was helping out in some capacity. Every night, Dad would bring home the hydroseeder, a giant, tank-like trailer that was filled with water and seed mix to spray on new lawns throughout the day. (Well, it *seemed* giant to me when I was a fifth grader.) My job most evenings was to go out to the driveway when Dad got home and spray down the hydroseeder with the garden hose as Dad asked me about my day at school. I was happy to help Dad, and even from a young age I saw the exhaustion in his face when he pulled into the driveway. My dad has broken his back multiple times over the years, but the moment he could feasibly lift something, he was back to work. He continues to work long hours, in the sun, on his knees, straining his back, and refusing to quit.

Working for my parents' landscaping business also included stuffing, licking, sealing, and stamping what seemed like endless envelopes containing invoices with Mom in her office, which over time migrated from the kitchen table to the small office my dad fixed up for her in our basement, to some property my family secured about five miles down the road at the height of the business. In the winters, my parents also operated a Christmas tree lot, where they would sell Christmas trees and handmade wreaths. The lot was located next to a local bison farm, so families could make a big day of it: they'd come see the Glezmans, buy a Christmas tree, pick out a wreath my mother had made, and feed the bison some hay through the fence. I was still quite young when Dad had the lot, but I remember visiting him there daily. Mom would bring a Crock-Pot of sloppy joes, and we'd sit in the camper and wait until a family came. Dad would help the family pick out their tree, my brothers would help move it and tie it onto their car, and Mom and I would ring them up out of the little white shack we'd decorated with Christmas lights, where we also sold our homemade hot cocoa. I was relegated to handing out candy canes, but it was still so fun.

Because of the landscaping business, the Christmas tree lot, and the simple fact that my family had lived in the area for a long time, we always ran into people my parents knew, especially my dad. It was a running joke that we could never get anywhere on time because of this. If we missed the bus to school and Mom couldn't drive us, the task fell to Dad, which meant we would be late. He absolutely *had* to stop at the gas station on the way to get his donut and two cups of coffee, and he inevitably ran into someone, which meant we'd be caught up in conversation for at least fifteen minutes. We always gave him a lot of grief because he made us late for school, but everyone knew Dad and had a story to tell about him—how for a family that needed wheelchair access to their house he had helped build a deck and only charged for the materials. How he'd saved the day by rushing over to someone's mother's house to fix a leaking toilet in the middle of his lunch break. Dad will still drop everything for anyone.

2

"Did You Walk Your Steer Today?"

All this wholesome childhood Americana, and we haven't even gotten to the cows. When I was in sixth or seventh grade, my brothers and I started raising animals as part of 4-H with one of our neighbors. When we decided to get into 4-H, which was a pretty big scene where I grew up, my family built a small barn out on our property together. The "pole barn" is a Midwestern institution that is, like so many Midwestern institutions, pretty much what it sounds like: a barn constructed out of poles. However, the phrase "run down to the pole barn," like so many Midwestern phrases, was not meant to be taken literally. It meant we were going down the road to the property, even though the barn that we kept our animals in was not, get this, a pole barn.

I started out raising dairy feeders and worked my way up to showing steers. My brothers started with a steer, but I was a tad too small to handle such a large animal. Steers are yearlong projects, and they're regarded as the big-shot project in the 4-H community. (Except for horses. Don't get me started on the horse people.) You'd buy the calf wild off a farm in August or September when they were very young, and you'd have it for about a year before you went to the county fair. When you got a calf, it was only about two hundred pounds, and it could jump and buck; by the time the fair rolled around, it was between a thousand and thirteen hundred pounds, and completely unmanageable if you hadn't started out strong—you have to start breaking them in and helping them trust you right away. It never failed that multiple kids would bring their steer to the fair only to be dragged around in the dirt by a wild animal they had never tamed. Whenever I got mine, we'd halter it first thing so I could begin taking it on walks. At the beginning of the project, this involves getting dragged around a lot, but if you gain their trust, they'll follow you anywhere.

Every morning before school I had to head down to the barn and feed the cows. After school or on the way home from extracurricular activities, I'd stop at the barn to feed them again. Then, every weekend, we'd have to take our steers on a walk. ("Did you walk your steer today?" was a common refrain in our household.) They had a pasture to roam in, but walking a steer on the halter was a show of dominance, control, and a showman's ability. Before I could drive, this meant my brother had to take us, but I spent a lot more time at the barn than my brothers did. My parents were always yelling at them to walk their steers, and I'd always get in fights with them because they never helped clean the barn. I know I'm making myself out to seem like Snow White communing with her woodland creatures, but there was a limit to my pure-hearted love of animals, and it irritated me that my brothers never cared about having a clean space for the steers like I did. Those animals had to live in there! And so did I, sort of! As melancholic as this sounds, I could often be found sitting around at the barn, even when I was done feeding and walking the steer. A lot of it was the result of not having many friends, but I liked that it was quiet there, and I liked when it was just me and the animal. Eventually, I could open the barn door and my steer would follow me around without a lead. Even though I knew the animal would be butchered at the fair at the end of the year, I always connected with it. It was another way to impress my parents, and to stick it to the country jocks who mocked me at school.

I still have my 4-H trophy—featuring a cow—displayed prominently in my office today, right next to my master's degree. But when fair time came around, I always felt so nervous and conspicuous. As you might suspect, the typical 4-H'er is a tough guy, or wants to be. They present very masculine, and I never did. (One of the most embarrassing photos of me from high school shows me in my giant, round glasses and a very bright blue Hawaiian shirt. I don't know why I wore Hawaiian shirts so much in school, but it's a documented fact that I did.) Nevertheless, I was very good at showing animals, and I took it very seriously. In addition to all my dedication behind the scenes, I went to showmanship classes to learn how to show the animal better; I learned the parts of the steer, the cuts of meat, and how to properly position their legs so the judge could see the animal's muscle structure. Maybe I felt like I could defend my difference and my weirdness by winning blue ribbons; I definitely enjoyed driving my brothers crazy with all my trophies and awards. Alongside the usual gossip, there were lots of rumors about fair romances, and I always had it in my head that my success would make girls turn their heads if they heard one of the Glezman boys was pretty talented when it came to 4-H. "Did he win first in his showmanship class? My stars!" they'd say, fanning themselves. I know giant cows aren't the sexiest thing in the world—they're more cute than sexy—but winning usually is. Right? (What kind of world did I think I was living in?!) Girlfriends weren't something I was interested in, I would soon find out/admit, but that didn't matter so much—it was more important that I be able to show my brothers that I was good at something they weren't, and if they didn't care so much about the steers, they definitely cared about girls.

My 4-H triumphs were not just about besting my brothers and collecting blue ribbons, though. There was also a financial component. My parents were pretty strict about money, and the 4-H model allowed me to earn some in absence of an allowance. Early on, our parents would buy us some of the supplies we needed for the project, but we'd have to keep a log of how much they'd given us so we could pay it back when the 4-H check came in after the auction.

There was no guarantee of breaking even, but in a good year, if the price of beef was high enough at auction, I could pocket a couple hundred dollars. Still, I was supposed to save everything that was left over for the next year's project. Hoping to buy a car, I was desperate to get a job and start earning my own money. In the summer, my brothers worked for my dad, installing sprinklers and hydroseeding lawns at his side, but in a classically Chasten way, I wanted to do my own thing. It was nothing against my father, or his line of work; I think I just wanted to be on my own. For years I'd bothered our veterinarian to let me come work at the animal hospital. *I'm so experienced with animals!* I kept reminding everybody, but to no avail, until one night when I was fifteen, the phone rang while we were watching TV. The vet's office told my mom that he was in need of a kennel technician. I jumped at the chance.

Since I only had my learner's permit at that time, my brother would drop me off at the kennel after school. I'd walk all the dogs and spray down their cages, scrub the surgery areas, and clean the exam rooms after the hospital had closed. When I was done, someone would pick me up and take me down to the barn so I could take care of my 4-H animal. In less than two years, I had saved enough to buy a car—an all-wheel-drive 1992 Mitsubishi Expo (you're gonna want to google that), which an old man down the street was selling for $900 cash. At that time it only had about thirty thousand miles on it, and my dad couldn't believe how good a deal it was. No rust, and it seemed to be in great condition. The only issue was that it looked like a minivan, which was a dark mark on a high school student. But I didn't care—I had my jobs to get to. Dad convinced me that it was an excellent investment because it wouldn't cost me much in repairs and it got great gas mileage. I bought it right away. My friends took to calling it the Mitsushitzu, and not because with its odd, hulking shape, it resembled that kind of dog.

Once I had the 'Shitzu, I got another summer job, as a busboy at a Mexican restaurant called La Señorita. I'd put in half my hours at the vet hospital and then run to make my dinner shift at the restaurant, stopping at the barn to feed the cows on the way. I'd put in some hours bussing plates and scraping burrito detritus off the tables at La Señorita, and then I'd head back to the animal hospital to finish my janitorial duties. I'd get home at around ten or so, smelling like bleach and salsa. I was known for picking up extra shifts at both jobs, and my work ethic paid off. Waitresses would tip me extra if I'd get to their tables fast. I was a really good busboy, if I do say so myself.

....

It would be easy to describe where I'm from as the "real America." That term dominates talk of pragmatism in Democratic politics, where pundits obsess over "coastal elites" and their supposed inability to appeal to "the heartland," also known as "flyover country." People from Massachusetts, California, New York? Not "real Americans." According to the stereotype, a real American is not a professor, banker, or artist living in New York City or Seattle. Real America is Dixie Chicks and wide open spaces, proud men and hospitable women, farms, trucks, guns, patriotism, building, rebuilding, independence, hot dogs. Real Americans do not live within a day's drive of the ocean. (Lakes are, however, totally acceptable.) Real Americans earn their living through honest work, like manufacturing, teaching, or professional wrestling. They are usually also conservative, and so they must be unfathomable to Democrats from liberal enclaves.

Of course, this whole dichotomy is absurd. If America is a "melting pot," surely anyone can be a "real American." (And even if we weren't a melting pot, surely anyone could be.) Nevertheless, the idea won't seem to go away. Being from Traverse City, Michigan, never seemed like an advantage when I was growing up there, but since finding myself in the middle of electoral politics at the highest level, I can't deny that it lends me a certain credibility as a "real American," as if an almost psychic insight is necessary to understand that people want jobs, healthcare, and livable futures. Michigan itself is a swing state, a phrase that will make any politician's ears perk right up, so my insider information is valuable. But even if the "real America" is a silly concept, the media's endless concern trolling about it hints at the divide between places like my hometown and places with populations in the millions, often ignoring the racial, economic, and lived realities of the very people they claim to speak for. Although I believe we can overcome—or *traverse* (sorry)—that gap, the first step is admitting it's mostly artificial. We assume it's impossible to understand one another, when in fact we're more similar than we'd like to admit.

Although I grew up with more proximity to a city than some people, Traverse City—known as TC, Traverse, and, in the summer, "Traffic City" because hundreds of thousands of tourists come *insert tour guide voice* to enjoy the natural beauty of the Great Lakes, the Sleeping Bear Dunes National Lakeshore, and the annual National Cherry Festival—is a hop, skip, and a jump away from rural farmland. The surrounding area runs the gamut of class distinctions, even if smaller towns and cities have specific class identities. Generally, the "fancy" people lived out on the peninsulas or in downtown Traverse City. Although these days your typical idyllic Main Street, USA, is more "craft brewery and combination bookstore/coffee shop (that also serves craft beer)" than "local credit union and soda fountain," Traverse City has always been very idyllic Main Street, USA, the kind of place where a nice lady on the street will notice that you look sad and invite you back to her house for a slice of pie, and it wouldn't be weird, because your mom went to elementary school with her. The town's wholesome image is bolstered by its status as the cherry capital of the world, and we lean into it. We produce 40 percent of the United States' annual crop of tart cherries, drop a cherry disco ball to ring in the New Year, fly into the "Cherry Capital Airport," and put cherry products in or on all possible foods both sweet and savory. My grandpa had a cherry farm, and right after high school I worked part-time at the downtown location of Cherry Republic, the source for all things cherry, including cherry-flavored "pop" (not soda), coffee, tea, bread, salad dressing, sausage, salsa, queso dip (questionable), and . . . ketchup. Unfortunately, I was too young to serve the cherry wine.

I liked Traverse City proper, which is why I was very particular about claiming I was from there as a child. A confession: I have been misleading you a little bit, because technically, I grew up outside the city limits in a place called "Chums Corner." Kids would tease me on the school bus that I wasn't actually from Traverse at all but a much lower-income area called "Grawn." They weren't exactly wrong. If you look at a map, you'll see that Chums Corner is much closer to Grawn than to Traverse City—only a few roads away. ("Roads" is one of the standard units for measuring distance in Northern Michigan; the other is "hours.") Even if they can't articulate exactly why, kids fixate on significant details, and I knew that being from Traverse City meant something different than being from Grawn. Something bad. Say it out loud, and in a Midwestern accent. The kids made it sound like slang for a type of mold.

Nevertheless, there was little I could do about the fact that my elementary school was in Grawn. Because all the towns in the area are small, you'd often talk to kids from other schools, so whenever I'd be out—for a football game or at youth group—other kids would call us the trailer trash school. It made me so mad, and maybe this was part of my sense that I never belonged. I was constantly trying to fit in with conflicting groups. Deep down, was I actually cultured and fancy? Or could I become as tough and rugged as the other "hicks"? This really just means I wanted to fit in somewhere, and that I feared my "true self"—whoever that was—would fit in nowhere. Still, this chip on my shoulder was eventually a boon for the community. In sixth grade, I got so upset that all the other "fancy" schools had school spirit murals on the walls of their gyms and ours didn't, so for a few months, every morning before school I would stand at the entrance collecting pop cans to raise money to put up a mural on *our* gym wall. Faygo, the infamous Michigan soda brand, was a particularly common addition to the mountain of cans and bottles I collected. Cans come with a 10-cent deposit in Michigan, so after a few months of hauling trash bags full of sticky bottles back to Prevo's, our neighborhood grocery store, we had a couple hundred dollars, enough to hire a local muralist to paint the school's mascot, the Blair Bobcat, on our gym wall. The press seem surprised that I was considered an "asset" as a fundraiser for Peter's campaign, but the fact is I'm a seasoned pro.

Lest you think this all sounds too quaint, even for the "hick school," don't worry—since my childhood, the lovely farmers' market on the corner of my street has been turned into an adult novelty store. I can appreciate my upbringing much more today than I used to, and not just because it gives me a weird kind of anti–street cred in national politics. Everybody I hung out with wanted to escape TC—there was never anything to do. I dreamed about moving to New York City and being in the theater, and I desperately wanted to be surrounded by culture. Not that I even know what I thought "culture" was. My access to theater was limited to what I could see on television and hear about in school, and the community shows at the Old Town Playhouse. I just always felt out of place, and I knew there had to be something else out there, even if I wasn't always comfortable enough in that knowledge to actually pursue that mysterious "something else."

We did of course have the great outdoors, but although I enjoyed fishing, four-wheeling, and 4-H-ing, I never felt like it was enough; being good at those kinds of things felt like I was rising to expectations, not developing my own. Now I know that suppressing a major part of your identity will make it feel like nothing is enough, but at the time I just felt uncomfortable in my own body, and my body was in Traverse.

My high school, Traverse City West, was also known as the "hick school," and that is best evidenced by the mode of transportation a certain percentage of students used to get there. In the wintertime, it was snowmobiles; in the summer, it was tractors. A major statement. At some point I believe the administration started requiring you to get a permission slip signed to do it. If you drove a souped-up pickup truck or a tractor to school, you parked in the "hick lot," for pickups, Jeeps, and ATVs only—the 'Shitzu dared not enter. Though they always parked their trucks there, I only remember my brothers taking advantage of the snowmobile policy a few times, and I did it once. I thought it would be fun, but mostly the ride was far too long, cold, awkward with a back-pack, and ultimately mortifying when we rolled into school. I was con-tent driving the 'Shitzu. Until the day the engine gave out, the car filled with smoke, and I rolled downhill into a ditch.

....

Like many places that project an atmosphere of upstanding Americana, Traverse City is very white—almost 95 percent white according to the 2010 Census—and Grand Traverse County is very conservative. I don't remember thinking a lot about politics growing up, but in Northern Michigan, not thinking about politics means you likely absorb a great deal of Being a Republican energy and probably become one yourself, at a young age, though you probably don't understand what that truly means. My family is Catholic and pretty conservative, in the sense that they cen-ter a lot of their morality and values on religion and tradition. My parents weren't especially forthcoming about their politics, and it wasn't immedi-ately clear to me the way politics could have real effects on our day-to-day lives. For example, we occasionally went across the channel to Sault Ste. Marie, in Canada, for my brother's hockey tournaments, and while there, my parents would always make sure to stop by a pharmacy to pick up cheaper prescription drugs, like Tobrex for pinkeye and amoxicillin for recurring ear infections and strep throat. But I never thought about this as a consequence of the American political system—that, like many other things, wouldn't become clear until later.

While Mom and Dad weren't very vocal about their political beliefs, many people in some of our social circles were *very* forthcoming about their conservatism, especially when it came to queerness. They often used their religion as a justification for their intolerance or unkindness. Even though I was starting to learn that I was gay, I witnessed a great deal of posturing and projecting from some of the people I grew up around, and I was rarely presented a different way of thinking, especially when it came to same-sex relationships. Instead, I believed that something about me was twisted, or wrong. Even though I knew many young people at school or CCD (Confraternity of Christian Doctrine class) didn't understand just how weighty their words and actions were, especially when it came to their blatant homophobia, the reality was that we were growing up in a bubble that made most of us feel we had to grow up to be one type of person. Eventually, of course, I would come out, and a close friend would tell me I was making an embarrassing choice leading me to damnation. The most common message in these circles was that God-fearing Americans and good country boys were tough-as-nails, *definitely* straight, and Republicans, and good, God-fearing American country boys were the only kind of boys to be.

Where I grew up, many people believed that being a Republican was also about a very visible and concentrated form of patriotism. Naturally, patriotism has something public about it—it just doesn't cut it to be a patriot in private. Sure, you can wear American flag underwear and eat hot dogs three times a week, but how does that serve your country? As I got older, I also understood that doing the most I could to blend in with those around me might help me fit in, and survive, at school; not only did silent approval quickly convey a set of acceptable values to other people, but it also meant that I could avoid having to figure out what my values actually were. These were preapproved, and if they were preapproved then they must be at least OK, if not perfect.

When George W. Bush was running for reelection in 2004, I was fifteen years old, and I begged my parents to take me to see him when he came through town. I was really excited that the president of the United States was going to be in my backyard. I didn't know anything about him—going to his rally was like going to see a celebrity, not a politician. (To be fair to Teen Chasten, the difference is often unclear to adults, even today.) Outside the Traverse City Civic Center, with Brooks & Dunn's "Only in America" blasting on the loudspeakers, Bush plucked the heartstrings of my fellow attendees. He spoke about the "forgotten" Americans who are taken advantage of and left with little to show for it, and about the importance of a strong country full of patriotic people just like ourselves. He knew us. He saw us. (Even though the feelings of being misunderstood and left out that I experienced weren't the same fears he was talking about.) I thought that if I got a John Deere–themed George Bush yard sign, maybe other boys, or even my own family, would think that I was serious and tough—one of them. I remember putting the W sticker on my car because that seemed to be the easiest way to signal "I'm just like you. Please leave me alone."

Of course, not all conservative views are necessarily moral deal breakers. But the political atmosphere in Michigan wasn't just a matter of differences of opinion about education policy and limited government. It wasn't uncommon to spot a Confederate flag decal on the back of a pickup truck in the grocery-store parking lot. And by *decal*, I don't mean bumper sticker—though of course there were some very aggressive bumper stickers. No, by *decal* I mean that the entire back window would be covered in a Confederate flag, sometimes with guns emblazoned over the flag, sometimes with some kind of "Come and Take It" language. Other trucks had actual Confederate flags waving from the cab. Never mind that Michigan fought for the Union in the Civil War and that Traverse City is much closer to Ontario than any part of the former Confederate South.

I wish I could say that from an early age I fervently objected to the presence of these symbols, but truth be told I had no idea what they meant. I was swimming in a sea of whiteness, and I didn't even know I was wet. At the 4-H County Fair, it wasn't out of the ordinary to see Confederate-flag belt buckles, and in 4-H-land, the belt buckle was prime real estate. Some kids would drive their accessorized trucks to school, or show up to class in a Confederate-flag T-shirt. I don't remember the school ever making a statement about that, or seeing anyone in a position of authority address it. Symbols like these were just around and accepted. Their presence was rarely discussed. I suppose it's telling that they weren't evaluated in school; that's how the system was designed. I watched as people described the flag as a symbol of "Southern pride," even though there's literally no reason for someone from Michigan to have "Southern pride."

I'm not saying this because I'm proud. In fact, I'm deeply ashamed. I'm saying it because there are so many pockets of this country where this kind of denial is encouraged and accepted, so much so that people don't even think to question it. I don't like admitting this, but I didn't fully grasp just how blatantly hurtful these symbols and rhetoric truly were when I was in high school. I was growing up in a system designed to keep me from questioning them in the first place.

There were a lot of lessons I needed to learn after high school, some of which required leaving the bubble I'd grown up in. I needed to be able to examine it from the outside.

3

How Do You Say "I Think I'm Gay" in German?

I would like to be able to say that my coming-out story begins with me seeing a bunch of naked Germans. But in fact it begins a little bit before that.

Around the time I started working, I also started getting really restless in Traverse City. Though I'd always suspected the world was not as narrow as it felt to me there, I wanted to know how not-narrow it was. I wouldn't say I was living in a bubble, exactly—maybe that I was living in a big bubble. I knew that there were some students at school who called themselves Democrats, and I didn't really understand what made me different from them. (Probably because I was not different from them at all, in my soul if not in my public persona.) The first time I noticed that the entire world was not as I'd been led to believe was one morning at school when a friend, who eventually became one of my best friends, asked me why I had a Bush sticker on my car. How could I support someone like him? "I thought you would know better," she said, passing me on her way to class. I remember standing in the middle of the pre-first-period rush of students feeling like an imposter. Someone had called me out for something I didn't even understand. Most of the families in 4-H supported Bush, and I thought that as a good country boy, I was supposed to, as well. I felt like I had made a mistake, despite the fact that I didn't even know what the mistake was. At the same time, I was ashamed because I knew nothing about Bush. Either way, I felt like I had committed some kind of irreversible act. Was I unwittingly—you might say ignorantly—sacrificing my values to blend in with other people?

That I wasn't sure exactly *what* values I thought I was sacrificing was the first problem.

When it came to identity in high school, I often felt isolated, floating between different groups. I never understood where I was supposed to fit, and I never saw a place that screamed "This is where you belong! Come! Be yourself!" I don't remember "seeing" any gay people in person growing up. I had an inkling that maybe there were other kids "like me" around, that they existed—the sense that perhaps a friend and I shared a secret, whether it was the feeling of just not fitting in or the deeper truth of growing up queer in an environment that told us not to be, but neither of us ever spoke of it. What I do remember, most vividly, are the words *fag* and *faggot* and *sissy*—descriptors for boys who were different, feminine, soft—being tossed around in the locker room and in the hallways. I dodged them daily. The classic move was to push me into a locker while calling me a "freak," but the comments about my sexuality were much more hurtful than this general term. Something in those insults told me other kids knew more about me than I did myself, and I didn't like it. They were most often hurled by other students who, I believe, were hurting just as much, in one way or another. The identity crisis that high school brings on manifests itself in many ways, but so often, it's in the form of taunts and bullying by those who haven't quite figured out who they themselves are just yet. When someone already feels low and alone, tearing down others feels like a step up. I think about the girl who always made fun of me with her friends from the back of the bus, calling me my brother's "sister" and "Chas-teen the crack-phene." It was so pathetic—at least come up with better jokes than that!—but we were all just trying to find our place, swimming in a sea of hormones and loneliness and confusion. Fighting the waves of exclusion, I often felt like an undertow was pulling me away from everyone and everything.

I remember being attracted to men from a young age, but I don't think I fully understood until about seventh or eighth grade that this might mean I was gay. I didn't have the vocabulary for it until it was presented to me in a pejorative way. Of course, like in the movies, it was gym class that made the world of a closeted and confused gay kid come alive! At the time, my grade was sharing locker-room space with the older boys during gym, and I became absolutely terrified because, when some of the boys were changing around me, it made me feel a certain way. I felt like I was experiencing the first symptoms of a chronic illness. Something was telling me that this wasn't right. From everything I'd heard, I knew this was a terrible secret that I had to keep hidden.

I feel almost heartbroken to think of how much pain my younger self felt at the prospect of being around other boys. Of course, there's a reason men's locker rooms are known to be places of gross, sweaty aggression. (Cue Donald Trump quote.) This was not an open, welcoming environment for anyone. But my terror mixed with a sense of deep shame to make me dread gym class more than your average preteen. The shower was strictly jock territory, so I never showered at school—like the rest of my other outcast/misfit/unathletic classmates, I'd just reapply deodorant, wipe my face, and rush out of there as fast as possible. One day, after gym class, a group of guys had just emerged from the shower in their towels, and as I was lacing up my shoes, they surrounded me and started taunting me. Out came the insults and accusations. "You like what you see, faggot?" "Stop looking at my dick, faggot." I gathered my stuff and hustled away. That wouldn't be the last time they'd gang up on me. Another time, on my way out of the locker room, a group of guys started pushing me around by the backpack. Before I knew it, my face met the floor. My brother happened to be walking down the hallway, saw what was happening, and got them to leave me alone. Though I was relieved, I was also overwhelmed with shame—while I knew he loved me and wanted to protect me, I could see that I was an embarrassment to him, too. I can only imagine what they said to him later. I didn't want to be what they were calling me, and I'm sure my brother didn't want to be related to one, either. Once the guys dispersed, he hurried away, and we never said a word to each other about it.

Based on the way people around me talked about gay people, I felt like being attracted to men meant I was repulsive, something to be shunned and feared, though I was the one who was scared most of the time. While they all likely had the same amount of exposure to out gay people that I'd had (i.e., basically none), the way my peers talked about "fags" and everything that was "like, so gay" made me even more fearful of both myself and what could happen to me if my peers knew who I truly was.

But what was so confusing was that the message wasn't just "Gay men are predatory swamp creatures." It was something more like "Gay men are predatory swamp creatures . . . who are also extremely vulnerable to attack." Alongside all the demonizing, there was a competing narrative of the gay person as victim, or the gay person as prey. The idea was that we were menaces who had to be vanquished. If a gay person was in the news, it was likely about how they'd been harassed, bullied, beaten up, or murdered. All the horror stories traumatized me, but I was especially affected when I learned about what happened to Matthew Shepard, the college student who was brutally murdered in Laramie, Wyoming, in 1998. His story wasn't exactly familiar, but it approached the edges of reality for me—it seemed like it could happen to someone like me in Northern Michigan. I had nightmares about him. As a result, I never would have suggested that I was gay—or even broached the subject of anyone else being gay, just, like, you know, hypothetically speaking—out loud to anyone, even people I trusted. Would the people I trusted turn on me, or worse? I didn't want to find out.

I now understand that this is how homophobia works: when people are scared or feel threatened, they puff themselves up, like certain funny-looking birds, to make what's threatening them feel small. At the time, it worked on me. I lived in a swirl of mixed messages, which added to the sense that I was some kind of unknown *thing*, whose characteristics were so freakish that they were difficult for even me to understand.

I know that there were certainly other closeted gay people around me, in school and in Traverse City. But they must have felt the same way that I did—unsafe, afraid, alone, and ashamed. My friend Garret, who was on the bowling team with me, also came out after high school. We must have seen something in each other, not romantically but that we were two outcasts who didn't blend in very well. We never discussed boys or our sexuality until much later in life. Even when we'd get together with friends to watch *The Rocky Horror Picture Show* or sing along to musicals, not a word was spoken. Ever.

My only positive exposures to homosexuality were mediated and re-moved. I watched a lot of *Will and Grace*, even as my parents or brothers protested and demanded *Seinfeld*. I wished that I could live somewhere like New York City, where it would be OK to be like someone on that show, where I could find friends and acquaintances who would be kind to someone "like that." (Also, I would gladly have lived in Will's apartment.) I remember the fear of laughing perhaps too enthusiastically whenever Sean Hayes's hilarious character, Jack, entered the room, or when an offhand gay joke was made. Would they think I was gay? Watching the show in front of my family was like torturous therapy. I loved seeing someone "like me" on TV, but I didn't want anyone to see that I loved it.

Another glimmer of hope came in the form of Ellen DeGeneres—I knew she was gay, and I also knew my mom watched her show with admiration. Still, gayness was something distant, almost like a luxury or privilege. People on television could have it—not an awkward high school student from the middle of nowhere, who worked two jobs and went to church and would probably live in the same place his whole life. It almost felt as if growing up somewhere like Northern Michigan meant it was impossible that I could be gay—gay people weren't found in places like that. If they happened to show up there, it was a mistake, and I was not going to be a mistake. There had to be some other explanation for my personality, my difference.

There was a lot of pressure in school and in my town to hurry up and achieve the "American dream." I was beginning to realize that, no matter how hard I worked, I was never going to be less gay, but it seemed possible that I could get smarter and achieve more if I put my mind to it. People without much money can always imagine they're on the verge of getting more; being gay did not feel like something I could get out of. (Now, of course, I wouldn't want to get out of it.) It was starting to feel like the thing that was going to prevent me from achieving anything at all—that is, if anyone found out. I was too afraid to think about my sexuality in a way that would help me understand it.

My sense of style was also hampered by my desperation to be a part of something solid and defined. I've already mentioned the Hawaiian shirts. For some reason, I must have thought that wearing Hawaiian shirts was a shortcut to popularity and acceptance? Dressing like a dad on vacation isn't the *least* masculine thing I can think of, but it's still hilarious to look at old photos and see me in a series of aloha patterns. I don't think I ever thought I would fully blend in with either the farm kids or the jocks, but I really didn't want to stand out, so the Hawaiian shirts were and are *very* perplexing. Perhaps I thought that they mimicked the beachy brands favored by the well-off kids. I could barely step into a Hollister without feeling like a total fraud. I remember begging my mom to let me shop at American Eagle because that's what all the cool kids wore, but the clothes were much more expensive than what was on clearance at Kohl's. Similarly, a jacket that only *looked* like a North Face would save my parents tons of money, but we all wanted the real deal because the cool, rich kids could tell the difference. (The look was to wear a hoodie underneath a North Face jacket. Remember, this was Northern Michigan—we had to feel warm to look cool.) I was usually shocked at how good Mom was at finding deals. I knew Mom felt a lot of pressure to give us what we asked for, but the truth was, unnecessary luxuries weren't reasonable. Kids are always going to judge one another at school, especially on their appearances, and Mom knew that a warm coat, and not a brand, was what was going to keep her kid warm. She's the reason I still check TJ Maxx first, always.

When it came to getting ready for school. I was so absorbed with making sure I looked "normal" (i.e., straight) that I would put on an outfit, go to the bathroom, look in the mirror, return to my room, and try another option. My brothers would poke fun at me for changing outfits so often that I would sometimes take multiple options to the bathroom so they didn't see me traversing the hallway as much. Once, during a school spirit week, the class council sold purple T-shirts, and because of the ridiculous gender stereotypes I'd grown up learning (purple being a "girl color"), I was so afraid that wearing the shirt would give away my big secret. Despite all this preparation and analysis, nothing I wore would help me escape my fear of rejection. I simply didn't fit with the "cool enough to wear purple" kids. (By the time I got married, though, that had changed—purple was one of our wedding colors.)

Still, I wasn't a total loner. I had a varied group of friends, a couple very close, and more that I didn't become close with until after college. Most came from what you might say were my eccentric extracurricular activities. Along with those I met doing community theater, I had a lot of friends from the bowling team. Yes, we had a bowling team, and yes, I was on it. Very on it. I was highly competitive, bowling six days a week, and in high school I had a decent average of around 190. I was also on a recreational bowling league, which gave me more time to practice. Later, when I was living at home and going to the community college, I bowled on a league with my parents. Most of the adults called it a "drinking league," but I was there to win. Young Chasten took bowling very, very (deep inhale) seriously. (Exhale.)

Another core group of friends belonged to a program called Odyssey of the Mind—"OM" for short—which was essentially a creative problem-solving competition blending many technical and performance elements of theater, forensics, and robotics. Each team had to devise an eight-minute skit that would satisfy a list of criteria. One team would choose a problem in the fall and have until spring to write the skit, make the costumes, build the set, and perfect the scorecard to ensure we could be awarded the maximum number of points in each category. An essential element of OM was that it was completely student driven, which meant that parents and coaches weren't "allowed" to help in the construction or writing. (You could always tell when *those* schools rolled into competition. No way those ten-year-olds had built that set.) (I'm not bitter.) One year, an element of our problem required our main character, the hero of the story, to communicate with animals and help them in some way. So we wrote a skit about a hero with the ability to talk to birds through song. While trekking through the forest, he and his knucklehead of a sidekick (enter Chasten) stumbled upon a bird living in captivity (a cage made of straws and cardboard) and had to fend off his captor (a woman hell-bent on collecting the feathers of rare birds for her elaborate outfits, which were constructed from the clearance rack at Jo-Ann Fabric). Then they celebrated the rescue with a song and dance (both generous descriptions of what we actually did in front of the judges). As a team we would write the script, build the set, and assemble the costumes.

My teams were always pretty good, and during my junior year, we went to World Finals, which was held in Ames, Iowa. Out of thirty-five teams, we placed fourteenth. (While researching this book, I discovered that all the World Finals scores are still available online. I have to say, I remembered us doing a lot better. . . .) Even though we didn't win, my mom, who made the trip with me, was very proud. The dissonance isn't lost on me now. There I was, in tights and a costume of old bath towels, winning medals for singing, dancing, and jumping around in a feather boa, while my brothers were winning medals for hockey and football. My family has been competing in OM for decades, but still, it's one thing to go to the World Finals for, essentially, being flamboyant, and it's another to sing Celine Dion in the basement. The first is a kind of queerness that can be explained away as a competition or performance; the second feels much more volatile. Most of the kids from Traverse City who had gone to World Finals went home early to attend junior prom, but I stayed in Iowa for the awards ceremony. I knew we weren't going to win, but I felt more at home there than I would have in the dimly lit gymnasium back home. Though some people would consider missing junior prom to be a crushing disappointment, I didn't mind at all. I got away with dumping my date and was content to spend more time with my mom, my drama teacher, and other OM competitors from all over the world. I did feel left out, a little less popular, but all in all, it made sense for me to not be there. I was getting a glimpse at what my creativity could do for me in the wider world. Now a part of me does wish I'd experienced prom—that I had gotten to dress up, watch my date awkwardly fumble with a boutonniere until someone's mom had to step in to pin it on me instead, and perform the YMCA along with my classmates as a chocolate fountain burbled in the background. In fact, I never went to a school dance. But ultimately I'm OK with it, because I wouldn't have been able to go as myself. I belonged in the arena with the other geeks.

Another safe space I found was the theater, both in school and at the Old Town Playhouse in downtown Traverse City. My first big break was in sixth grade for a local production of *The Best Little Christmas Pageant Ever*. I was cast as the lead, Charlie. This was a big deal, and everyone in my household heard me talk about it *ceaselessly*. The night of the auditions, a local production company was also scouting kids to be in a TV commercial for a waste management company. (Sexy, I know.) Not only did I get the lead in *The Best Christmas Pageant Ever*, but about a week or so later, I got the call that I had landed the commercial gig. A hundred bucks, an entire day off school, and I got to see myself on television for a few months, happily riding a bike around Traverse City. Behind me, early CGI transformed items around town into the products from which they had been recycled. You would think that appearing in a recycling commercial would result in extreme teasing, but some of the kids at school thought it was pretty cool, rushing up to me in the hallways to tell me they'd seen me on TV the night before. Not in a cheerleaders-hanging-on-the-arms-of-the-quarterback way, but I was still, like, pretty cool. At least for a few weeks.

In retrospect, I would have seemed out of place even ignoring the fact that I was, unbeknownst to even myself, gay: I was a farmer/actor/nerd you might have recognized from the Christmas-tree farm or the recycling commercial, who could often be spotted wearing Hawaiian shirts while driving his fifteen-year-old minivan to his job as a busboy at the Mexican restaurant. I was clearly a little different. Besides bowling, Odyssey of the Mind, and theater, I could be found at home reading, organizing my extensive flag collection, or down at the barn taking care of the animals. Once I started working, my schedule was packed enough that I didn't have much time to feel lonely or ostracized. Looking back, though, I don't remember a lot of joyful high school experiences, just isolation. Once during Thanksgiving break when I was in college, I met up at a bar with some former classmates, whom I'd gotten close with after graduation. Gathered around the table sharing our memories from high school, I realized I didn't have much to offer by way of crazy nights and ex-lovers. I listened as they all reminisced about stuff I'd thought only happened in movies: times their parents had gone out of town and they had thrown huge parties. Kids puking in the sink and making out in the hot tub. Who got drunk? Who was in the hot tub with whom? Remember when his parents came home and the house was completely trashed? All I could think was that I could have never imagined doing those kinds of things in high school. I couldn't even believe that other people had done them. I'd never thought of myself as a prude, but, like, *was I?* How did I not see (or get an invite to) any of this? The nights I remembered were double features at the movies, playing

Nintendo or SimCity at Garret's mom's house, and staying home alone, when I would close my bedroom door, climb into bed early, and just stare out the window at the bright Northern Michigan stars, dreaming of an escape, wondering what, if anything, was in store for me.

....

And then, an opportunity presented itself one day in German class during my junior year of high school. I had started taking German in the seventh grade, and in my junior year I applied for the Congress-Bundestag Youth Exchange program, a joint effort between the American and German governments that allowed a group of high school students to spend their senior years studying in Germany, living with German host families. When my high school German teacher, Frau LaBonte, told our class about the program, it seemed as if someone were waving a golden ticket in front of all of us and only I could see it. I asked her to clarify that the year was free as I took a flyer from her and immediately began preparing the sales pitch for my parents.

As soon as I told them about it—even that it was free!—they were wary. They were probably worried it *would* end up costing a lot of money somehow, but they also thought it would be dangerous. Neither of them had traveled overseas before, and my mom didn't want her "baby" to be gone for a year. I had a great relationship with my parents in high school, and I think they saw my desire to leave as a betrayal, or a rejection of what they worked so hard to build for me at home.

Like many, my parents had lived in the area all their lives. In the circles I grew up in, leaving was considered suspect, as if you thought you were "too good" for everyone else. Everything you could ever possibly want or need was right in our backyard. You were supposed to be grateful for what you had. My family was an entire world of its own. If I had one eye on a different, "wider" world, what would that say about them?

I dreamed about Germany for weeks. In class, I would imagine flying in a huge plane across the ocean, arriving in a new place, making new friends, going to a new school (where I would no doubt be known as the exotic exchange student others admired), and, most importantly, being in a safe place where I would fit in. In what could have been my first act of rebellion, I forged my dad's signature on my application for the Congress-Bundestag Youth Exchange program and waited with bated breath.

This was highly unusual. I did *not* disobey my parents. When they said to call home at 9 p.m., I called at 8:50. If they said be home at 11 p.m. and I pulled into the garage at 11:10, I would apologize profusely. I had seen enough of the aftermath of their "disagreements" with my brothers to know exactly what my fate would be if I broke the rules. When we were in high school, it was the revocation of driving privileges, and no fun on the weekends. I couldn't stomach the loss of my Saturday morning bowling league. But I didn't feel like I was breaking rules when I sent in the application. In part because I just wanted to apply as an experiment, to see if the program would even take someone like me. On paper I didn't seem like the outcast I felt in school; I may have been testing the waters to see if I seemed like a freak to a panel of strangers assessing my adaptability to a German host family. What was the worst that could happen? I'd only have to tell my parents what I'd done, but their disappointment in me would have to be mitigated by pride and how excited I was to get the opportunity. Only one hundred kids got to go each year!

Soon enough, I got a letter from the program inviting me for an interview, so it was time to tell my parents the truth. I adopted a strategy of nonchalance, downplaying that this event had resulted from any action of my own. Hey, Mom and Dad, the German program invited me for an interview—isn't that cool? Mom was very skeptical, and I think a little heartbroken, because she understood I would probably be accepted. I had good grades, I had studied German for years, and I think she knew that, although I didn't fit in at school, I was well suited for this type of program, which required independence and responsibility. She knew I wanted to leave the nest—the nest she had worked so hard to build for me.

A few weeks after my interview, I got a letter from the program letting me know I'd been waitlisted. When I called to find out exactly what that meant, they told me that I was on a list of kids to whom they would offer a spot if any of the accepted students dropped out. As soon as they started explaining it to me, my heart sank. I knew no one would ever drop out, especially kids like me who couldn't afford to study overseas otherwise and were now essentially being handed a way out of their small towns.

I was crushed. But then, a few months later, I came home from school and my mom and dad sat me down. The program had called while I was at school. Someone had dropped out, and my name was first on the list. I could tell they were very proud of me, even as my mom hugged me, wiped her tears, and retreated to the kitchen to make dinner. For all the dreaming I had done about running away from school, I also felt guilty seeing just how much they were going to miss me.

The program brought us accepted students to Washington, DC, for a week of orientation before we headed off to Germany. I had been so excited about my adventure to another country, I was unprepared by what an adventure it was just to see the capital of my own. We toured the monuments, met with our representatives, and discussed the importance of representing the United States while abroad. While some of the students seemed miffed by the slow build to our departure, I was overwhelmed with just how dramatically my life was changing, and I hadn't even left the country yet. Every night that week I used a phone card Mom had sent me with to call home and tell my family about what I saw.

At the end of the week, about a hundred of us got on a bus and headed to Dulles Airport. (There's a joke to be made here about this being the first time anyone was excited to go to Dulles.) I stayed awake the entire flight, watching the plane icon move slowly across the flight map on the little television screen on the back of the seat in front of me, thrilled that life was whisking me so far away. When we landed in Frankfurt, I caught a connecting flight to Leipzig, and from there I rode a train for the first time in my life, north to the small town of Zerbst, just outside Magdeburg. A small group of us would live in and around that town for the rest of the summer while we took intensive language training five days a week.

Stepping off the train with my bags in the July sun, I nervously scanned the platform for a host family I had only seen in pictures. They lived in a small village about a three-mile bike ride outside the city, and as soon as I met them, it became clear that my German was not as good as I had thought. You can study a language for years, but some things just don't feel natural unless you have to speak it. The awkward silence that filled the car as they drove me from the train station home was enough to fuel the production of many flash cards. When they showed me to my room, it hit me that I had just upended my busy but regimented life for something really unknown. That I was on the other side of the world, far away from my family, far away from my friends, and that because I had done this I was now responsible for getting to know people whose language I didn't speak very well but whose home I would be living in. I suppose teaching kids this responsibility was the point of the program, but still. The bed was as hard as pronouncing the German word for ice skating. (It's *schlittschuhlaufen*—good luck.) I set my bags down, took a deep breath, and walked into the kitchen to ask for a glass of water, mostly because that was a sentence I knew how to say.

Our language courses were held in a local school building, a former monastery that dated back to five hundred years before the Declaration of Independence was signed. Just down the street, a hollowed-out church stood towering over the main traffic circle, a reminder of more recent history. On lunch breaks, we would walk to the corner bakery, where each day the kind woman behind the counter would enthusiastically greet the flock of culture-shocked, carb-loving teenagers flooding her store. We ate *a lot* of pretzels. In the evenings I would bike a few kilometers home, have dinner with the family, and then read or study quietly in my room. My host brothers didn't seem to want to hang out with me—I don't think I was the cool American they had thought they were getting. I didn't really have the words to hang out with other boys in English, and I most definitely didn't have them in German. "So, uh, what's up? Would you like something to read?" was about the extent of my small talk at that point. Sorry, *Jungs*.

After the language program was over, we went off to our full-year families. Mine lived in Mecklenburg-Vorpommern, the lakes region of northern Germany, and I was very excited to move in with them. Before I left for Germany, my future host brother had found me on MySpace, and we'd been chatting for a few months; he had recently returned from an exchange year in the States. But as is usually the case with culture clashes, things began to derail as soon as I arrived at their house. Since it was still summertime, the family was very excited to take me to the lake where they had a little piece of property. This sounded good to me; I told them, in my improving but still not great German, that we had lots of lakes where I was from, too.

What we don't have as much of in Northern Michigan is public nudity. Anyone who's spent time in Germany, especially the former East Germany, may know where this is going, but although I'd been treated to many *"Kultur"* lessons in my five years studying German, I had not been introduced to this particular custom. I had barely been able to change in the company of others in the locker room at school. As soon as we stopped the car, my host family— mom, dad, son—went down to the water, stripped completely naked, and jumped in. I was torn between competing impulses: *Am I supposed to do this?* and *I cannot do this*. I later learned that naked swimming—as well as naked sauna and naked hiking—was part of a larger popular German movement called *Freikörperkultur* (literally, "free body culture"). At the time I just felt like I was a test case in culture shock. I dragged my suitcase out of the car, brought it inside, and dug through everything I'd brought with me until

I finally found my swimsuit. When I emerged from the house, I saw the family trudging back up the lawn with their towels. While toweling off bare-ass naked right there in front of me (an entire hour after our first meeting), the mom said, "Something something eating cake," so I decided to forgo the lonely swim and sit down and eat cake with them. In my swimsuit. The cake was dry, and so was the conversation. They had put their clothes back on, but I was still too embarrassed to make eye contact with any of them.

A few times during the year, all the exchange students would get together for conferences and trips abroad, and there was one guy in particular I hung out with a lot. One night, a group of us were hanging out enjoying some drinks at our hostel, and while everyone was chatting and laughing, he reached over and touched my leg. I was so nervous—not only because that's usually what happens when someone you like touches you, but also because I definitely liked it. My enjoyment of the drunken leg grazing seemed to prove just what I was so afraid of. Later that night, on the way back to our rooms, we ducked into a private corner in the hostel and kissed each other. This was not a romantic thing you see in the movies, where a couple mischievously finds a secret spot to steal a kiss. Oh, no. This was sloppy and scary and thrilling and humiliating all at the same time. It wasn't just lips meeting lips; it was more teeth meeting teeth. (Thank God neither of us had braces.) I think we were both embarrassed about how bad we were at it. I don't know how we both made it out without black eyes.

But then it was over with, and we both had kissed a boy.

I went to bed filled with joy and dread. Unfortunately, I sort of had a girlfriend at the time, another American in the program. I hadn't really been in any relationships before, and I think she knew I was gay, even if I wasn't ready to admit it yet. Nothing about our relationship was romantic, but we enjoyed hanging out together and traveling together and being there for each other. I wasn't pretending to like her—she was wonderful—but I was obviously pretending to *like* her. I wanted so desperately for this *thing* inside me to be untrue. But it was becoming increasingly clear to me that I was gay, and that I was hurting her, and I felt terrible about it. I was also hurting myself by not being honest about who I was and what I was feeling. I was consumed by my anxieties about being gay, and no matter how loud I screamed or how hard I cried, they wouldn't go away.

Some part of me had started to feel like I had wasted my time in Germany by trying to keep my real self hidden. I was still attached to the idea that if I could just push myself hard enough to date a girl, to kiss a girl, to be with a girl, I could change. I had run so far away from home to escape my doubts about all that, but what I didn't understand at the time is that you cannot run away from those things. Your soul, your truth, your identity, your fears—they all follow you.

I ended up bouncing around with a few host families throughout the year. My second-to-last host family decided late in the year that they didn't want an exchange student anymore, and it really hurt. I felt like I was finally adjusting not only to being far away from home but to the truth I was beginning to discover about myself. Their rejection came just as I was peeking around the closet door, and I was fearful that going back home would mean more than just leaving Germany. However, with just a couple of months left to go, I landed in my last family, thanks to some tireless advocacy from one of my dearest German friends, Franzi. Franzi was wonderful, and very German in every way: she was super-straightforward, with the driest sense of humor, and engaged in the typical northern German custom of wearing a raincoat even when it was sunny. She was also focused on being there for people emotionally. She convinced this last family to take me in even though they usually only hosted people for a month, and she made sure I had plans on the weekends and people to hang out with. She pushed me to improve my German by only speaking German with me (unless I confessed my brain just couldn't take it anymore). She was a staunch ally and a great teacher.

At my last host family's home, back near Zerbst, where the year began,

Mutti and *Vati*, as I came to call them, made a big effort to make me feel welcomed and loved. Mutti was an exuberant and loving woman who wore parts of her hair dyed different shades of red. She was the most accommodatingly strict host mom you could imagine, always sending me to school with sweets and making my favorite dishes for dinner even as she demanded I perfect my pronunciation and grammar. It often took me twenty minutes to finish a story at her dinner table because she corrected every word.

Still, when I moved into their home, my depression was deepening, and all I can really remember is feeling completely deflated. It was strange: I missed home desperately, but I was also dreading going back. It felt like something inside me had torn open in Germany and I couldn't mend it. All the logistical and interpersonal drama I experienced there didn't help, but ultimately I knew all the relocations and language bloopers had little to do with what was actually bothering me.

One day Franzi and I were hanging out in my room, sitting on the mattress and talking. I told her I felt like something was eating me alive, consuming all my possibilities, focus, and will. Since Franzi was so supportive (and, ultimately, lived thousands of miles away), I told her that I had such a strong attraction to men that I thought I might be bisexual. She replied, in the lovably direct German way, that maybe I was just gay, adding that there was nothing wrong with that at all and that she would still love me. I just *knew* that if I came out, I would lose my family and my friends, but something about having been away for so long meant I couldn't just go back to how I'd been before.

Franzi's frankness was almost profound. "Maybe you're just gay." It felt almost illicit to hear her say that. It might have been embarrassing if it wasn't so shocking. I'd never heard anyone say it so matter-of-factly before—what do you mean, you can just *be gay*? I had only known it as a terrible fate, something you should resist with all your power. It was striking to hear someone talk about it as if it were just another thing you could be.

4

Running: Part One

I realize it's a little cheesy to say that travel changed my perspective on myself, but often sentimentality shows up when we need it the most. Luckily or not, I didn't have time to dwell on it. Despite not working out as I'd imagined it, going to Germany was ultimately freeing, and I mean beyond the usual things people say about Europe: that it's more socially liberated, that class differences are ironed out a bit because of more robust welfare systems, that people are more comfortable interacting with other cultures and customs. (All these things are true, or true to a point; the waves of nationalist populism sweeping the continent have shown that we shouldn't take them for granted.) But I'm talking about something else. When I was there, I stood out for an obvious reason—I was American, and I spoke German imperfectly, with an accent. This meant that the more subjective ways I stood out at home, for being an oddball and a "sissy," seemed less significant by comparison. My Americanness was awkward but not prohibitive; I was in Germany in order to "promote cultural exchange" between Germany and the States, after all, so in fact my difference was treated as a good thing—in theory, at least. Nobody there noticed the things that made me seem different in Michigan. I saw something that I'd intuited by watching

Will & Grace and bingeing on musicals: being gay didn't necessarily mean the same thing to everyone as it did to my conservative community.

This, plus the distance that allowed me to gently experiment with kissing a boy (or maybe what I mean is the distance that allowed me *to drink enough alcohol* to gently experiment with kissing a boy), allowed me to return home understanding that I was gay. I had attempted to date a girl and failed. I had attempted to kiss a boy and succeeded. The former made me feel horrible and the latter made me feel like I wanted to do it again (minus the awkwardness). Oh, and I also got really good at German.

But knowing I was gay didn't make me feel any better. In fact, I was a complete mess. Whatever joy and confidence I'd gained from being accepted to the exchange program, making friends in a foreign country, and kissing a boy for the first time were contaminated by my conviction that my family and community were not going to accept the new me. As soon as I had gotten a little comfortable admitting what I'd realized about myself, I had to go back to a life where everyone else made me feel I had to keep it a secret. It seemed that I could either be honest and lose everything, or continue living with this fundamental part of myself buried under my trademark cheerful responsibility and agreeableness, the stress of which would gnaw at me until there was nothing left.

I already felt like I'd disappointed my family by going abroad in the first place. Coming out would not only disappoint them once again; it would also confirm their suspicions that venturing outside Traverse City wasn't a good idea. *He shouldn't have gone*, they'd think. *The Europeans must have radicalized him!* The possibility that they would think Europe had made me gay was additionally upsetting. If they took me seriously, they would think I was a predatory swamp creature, a sinner who deserved to be cast out; if they decided my coming out was just a phase, residue of Europe's influence, they would be denying all the pain I'd already felt about my sexuality. The prospect of being doubted or waved away was humiliating. I felt totally trapped.

This is a trap many queer Americans find themselves in, especially those living in rural, red places. Most often, the fear of rejection, or worse, pushes people further into the closet. In many places, it's unsafe for queer people to be out. That's not up for debate—it's just a fact. While traveling the country on behalf of the campaign, I met couples who had been together longer than I've been alive, tearful to see me in person as the husband of an openly gay man running for president. I didn't have to say much of anything—the simple fact that I existed was, to some, a miracle. But then they'd lean in and tell me they're not out. They couldn't be. Sometimes they would tell me they drove for hours to attend one of my visits, out of excitement, yes, but also just for the safety of distance. They couldn't risk anyone seeing them waving a rainbow "PETE" placard. These interactions always left me with such a sense of obligation and gratitude.

....

I came home in June, graduated from high school, and prepared to start classes at the local community college in the fall. While I was in Germany, I had lost all motivation to continue with college applications to Michigan State, where most of my friends were headed and where I'd wanted to go for most of my high school career. I knew that if I came home and then rushed off to college I would break my mother's heart, again. With that, I knew there was much too much to deal with internally and *for me*. Before I returned home, I'd settled on attending community college in the fall.

I only lasted a few months back home before I decided I had to tell my parents.

Thanks to those early conversations with Franzi, it was much easier to slowly come out to other close friends at home than it would have been. I remember being nauseated and terrified when I told my friend Erin, but at the same time, I knew that being gay was OK—not some kind of incurable disease. But I still dreaded telling my mom and dad. It was right around the time my community college classes started, in August or September. I didn't concoct an elaborate plan about how I would do it—this wasn't a time for celebration, and there was no way to make it perfect. I anticipated that my life would explode as soon as it was over. When I came home from Germany, I'd told a couple friends that I thought I was bisexual, and like Franzi, they'd assured me that it was OK if I was gay. I knew that some people in my life would understand, but I could sense nervousness in even their support of me—it was still unsafe, and just extremely difficult, to be gay in Traverse City. I loved my parents so much, but I had a firm belief that I would be loved only conditionally in return. This turned out to be completely unfair of me, but at the time I thought for sure that my coming out would be an immense disappointment to them. I felt like I was destroying the dream they'd had for me: that I get a good job, marry a woman, and live nearby so that they would have full access to spoiling their grandkids. In those days, being gay didn't just mean I wouldn't marry a woman—it meant not getting married at all. Having kids as a gay man seemed even less likely.

I'd already packed my bags and started moving out of the house before I did it. I told a friend that I planned on telling my parents, and she told me that if I needed a place to go afterward I could come sleep at her house. I told her she should definitely expect me, because my parents were going to disown me. I slept on her floor the night before, if *slept* is the right word. I stayed up wondering how there could be anything next for me, counting down the hours until I lost everything I knew. That's how I thought about it—I never considered the freedom I'd feel once I was able to be myself in front of my parents and friends. I never fantasized about meeting a hot guy, falling in love, and traveling the world together. I didn't think a weight would be lifted off me. It was pure dread.

The next day, I went out into the living room with a letter for my mom. I don't remember exactly what it said. She was sitting in her chair, watching TV. The windows were open. It was sunny outside, and the wind was blowing through the screened windows. The dogs circled in the living room as I tearfully, shakily, handed her the letter. She read it slowly. When she was done, she looked up and began to cry. She asked if I was sick; I think she might have thought I had AIDS. I told her no—nothing was wrong. She asked if I was sure about this. I *was* sure. I don't remember where my dad was—I think she told him later.

My brothers' reactions were more straightforward: I remember feeling like they were embarrassed of and disgusted by me. They had no questions. This definitely wasn't the coming out that some children experience with their families. My brothers had always picked on me for being a sissy, and now in their eyes they had confirmation it was true. Not just any confirmation—I was daring to claim it as an identity myself. Though I was deeply ashamed, they saw my coming out as an act of defiance—they thought being gay was shameful enough that I should want to hide it forever.

Shortly after, I left.

....

Now, what comes next is not my parents' fault. I don't believe it was my fault, either, but the crucial thing to remember is that, while they have come a long way from what they believed the moment I came out, my parents never kicked me out. They never said, "Get out—you're not my son." My mother was mad that *I* was so set on leaving that I actually did it. Moments after I left, she called and demanded to know why. My dad even told me he loved me when I was on my way out.

Why did I do it? I'm sure my parents were confused and frustrated by my explanation at the time: I said that I was sorry, but I was such a disappointment that I couldn't stand to be in the house. We can call this a product of homophobia and the messages our culture sends to gay kids. I left because I was so embarrassed that I had to get away from them; I assumed that they were mad at me, that they wouldn't want to talk about it unless I somehow took it back, relegated it to temporary European radicalization. I couldn't stop thinking about all their conservative friends from church: while my parents weren't the type to talk about Jesus or openly proselytize, they had friends who did, and once those friends found out, I thought my parents would feel burdened by all the uncomfortable, scolding conversations they were going to have to have about me. I knew it would be an absolute embarrassment to my brothers as well. Some of their roughneck friends had made me feel so small and awful about myself already that I worried they would beat me up on behalf of my brothers. They didn't, but it wasn't that far from the realm of possibility.

That first night, I slept on my friend's couch, and after a couple of days she set up an inflatable mattress in her office. But she was studying for a master's at the time, and I felt like such an imposition that I sometimes slept in my car. The backseat of my Saturn Ion—purchased after the Mitsushitzu caught fire—was no Marriott, but it was solitude, a space away from all the noise. Completely alone and, at least what felt like it at the time, safe.

This went on for a couple of months, until one day my mom called me and told me to come home. I was completely exhausted and burst into tears. I felt like I hadn't exhaled in months. I said I missed them and I was scared. They said they wanted to make it work.

Early on I remember my mother saying, "I just don't know why you would choose something so hard." Even though I know my mother was well-intentioned, her response encapsulates the attitude well-meaning but less-informed people most often have when their kids come out: Why would I choose to be made fun of and demeaned and picked on? Why would I give up the possibility of family, "real" love, and a career?

But here's where my good fortune truly saved me. Even though it took a little bit of time, my coming-out story has a happy ending, and that made a world of difference. My parents welcomed me back into their home. My mom and dad asked questions and listened to me, and they welcomed my feedback, even when it was hard. Once they really understood, my parents could see it was just who I was, that it wasn't a choice for me. What *was* a choice was that we all decided to discuss it in good faith, to not jump to conclusions or accusations or fall back on stereotypes that had no basis in fact or experience.

A few months after I came out, I decided it was time to tell the only grandparent I had. My mother's mother, Wanda, was a force to be reckoned with both on and off the bingo field. She was a deeply religious woman, a devout Catholic who took tradition and family very seriously. (Though she'd sometimes lean over while we were kneeling and praying in church to tell me to keep walking after we took communion so we could beat the other families and get a good table at Big Boy.) I adored my grandmother. I spent a lot of time with her growing up, and in high school I'd drive by to check in on her and listen to her stories about the cherry farm or my mother's father, Jim, who passed when my mom was just thirteen. I loved to hear about all the adventures they had together during his years in the Coast Guard.

One evening, while Grandma was visiting, I asked if I could take a walk with her. We made our way outside and eventually found ourselves sitting in the front seat of her Buick Skylark. We sat in silence and I stared at her rosary dangling from the rearview mirror. The tears began to well as I fought to get the words out. I started to say, "Grandma, I . . ." but I choked. She immediately reached her hand over and rested it on my forearm. I felt her rings pressing into my arm as I struggled to get any words out. "I know, Chassers," she said. "And I love you just the same."

Of course, I eventually learned that being gay doesn't necessarily prevent you from having a family, love, and a career. But it did take a while— much longer than it needed to.

....

Looking back on my journey, I know I was lucky in so many ways. But in others, this was also a bad time for me to come out, and it set me on a pretty dark path. Of course, I don't regret doing it at all; I couldn't stand being in the closet, so I don't feel as if things could have gone any differently. But for the next few years, I couldn't see more than a couple of steps in front of me. There was a lot I didn't know how to figure out on my own, and I never allowed myself to imagine a future, much less start working toward one. After a year of upheavals in Germany, some of which were unrelated to my homosexuality, I had just started college, which was a waste at that point. I wasn't in a good place mentally or emotionally to be curious or to think about what classes would help me in any future job. I was disappointed in myself that I hadn't managed to complete my applications to the bigger schools, and I felt left out as my friends from high school began having all those freshman-year experiences that I was missing out on. All I could focus on was what my friends and parents thought of me and whether this new information would fundamentally change our relationship. Would I ever have a meaningful relationship with them again? What comes next?

One of my biggest regrets about those years is that I was so hard on my-self in every respect. Even after my parents and I made up, I was so obsessed with how people would react to me that I incorporated the horrible things I suspected they thought of me into my self-image, regardless of whether they actually expressed them. I never stopped to consider what *I* believed, what *I* thought, and it prevented me from making good choices for myself in many areas of my life. At the time I didn't know that what I was feeling were common symptoms of internalized homophobia. *Surely I don't have value*, I thought. *My feelings and emotions are not valid. I am an embarrassment.*

A few weeks after I returned from Germany, I picked up a job at Cherry Republic, the region's source (and tourist trap) for all things cherry. Feeling that a career in theater and the arts was out of reach, I decided to study nursing and go into healthcare. My mom had worked part-time at the hospital as a nursing assistant since I was young, and I thought I would be suited to caring for people the way she did. Soon, I got a job as a home health aide working with a nonverbal sixteen-year-old boy with cerebral palsy.

I really enjoyed taking care of him. I'd meet him at his bus stop and take him home, and his daily stretching session coincided perfectly with when *Ellen* came on TV. We'd laugh together at all her jokes. Soon, though, a job as a nursing assistant at the hospital opened up. It was a hard gig to land—the pay could push me over ten dollars an hour, especially if I was able to pick up overtime on overnight shifts—so I transitioned out of both other jobs so I could take it.

I loved working at the hospital. My responsibilities required taking patients' vitals, helping them to and from the bathroom, and a lot of cleaning. On my floor, many patients had been in surgery, and I liked being the nice guy who came in and made them laugh while they were down or hurting. I was also fast on my feet; I could finish double the sections other nursing assistants could, which meant the charging nurse didn't have to worry about giving me a high patient count. Many nurses liked me because I was meticulous and didn't cut corners but I wasn't annoying about it. Or maybe I was. All I know is, they never yelled at me for occasionally eating the ice cream that was supposed to be for patients.

Sustaining a full-time job at the hospital was the easy part—navigating college while trying to figure out who I was was another thing. Neither of my brothers lasted very long in community college, and as first-generation college students, we didn't know as much going in as some of our peers might have. For everything my parents had done to try to prepare me for a life after school, college wasn't necessarily the easiest puzzle to solve. The college experience certainly goes much smoother if you're equipped with mentors, an understanding of money, and a game plan. I know I was lucky to have blessings that many first-generation college students don't have.

I was starting to get pretty bad at the *school* part of nursing school. If I'd been at a different point in my life, I probably would have finished, but I wasn't talking to my family at first, and then, when I went home, I was in no position to focus on anything but surviving. I couldn't figure out who I was, and I couldn't focus because I was so exhausted from working full-time and, for a while, not having a stable place to sleep. I was also beginning to date men, which, as anyone who's done it knows, is no simple feat. Though I had found a community of other gay folks in Traverse, I also seemed to attract people who wanted to take advantage of me.

I decided I needed a change. With some community college credits under my belt, and with my parents back in my life and the stability of living with them helping me to feel slightly more secure, I transferred to the University of Wisconsin–Milwaukee. I seemed to be attracted to the peculiar and unique, so of course I found a college in . . . Milwaukee. If this seems kind of weird, that's because it was. I found a house that I could share with three or four other guys; it had an illegal bedroom in the attic, you just had to walk through an unfinished part (carefully) to get to it. There was no heating or cooling system, so I would have to use a space heater and descend a rickety staircase to use the bathroom. No big deal. I had wilderness skills. I wanted something completely different from what I knew, and I was going to get it.

My parents helped me move to Milwaukee, and their reaction to this illegal attic bedroom I found on Craigslist could be best summed up as "What the fuck?" I'm sure they did not want to leave me there. And I can only imagine how my mother felt driving away from me. Even though I did my best to assure her I was fine—I could afford it, and it was just two blocks from campus!—I know my parents struggled to understand why I was hell-bent on this college dream, when the comforts of home, and any number of respectable full-time jobs, were waiting for me back in Michigan.

Wilderness skills did not prepare me for having to cover utilities bills or for roommates who don't pay their share or wash their damn dishes. By the time I got to classes in biochemistry and chemistry for nursing, I was seriously behind. After just one semester at UWM, I failed and came back home, once again ashamed that I couldn't prove that the life I wanted could work out. I moved back in with my parents, re-enrolled in the community college, and got a job at Toys "R" Us. My attitude toward all this was surely darkened by my frustrations with failing at school and moving back home. I sat at the cash register, where my job included inundating customers with dumb questions as their screaming kids demanded to be allowed to play with the toys they were about to pay for. "Would you like to sign up for a two-year warranty for your light-up piece of bullshit?" "Would you like to join our birthday program?" "Can I interest you in some batteries for that obnoxiously loud electronic action figure that's going to ruin your life?" Because the customers disliked this as much as I did, they usually responded by yelling at me. I had to work on Black Friday. Enough said.

This lasted only for the holiday season. At some point, I decided that part of my inability to focus was due to a suppression of my true passions and identity. *Fuck it*, I said to myself, thinking of all the teachers who'd encouraged me to be practical, *I'm going to study theater, because that's where I've always felt like I belonged.* I looked at going back to Wisconsin and used a Midwestern university exchange program for tuition discounts to go to the University of Wisconsin at Eau Claire, where I enrolled as a theater major.

By now I had a plethora of random credits and an impressive amount of student debt. The decision was a typical early-twenties one—based on vague associations I had that didn't especially correspond with reality. I didn't want to be at home. I was embarrassed to go to a school where my friends were; I think I was afraid of rejection or being judged for not having done college the "right way." I wanted to be far away. And looking at my options, the getaway I was looking for was waiting for me in . . . northern Wisconsin.

Stop laughing. That's important. They have really good cheese there.

If I'd had people close to me who could have advised me on these kinds of life decisions, they helped me make sure I was prepared before I took a leap and went to college. On top of having a sink-or-swim attitude toward us kids once we turned eighteen, my parents didn't know much about the ins and outs of going to college, despite all the wisdom they gave me in other areas of life. They didn't go to college themselves, and everything from filling out a FAFSA form to selecting the right school was foreign to them.

The idea of just going to school full-time was outside their experience, though they didn't disapprove of it. They were wildly proud of me for trying. I was operating on borrowed wisdom, without a close academic counselor or mentor, as well as borrowed money. The notion sold to me in high school was that if I could just get a bachelor's degree, everything would work out.

I put everything I owned into the back of my car and drove north, ready to try, one last time, to make my dream of graduating from college come true.

Two

5

How to Succeed in Wisconsin
Without Really Crying

While I was studying, student loans kept me from sinking below
the level of constantly broke. Afterward, having to pay them back
kept me from rising above it.

I started taking out loans when I enrolled in the local community college at eighteen, and I had no idea what I was getting myself into. I took the
words *financial aid* at face value: I needed aid with my finances, so I went
to the relevant office and asked for this. I sat down at the desk and looked
at the counselor with tears in my eyes and asked how to make it all add
up. Even though I had shelter at first—whether in my car, on my friends'
couches, or, once we reconciled, in my parents' basement bedroom—I
couldn't understand how other people made it work. It was very simple
arithmetic: The money I earned working part-time at the hospital was less
than the total cost of all my bills and expenses. Tuition, books, gas, car insurance, and food were the bare minimum. The Mitsushitzu had recently
met its fiery end, too, so I had a car payment to deal with. I had splurged on
a 2004 black Saturn Ion, a car so luxurious that the company that manufactured it dissolved just a few years later. But there was no getting around the

fact that buying and maintaining a car was more expensive than not having a car, and no getting around the fact that I could not get around to class and work without one in Traverse City, Michigan.

The people working at the financial aid office told me I could use a loan to pay for books, gas, tuition, and whatever else I needed, so I took out a couple thousand dollars. Because I didn't have to pay rent, and I had a decently paid job at the hospital, and community college tuition is less expensive than most, that relatively small amount helped me a lot. The relief I felt when I had money in my account—even money that, technically, wasn't mine—was probably what kept me going at the beginning of my college career. Owing that amount of money was manageable, and since I'd always worked as much as I could in high school, I had no reason to assume that policy wouldn't continue throughout my college years. I just needed a little help starting out.

Like so many others in my generation, I found out that just getting on my feet cost a lot more than I imagined. When I moved to Milwaukee, I immediately needed to cough up about $700 for a security deposit and first month's rent. The next day I went to the college bookstore and spent more than $500 on textbooks and nursing school supplies. Then I went to the grocery store for the first time on my own and remembered shopping with Mom as a kid. Mom was scrupulous with coupons and kept to a list. I learned very quickly to make a budget at the grocery store, and Mom helped me with recipes that would stretch my dollar. This included a lot of peanut butter, but it had to be Jif. Sherri is known for cutting costs, but in our house growing up, Jif was an absolute must for Dad.

Dad knows a thing or two about peanut butter sandwiches. When my mother met him in high school, he was living off them. Dad was on his own from the age of seventeen, splitting his time between flirting with Mom at high school and flipping burgers at a local diner four nights a week. Dad would close the diner and then walk eight miles across town to a trailer he was sharing with a friend. Dad never had pocket money when he met my mom. When Mom found out he was wearing his coat at school every day because he didn't have clothes to change into, she started using her waitressing money to add to his wardrobe. Grandma was suspicious. The year they first met, Mom made a birthday cake for him. It was the first time he had ever blown out candles on a cake with his name on it.

So when we were growing up, my dad always joked with us that if you had Jif peanut butter on the shelf, you were doing just fine. Eventually, after years of hearing him repeat this mantra, I learned to appreciate this lesson in frugality and humility. In fact, I have two tattoos, one for Mom, an infinity symbol on my right calf, which I got after her cancer diagnosis, and one for Dad, the Jif logo on my left bicep. (Without the lettering, though—most people think it's a flag, but they can never quite guess the country.)

Shortly after moving to Milwaukee, I knew I needed to secure a regular source of income, but finding a place hiring full-time college students and a position that would work around my class schedule was difficult. After two months in, I knew the initial aid wasn't going to cut it, so I applied for more. Eventually I found a gig waiting tables at a new restaurant, but most nights we barely had any customers. The restaurant didn't last long. I felt like I should find a second job, but I was doing too poorly in my classes to add any hours. The lessons were really hard, and I was too exhausted and stressed from work to give them the attention they needed. Transferring had added costs, too—miscellaneous stuff you need to buy when moving. And even though I was living in an illegal attic bedroom, I still had to cover my share of the rent and utilities.

Figuring out how to make it all work on my own just became totally overwhelming. I would sit in anatomy and physiology lab nervously wondering if my tips at the restaurant were going to cover my car payment for the month.

The immediate pressure of having to cover bills and feed myself crowded out any thoughts of future obligation, and this cycle continued throughout my college career and all the tumultuous transferring I put myself through. I thought that going to college was what I was supposed to do, and that taking out loans was how I was supposed to pay for it if my Pell Grant didn't cover everything. I can't believe now how benign the process seemed to me at first, but I never thought to question it at the time, and neither did anyone around me.

I never discussed my financial situation with friends. I remember being at a theater party one night when a cast member was bragging about their dad's credit card. (The booze that night was on them.) While my parents would occasionally send pocket money or a care package, I also never asked for their help with bills. I didn't want to add to their stress, and I wanted to do this on my own. I wanted to prove that I could do it, and make it, on my own. I also didn't have anybody in my corner telling me how to make it work, or telling me to be careful taking out loans. I never questioned any advice I was given. I never expected that the people working in various financial aid offices were more interested in getting me out of their hair—and in getting their institutions paid—than in helping me make smart choices about my future. Many of these employees were very nice, and I don't believe they wished me harm. But I've since learned that a person might exhibit friendliness, a soothing affect, and basic courtesy without actually caring what happens to you in any meaningful sense. I expected that once I graduated, I'd have a job and pay it all back, because that's what everyone else seemed to believe, and certainly the student loan providers' cheerful assurances that they had my back did nothing to suggest otherwise.

But that's not how it works. I had no idea I was rapidly dooming myself to decades—if not a lifetime—of financial insecurity. (Peter would say on the presidential debate stage that he was the least wealthy candidate in the race and mention our household's six-figure student debt. It was true that, even without the debt, he still would have been the least wealthy candidate, but the debt was all mine.) Nevertheless, I see now that my experience with money till age eighteen was circumscribed and protected. To a certain extent

I just trusted that saving and spending was a process that would work out if I was conscientious and hardworking, because that was what my parents had taught me. And because, you have to admit, it makes a lot of sense. I watched my mother cut costs and stress about spending, but she always shielded us from the worst of it. She also had no conception of what college cost, both in terms of the sticker price and in terms of the limits it placed on how much you could work. The fact is that most people can't afford to spend an extra few thousand dollars (at best) every few months for several years, and most people can't afford to decrease their hours at work to give themselves more time to study. When my parents loaned me money to complete my 4-H projects, they had known how much the supplies I needed cost and how much I could reasonably expect to earn to pay them back; they were responsible lenders. Though big banks and the federal government *also* know how much things cost and how much students can reasonably expect to be accountable for to pay them back, they are *not* responsible lenders.

My finances—and my worries—were at their worst once I got to Eau Claire, the small art school in the Northwoods of Wisconsin. Before I arrived, a series of bad service jobs and hasty moves had left me with little to show for my bank account and my mental health.

As soon as I arrived, I felt like I'd found a little shelter from the storm—a secret college getaway populated entirely by "my people." Immediately I met some kids from the theater department because a professor walked me over to the greenroom, *the* place for theater kids to hang out, and introduced me (Midwestern hospitality at its finest). My visit was well timed. They invited me to audition for one of their student-written plays. Auditions were that night, so I decided to stick around. After auditions, I joined the theater troupe for a beer down the street at the hipster dive The Joynt, which was so familiar that I felt at home. A neon sign above the bar read "No light beer," the cigarette dispenser still worked, and a gin and tonic was $1.25. We all piled into tables in the front of the bar, where Eddie, the director (who would quickly become one of my closest friends and one day, a groomsman in our wedding), informed me that I had gotten the part. (It required playing a straight businessman, if you can believe it.)

I'd always felt like theater was a safe space, and finding it at this moment in life was so much of a relief that I committed to Eau Claire and switched my major to theater immediately. I knew nursing wasn't going to work out. Theater was home, and I was going to do my best to feel at home again. I even moved a month earlier than I thought I would in order to rehearse for the show.

A few weeks into my first semester at Eau Claire I felt like I was finally on a train headed somewhere. One evening, very early into my first semester, my professor and director, Dr. Jennifer Chapman, invited me into her office to chat after a rehearsal. I hadn't come out to any of my classmates just yet, but Dr. Chapman could sense I was in need of some guidance. As our chat ended, she pulled out a stack of DVDs. "I have something I want you to watch," she said. I went home and popped one into the computer, eager to see what she thought I should see. I stayed up late watching *Hedwig and the Angry Inch* and *The Adventures of Priscilla, Queen of the Desert*, just to name a few. Poking my head into her office the next day, I said, "I think you know something about me." She smiled. It was the first time an advisor had made room for me and asked me to open up about what I was feeling. Her mentorship and friendship got me through the rest of college.

Sitting in the greenroom I would look around and marvel at the cast of characters I had stumbled upon. I was making friends who were genuine and easy to talk to. For the first time, I was able to seek counseling for my depression, and I eventually found the strength to tell my friends what I was feeling as well. I had spent the first two years of college believing that I didn't belong, but more than that, I was also convincing myself I was unworthy of the big things I was chasing.

The theater community at Eau Claire was just what I needed to finish college. I was finally surrounded by other people who were interested in the same things I was, and the friendships that grew from all of those late-night rehearsals and study sessions made me feel like it was OK to be myself and to take on hard challenges. I started to feel like I wasn't alone and that I had worth.

The finances continued to be what they were. I was probably not as austere as I could have been. My budgeting strategies consisted of picking the cheapest sandwich at Erbert and Gerbert's—the sandwich chain founded in Eau Claire—and calculating how many extra ounces per dollar I got for purchasing the economy-sized Yellow Tail wine. It's hard to think about your budget when everything in your life feels tenuous and conditional; it's hard to resist small pleasures, like a burger or a fancy coffee, when you feel like life's bigger pleasures (love, stability, a sense of possibility) will remain out of reach forever. "If only they'd stop buying $5 lattes" is, of course, a common argument for the reason millennials can't get ahead in life. And on top of the random expenses and very limited cash flow, I was way too generous. If friends said they couldn't afford something, I'd put their groceries in with mine or pick up the bar tab. I knew what it was like to run out of money, and I felt for them. If you caught me at the right time of the month, I would have the money—and then suddenly I wouldn't.

Figuring out college alone was tiring, especially when it came to learning how to manage money. I hid a lot of it from my parents, eager to prove I could do this on my own. So often, the money part was more overwhelming than the studying part. Like many other middle-class kids who are lucky enough to even think about attending a four-year college, I felt like I leapt from the nest with no real idea what it would take to fly on my own.

....

In an effort to keep the loans to a minimum, I kept getting part-time jobs. The most notable was at Scooter's, the well-known gay bar in Eau Claire with a stage for drag shows and plasma TVs for Packers games. (Gay, but make it Midwestern.) If the theater group had a night at Scooter's, we went wild. (Because of course we did.) But although performance was our forte, we didn't dare try to outshine the local queens.

The first time I went to Scooter's, I flirted with the bartender for too long before he let me know he had a boyfriend. Still, he said, I was cute and should try to get a job there. "Yeah, totally," I said, thinking he just wanted more tips. I must have been underestimating my charm, because soon after, he found me on Facebook and sent me a message. He said he was planning on leaving Eau Claire, and Scooter's needed a replacement. I should interview.

They did not interview me. Instead, they told me to start whenever I wanted. The uniform was simple: be cute. This usually meant a V-neck and some shorts. Preening didn't come naturally to me—I was more chatty than cheeky—but Felicia, the drag queen I was working with, gave me tips on working the crowd as well as tending bar. She was tough, but I know she was looking out for me. "Uh, Felicia . . . ," I'd say, nervously approaching her with the cocktail shaker in hand, "how do I make a cosmopol—" She'd whip around, almost knocking off my glasses with her wig, point her nail at my chest, and say, "Kid, I'm only going to tell you how to make this once—am I clear?" I still know how to make a cosmo.

The bar was a beacon in remote northern Wisconsin: the clientele was generous, and the atmosphere always welcoming, and the queens were encouraging. Nevertheless, I was out of my element. I could mix drinks and manage ten orders at a time, but the flirting and the late nights didn't mix with my study habits. I lasted about six months. As is probably apparent, this was not exactly a labor-conscious environment, though the tips were good, and helped me stay above water for the length of my employment. The cash was nice at the end of the night.

But I didn't last long, and soon I needed a new job. The semester was starting again. To hold me over for the few months before I graduated, I took the first thing I found, another seasonal gig, this time at Eddie Bauer. Understanding that I would only be there for a few months, the manager assigned me to the role of greeter. When people would come in and ask where they could find a men's coat, I'd have to radio for a more senior employee to escort the customer over to the parkas. Customers would get irritated waiting for another employee to appear, torn between waiting and just walking over to the very visible coats themselves. They would ask, politely or sarcastically, if I couldn't just take them there, and I would have to say, seriously, no. But it was a job. And with the employee discount, you know everyone got an Eddie Bauer blanket or thermos that Christmas.

In many ways, I thrived in the theater community at Eau Claire, and I was so happy to have found the college experience I'd seen on TV and in movies, with all the curiosity, lifelong friends, love interests, and late nights at the bar I'd imagined. I got the opportunity to play some of the most exciting and challenging roles on the stage, like Louis in Tony Kushner's *Angels in America*. I spent so much time in the greenroom in the theater department at the Haas Fine Arts Center that it became my second, and very possibly preferred, home. It had a kitchenette, so during lunch or dinner you could often find me making mac and cheese on the stove. (Though the laundry room was always locked—rude!) Whenever the janitor would come around and empty the trash at night, she'd lock the door behind her and tell me to turn off the lights when I left. Some nights, when I stayed especially late to work on a paper, rather than walk to my apartment at 2 a.m., I'd sleep on the couch because it would make it easier to show up for my 8 a.m. class the next day.

I kept a collection of cereal bars, ramen noodles, and a ream of paper for printing an inordinate number of scripts and assignments under my chair in the greenroom. My friends started calling me the greenroom "hermit," but I didn't mind. I wanted to finish college so badly; I was so mad and embarrassed that all my vacillating had meant I wouldn't be able to finish in four years. I wasn't going to finish with honors, either, but I was determined to be the first in my family to graduate from college. During my last three semesters at Eau Claire, I got waivers to take on additional coursework, and tacking on classes during the summer and winter breaks, in an attempt to finish on time, but I ended up being one semester off. Having attended three different schools with three different concentrations, I was set to finish in the winter of 2011, after starting in the fall of 2007.

I thought I was going to graduate, and based on that assumption, I got a job at First Stage, one of the nation's premier children's theaters in Milwaukee. I was hired as a part-time teaching assistant, making $25 per class, with the initial agreement to teach two to four classes per week. This was in no way a job that would sustain me, but I was thrilled: theater had seemed so impractical, yet I'd gotten a position doing exactly what I'd gone to school to do. I knew this was the foot in the door I needed.

Then I was informed I had failed a class. I had taken a world history course packed with 150 other students, had missed a test, and had foolishly forgotten to make it up. Earlier in the semester, I had gone home to be with Mom because she'd had to have a skin cancer surgery, and the professor told me it would be OK to make up the test when I was back in Eau Claire. When I found out I'd failed the class, I panicked and emailed the professor, who didn't respond to any of my increasingly distraught messages. When I appealed to the administration for help, they told me the professor wasn't obligated to respond because that had been his last semester.

I was absolutely crushed and embarrassed—not least because I knew that meant my dream job was going to slip through my fingers. But when I approached the academy at First Stage to tell them that it wasn't going to work out, I was shocked to find that they didn't care about my lack of degree at all. "I'm sure you'll figure it out," they said. "We're excited to have you. It's fine."

For years I'd been moving around, living precariously, racking up tens of thousands of dollars in debt that I was somehow too overwhelmed to keep track of, all on the belief that I absolutely needed a bachelor's degree to get a decent-paying job, especially one in theater education.

It turns out that's not exactly how things work.

6

Ma'am, This Is a Starbucks

I don't regret going to college at all. I only regret that it costs so much, and that it's presented as a necessity. But I also know that my life at the time wasn't suited to academics. Looking back, I shouldn't have gone to college until I was ready financially and emotionally. I just wasn't ready to study. I would eventually receive my bachelor's degree, but not until sometime in 2014, when I was able to finish a class online. One stipulation of part-time financial aid was that you had to take a minimum of three classes, not just one, so I ended up taking what amounted to almost an entire extra semester in order to get my diploma.

I was unprepared for the student loan statements that started arriving a few months after I left Eau Claire. When I opened that envelope, the number felt like a direct punch to the gut. They were going to want their $70,000 back.

So after college, I continued living paycheck to paycheck. If I needed to put new tires on my car, a new set was out of the question. I just did it one by one. I once got a flat tire in Milwaukee, and the cheapest option, the mechanic informed me, "might get ya another week or so." I took the tire (and the risk). In college, I could reasonably pretend that I was just putting off dealing with my finances until I was in the stable position of being a college graduate. Now I had to realize that I might never be stable on this path. It was impossible to think about and impossible not to think about, as if the loans had cratered a huge hole in my life, and it was so deep that I didn't know if I would ever find a way to climb out of it.

I had just moved in with my friends Matt and Jeremy, who graciously allowed a part-time theater teacher to live in their basement bedroom. Spiders included in the utilities. The pay and (lack of) benefits package for a job at a nonprofit children's theater being pretty much what you'd expect, I had no health insurance and, on top of that, would need a significant supplement to my income. I hadn't had health insurance through college; Obamacare still wasn't in effect. (I hoped to stay a step ahead of any health issues throughout my studies; for prescription necessities, my mom would send me home with my backpack full of cold medicine and some leftover antibiotics just in case. I knew that if I couldn't stay healthy, I would be on the hook for medical bills that I couldn't afford. As it would turn out, luck would only last me so long. Eventually, this would catch up with me, and I'd acquire an inordinate amount of medical debt on top of my student loan debt.) Like millions of fellow Americans, I was living in the middle of our failure to provide. I became fastidious about washing my hands and covering my mouth when I coughed. But between the time I went to Germany and when I finished college, my mother had developed a rare and serious form of skin cancer, and watching her deal with the nightmarish billing process drove home to me the importance of having some kind of insurance, even if insurance couldn't be counted on to cover everything she needed. After I finished (but didn't graduate) college in the winter of 2011, I knew I needed to get coverage.

I'd heard that if you worked a minimum of twenty-four hours a week at a Starbucks, you would qualify for their employee benefits package, so I applied to one down the street from where I lived. I submitted an application online and waited.

I didn't hear anything, but I knew I had to get this job. Starbucks was seen as a great company to work for at the time, and although I already had a cool job at the bottom of a ladder that seemed worth climbing, I needed the relative emotional security that Starbucks could provide just as much as the extra income. I printed out a copy of my résumé and showed up at the store, where I asked to speak with the manager. I told her I'd applied online, she asked me to tell her more about myself, and then she took my résumé and said she'd be in touch.

Once again, I didn't hear anything. After a few days passed, I called the store and asked to speak to the manager; she said she hadn't had time to review my application yet. A few more days passed—nothing. I called again. (Like I said—I really needed the job.) Again the same response: she'd be in touch. After I called a third time, I was brought in for an official interview.

Later, the manager revealed that the only reason she'd hired me was because I'd been so persistent in meeting with her. Because of this, she knew I'd be a reliable worker. Once I started work, I realized how competitive getting a Starbucks job was; indeed, she said later that she hired only people who called at least twice. A sad but maybe useful tip for anyone applying for jobs.

Although I needed only twenty-four hours per week to qualify for benefits, I ended up putting in as many as possible. Indeed, my schedule at First Stage was robust: It involved me teaching in classrooms in Milwaukee from 8 a.m. to about 3 p.m., and then doing a couple of after-school sessions two or three days a week. I'd wear khakis so that once my teaching was over, I could arrive at Starbucks by 3:30 or 5:30 depending on the day, already half-dressed—our uniform was black pants or khakis and a black polo, which I'd bring with me. I'd work until close at 10 or 10:30 p.m., at which point I'd go home and crash so I could be back in the classroom by 8 a.m. the next morning. In total, I would work thirty-five to forty hours a week at Starbucks alone; I always worked weekends, and tried to pick up other people's shifts whenever possible. There's a "free caffeine" joke to be made here, but caffeine can't get you that far.

Working at Starbucks was an eye-opening experience, and not always in a good way. Our location was next to a private high school, and every afternoon we'd be subject to a steady stream of privileged teenagers messing around with their iPhones as they paid for their vanilla bean Frappuccinos with Starbucks cards. A thought I had not infrequently was *I'm (basically) a college graduate working forty hours a week serving milkshakes to teens who have more money in their bank accounts than I do.*

This frustration was not unique to me. Almost all my coworkers at the Kinnickinnic Avenue Starbucks in Milwaukee had college degrees; several had or were working toward graduate degrees, and many of us had more than one job. One day, a customer at the drive-thru was giving a coworker such a hard time that she ripped off her headset, took off her apron, yelled "BITCH, I HAVE A PHD!" and walked off the job. She was my hero in that moment; there was always that one customer who seemed to think the drinks were so expensive because treating us like shit was included in the price.

Working at Starbucks may seem kind of prissy, but like all service positions, it's a rough job: anything that requires you to talk to a constant churn of people who want something from you is draining as it is. And something about Starbucks makes customers feel especially entitled to inhumanity. It's like the corporate obviousness of the place encourages an abandonment of all pretensions, including decency. The imprecise quantity and distribution of delicious supplemental flavors is a particular trigger for many patrons of the Siren. Caramel Frappuccino perfectionists are a whole breed of human being, the kind willing to remove the lid of their specialty sugar drink, dramatically inspect it, and throw a tantrum if they feel the amount of caramel sauce is lacking. I know that people are struggling to get by, so little treats like caramel Frappuccinos feel essential; if they're not exactly right, then the day's saving grace is ruined. Nevertheless: there was a customer who came in every day—Every. Single. Day.— paid for her nonfat latte in change meticulously counted out from her fanny pack, and requested a "whisper" of nutmeg every time. No one knew exactly what a whisper was: sometimes she'd take a sip and be satisfied; other times she'd hand the cup back and say, falsely apologetic, "I'm sorry—I said 'a whisper.'" Did that mean more or less than what we'd done? No one could tell, and no one could tell why sometimes she'd request we add the whisper and other times she was content to walk over to the milk station and add it herself. But she was preferable to the Foam People, who would scream at you if you accidentally included foam on their no-foam order, and then scream at you again if you did the efficient and scientifically sound thing of scooping it off the existing drink instead of making an entirely new one. (I know this may seem over-dramatic, but this is not exaggeration: these adults would have full-blown, toddler-esque meltdowns.) Everyone wants a new drink, because everyone wants to be so important as to deserve one.

Then there was a woman I'll call Cassie, whose loud car would roll up to the drive-thru multiple times a day. "Hiiiii, it's Caaaaaaassiieeeeee," her script began. We knew her order by heart: triple venti zebra mocha with extra mocha, extra mocha drizzle, and extra whipped cream. Around Christmas, Starbucks offers mocha shavings—they're festive—so during the holidays she'd request those, as well. In practical terms, this drink involved a good inch or two of mocha sauce and a mere five or six ounces of milk and espresso, and the remainder consisted of whipped cream and drizzle. Nevertheless, it was not uncommon for her to swing back around a couple of minutes later and say into the loudspeaker: "Hiiiiii . . . there's not enough mochaaaaaaa."

Despite all this, I liked working as a barista and bartender. The horror stories are the ones to tell at the bar (or in your memoir!), but there was a lot to like about these jobs. I've always enjoyed talking to people and serving them. I firmly believed in some of the Starbucks corporate mantras, borrowing as they did from old-school café culture, like *Surprise and delight the customer* (they would often at least surprise me in return). The café was supposed to be a space between home and work, a "third space"—that is so important, especially these days, when usable public space is shrinking. More and more cafés are morphing into second spaces for remote workers and people who just prefer to do their business meetings over Skype loudly and in public, but still. I think it's important they exist, even in this mutated corporate form.

I maintained this nearly impossible schedule for about two years. At First Stage, I quickly moved up from teaching assistant to teacher, and then I got a job in the education department, which involved traveling to Milwaukee-area public schools in the region to teach theater lessons. A few months in, the education department brought me on as an unpaid intern so I could be in the education office, learning the ropes and helping out as much as possible. Technically, I was working full-time there, too, but because I was split between two departments, they didn't consider me a full-time employee. I always hoped to move up in the company, which is why I let this slide. I loved teaching so much, and I thought that if I kept putting in work—extra hours, being there for everyone, anytime, getting positive feedback from my students—I would get promoted when the time came. Not only would I get to have a job I loved, I would have a viable career path. I would be taken care of—less so financially than spiritually. I would be able to imagine a future.

Around the fall of 2013, the company put out calls for a full-time teaching artist in the academy, and I knew this was my chance. I submitted a portfolio, CV, and formal application. I went through a few interviews with staff members I'd known since I started as an assistant. The job went to the other guy.

I was more than frustrated. I thought I was doing such a great job at First Stage. My coworkers loved me, my students loved me, and I was improving all the time, despite working seventy to eighty hours a week and sleeping in the spiderweb that was my basement bedroom. When I didn't get the job, it was the first time I felt the full weight of all the debt I'd taken on. I was starting to get scared I would never get out from under it. I knew it was very unlikely that I'd advance to a position to be comfortable making my minimum payments, much less ever actually get rid of the debt all together. Not getting the job made me feel like I'd made a huge mistake, and I couldn't stop fixating on what to do next: Did I need to go back to even more school to get a nursing degree? Before, I'd been able to compartmentalize, focusing on working hard and telling myself something would come along. I knew it would be difficult to have a career in theater that also allowed me to support myself, but other people seemed to do it, so why couldn't I?

Well, there are all sorts of answers to that question. The top two are that most other people *don't* make their living from working in theater alone, of course, which is where the stereotype of the perennially auditioning New York waiter comes from. But how was I supposed to know that? Many of my friends from Eau Claire had gone to New York or Chicago to try to make it, and although I had always been glad I had never done that, sure as I was that I would only crash and burn, now I figured they were on to something. I decided I should move to a bigger city, where I was certain more opportunities would be waiting for me. I applied for a transfer to a Starbucks in Chicago, sold the Saturn for $3,000 cash, rented a U-Haul, grabbed my boyfriend and a bag of cheese curds, and left Milwaukee.

7

Patience and Healing

Wait a minute—boyfriend, you say? We should probably back up.

Well, yes. Dating was, in fact, part of the point of coming out, though the difficulties diving into those murky waters presented me were not what I'd expected. I hadn't really thought a lot about what being in love would feel like, but I guess even then I knew it was something I wanted—maybe even needed. I expected absolutely nothing. I was so nervous to come out that I hadn't imagined anything except that total destruction would follow, and the character of that destruction was familial shunning, widespread discrimination, and other unavoidable disadvantages. My fantasies about dating were about true love, children, and a cozy, welcoming home, and I thought that being gay exempted me from all those things, except maybe the cozy, welcoming home. (I do have a flair for *Gemütlichkeit*.) I had no conception of the typical annoyances and despair dating included. I had never talked to anyone about the ins and outs of their up-and-down love lives, because I didn't want to let the cat out of the bag that I was gay. I just thought my life was going to be loveless and hard.

I had no idea my life was going to be loveless and hard because *men are terrible*.

My romantic history did not get off to a good start. The summer I came out and was still living in Traverse City, I finally discovered a community of like-minded individuals, i.e., other gay people. It turns out there's a gay bar in Traverse City. It's the only gay bar in Traverse, but it works. Imagine a stripped double-wide trailer with a dance floor in the middle of it. It had a pool table, a dartboard, and not much else. Being the only gay bar in town, Side Traxx was generously accommodating (no relation to Sidetrack, the gay bar in Chicago): it was open to ages eighteen and up. The first time I entered, nervously showing my ID to the doorman, it was like telling a secret to a stranger who knew me better than I did. It was the first place I ever really danced—without abandon, letting my worries sit on the sidelines for the moment.

As I peeked around the corner of my new identity, I started to meet other members of my community who were out. One couple were tremendously kind. They'd often open their home for gatherings on holidays, especially welcoming people who didn't have a home to go to. They knew how scary it was to come out, and how hard it was to make friends when you were too nervous to introduce yourself to anyone. A wide variety of misfits and lost souls—singles and couples, those who'd been out for a month and those who hadn't seen their biological families in thirty years—rotated in and out of their place. They say you choose your own family after you come out, and these people became part of mine.

But it wasn't all potlucks and drag-queen bingo. Within the nuclear Traverse gay community, there was one guy whom everyone seemed to know, Mark. Older and taller, Mark was like the subject of a Shania Twain song. The problem was, it actually did impress me, very much.

Strangely, he often seemed to be flirting with me, though I also knew that he could never possibly be interested in someone like me. Shy and tentative when it came to people outside my close friend group, I didn't really feel like I fit in with the scene. I didn't even know what a scene *was* at that point. At every party or gathering, I buzzed with anxiety about being an imposition or getting in the way. I wanted so desperately to blend in, but I didn't know what would work best: Should I try to regale them with tales of my outdoor exploits and farming successes? Jump on a table and sing a lively rendition of "(You Drive Me) Crazy" by Britney Spears? Buy a beret and start brooding in the corner of the bar, reading a book in German? I now can see that the group was too insular for me to have been truly excluded. But it was completely daunting at the time. I couldn't stop worrying about who I should be for them rather than asking myself, "Who am I?"

One night that fall, after I'd been out for a while and was back living in my parents' house, I ended up at a party at Mark's house. A part of me was exhilarated to finally be taking part in a social life that was recognizable from movies and television—and that it was with older people, most of whom I treated with a combination of awe and fear. I was uncomfortable drinking underage; though I'd gotten drunk in Germany, I had limited experience with alcohol in the United States. I always thought I was on the verge of getting in trouble. Still, I did it anyway, because after spending high school feeling like a freak and desperate to feel part of a group, I finally saw that I had a chance to fit in.

I had gotten word of the party from some friends but showed up alone. As I walked through the house, following the yelling and singing from the back room, I was nervous to see Mark. I both really wanted him to flirt with me and couldn't bear to think about it. Once I arrived, I looked around for a friendly face: there he was, flashing me a smile. My face must have turned purple: a guy was happy to see me! As if on cue, disco lights turned the walls into a rainbow.

The night went on, the drinks continued to pour, and at some point I found myself deep in a couch talking to him. The rest is blurry, not least because I've tried my best to both make it disappear and never forget the details. We were talking about who knew what when Mark took my hand and told me to follow him. We ended up in a bedroom, where, as soon as the door was closed, he became someone else. If I'd been confused about whether I was interested before; now I knew for sure I was not. This was my first sexual—or rather para-sexual—gay experience; at this point I'd still only ever kissed an acquaintance in a closet bathroom during our German exchange program.

Unfortunately, this first sexual experience was a very negative one. I was thrilled for the kiss from Mark, but something was off: it was too harsh, too fast, out of sync. He grabbed at my clothes and body, and when I tried to move my hands, he forced me back down. For a few moments I thought it was supposed to be that way, but I soon realized that something wasn't just off—it was wrong. I'd had a few drinks, but drunkenness didn't explain it. It was as if, when I asked him to stop, it went in one ear and out the other. First, I was gentle—I didn't want to hurt his feelings. But when he kept ignoring me, I got frightened, so I said it more firmly. *Stop. I don't want to. Stop!* But he kept pulling on me and trying to pin me down. Finally, I slapped him. He stopped and looked at me with an almost adolescent disgust and shock—it was like I'd unplugged his video game and smashed the television.

My mother and I had a deal that if I ever needed help and was drunk and unable to drive, I should always call her. I'd always laughed when she brought it up; I never thought I'd need my mom to bail me out of a party, much less want her to. I left Mark's room, grabbed my stuff, walked out of the house, and headed down the street, trying to physically distance myself from the sense of violation I felt. Mom arrived in her pickup truck soon after, I got in, and we barely spoke.

This experience set me up for a lot in my life. Before, I'd been lucky—although I'd been bullied and teased, I'd never been taken advantage of. My parents were generous and straightforward, and so were my teachers. I'd never had to suspect that someone was treating me with kindness in order to get something from me. After it was over, I felt profoundly unstable—I became more suspicious, less trusting, less open. I suppose this is a lesson that everyone has to learn sooner or later, but I don't think that it has to be so violent, or come intertwined with love and intimacy, two of the things in life that are supposed to be among the most rewarding and fulfilling. During the hearings surrounding Brett Kavanaugh's appointment to the Supreme Court, watching Christine Blasey Ford's remarkably open and vulnerable testimony, I felt something turn; I felt ready to open up about my experiences, too. I'd never allowed myself to talk about it out loud before. Over time it became clearer and clearer that this was a foundational experience for me, in the worst way possible. I've never forgotten that evening, and what he did caused me to be skeptical and fearful of love and affection for years. It took a lot of work, and years of patience and healing, to make amends with what he stole from me.

....

I found Adam later that fall. I don't remember how we started talking, maybe at Side Traxx, but soon enough, we were dating. By which I mean "dating." I don't think we ever held hands in public or canoodled in the movie theater—that was still scary—but we could go back to his mom's house together because she was OK with us hanging out. We would de-camp immediately to his bedroom: not even his bunk bed could stop us from awkwardly attempting to cuddle.

Everything about the relationship ("the relationship") was painfully awkward: the kissing, the cuddling, the talking, the *so what are we doing today?* The main reason Adam and I got together was that we were both gay. Neither of us knew how to be romantic and in love, which was sort of good because we weren't going to feel that for each other. My feelings, at least, were defined by the disconnect between what I wanted to feel and what I actually did: I'd fantasized about the romantic-comedy kind of intense, nearly obsessed relationship for so long that when I finally found another gay guy who wanted to be boyfriend-boyfriend, I jumped at the chance. As most people know, having the same sexual orientation does not necessarily make a relationship, but I suppose this is a lesson that most people have to learn sooner or later.

Not that it was all bad. It was often very sweet, even if it's mortifying to think about now. (I guess this is also pretty standard when it comes to teenage relationships, but still.) Adam was the first person who just wanted to hang out, cuddle, tell me nice things about myself, and make me feel good. The first time we lay in the same bed, all we did was stare at each other. I had only been out for a few months by this point, and we were both uneasy. There was a tiny Chasten jumping up and down in my mind yelling: "WE'RE TWO GUYS! TWO GUYS! IN THE SAME BED!! IN PAJAMAS!!!" In reality, I'm sure I said something like "Your eyes are . . . cool." The fact that our connection was not intimate was completely overshadowed by the magnitude of the sense of *Holy crap we're doing this*. It felt scandalous enough just to be in the same bed. (For both of us, I'm sure, as it wasn't like he was making a move, either.)

My overwhelming joy alternated rapidly with extreme anxiety until the two were indistinguishable. How do you cuddle? How do you make out? How long are we supposed to do this? Why is putting your arm around someone else in the movie theater so uncomfortable after five minutes? Now I know that gay couples laze around romantically more or less the same way straight couples do it in movies. But then, gay or straight, I had no idea what "being a couple" was supposed to feel like.

I also wondered if I was supposed to say I loved him. My friends had talked about being in love as if it were the most natural thing in the world. Love had always been part of my white-picket-fence fantasy; it was the foundation for the happiness I wanted to feel. But even as I desperately wanted to know what they meant, I felt like *I love you* couldn't possibly mean anything in this situation. Even the word *boyfriend* rang false; Adam didn't seem like a boyfriend, he seemed like *a person I was hanging out with a lot*. (Another short German lesson: they say *Freund* to mean both "friend" and "boyfriend." While it's less confusing with context—"a friend" generally means something platonic, while "my" or "her" friend something more romantic—I'm sure it's still frustrating for people who are trying to assess their chances with each other. Nevertheless, in this case, it really made sense.)

I was experiencing intense emotions all the time, but very few were directed toward Adam. I now see that my interest in him was only affectionately platonic, tangled up in my excitement about being with a boy at all and my nerves about being inexperienced. I also see that I needn't have felt such dramatic life-or-death, push-and-pull emotions about it. The disproportion between my excitement at the simple pleasures of doing things for the first time and my deep-down sense that something was off made me feel constantly frantic. I wish that I could have just enjoyed my first "real" boyfriend for what he was: a like-minded individual, another scared, excited young man starting a new and unfamiliar life.

....

Adam and I dated for a few months or so, and things fizzled out more or less naturally. Soon after, I got to know Brad. Brad was a professional with things going on in his life: a lively group of friends, a nice apartment.

We went out for over a year, and things did not end well. My memory from this time is frustratingly hazy; I don't recall a lot of good times with Brad, though that could be unfair to him. On my end, I was really struggling to keep it together financially, academically, and emotionally. Every day felt like a barely surmountable challenge, and it was difficult for me to be around someone who seemed to be doing everything right. At first, he seemed so attractive, funny, and exciting—magnetic. I couldn't believe someone with his shit so *together* would be interested in a shit *show* like me. Every time I showed up to his apartment, I instantly forgot about my less-than-welcoming studio that smelled like the Chinese restaurant next door. He'd take me out to dinner and pay, and he could be romantic; he liked going for walks and being intimate. But by the end of the relationship I felt like a burden to him— unaccomplished and embarrassing. At that point I was two years into my undergraduate degree, trying to wait tables while failing nursing school. It seemed almost ridiculous for me to be dating this slick, charismatic professional. At the time, I had no purpose or drive, though I desperately wanted both. I think I probably wanted to use our relationship as an anchor, because being with someone like him made me feel good about myself and my future, and about being gay in general. It was easier to find confidence in myself when I was attached to someone so confident with their own identity. I saw in him the possibility of being loved and cared for. Having a man as more than a friend felt normal if the man was him.

But most of that was superficial, external. Within the privacy of the relationship, things were very different. Brad was not supportive of me at all during this hard time; I'm sure he *did* think I was a burden. He often seemed to be trying to exert power over me by emphasizing the age difference between us, belittling my concerns and problems in the process. I don't think he ever faced the type of coming-out experience or self-doubt I did at that age. Of course, there *was* an age difference between us, but there was no need to make someone feel bad for being twenty years old; you could teach them stuff without making them hate the random year in which they happened to have been born. Brad was verbally aggressive, always letting me know that it was his way or the highway. Indeed, it made sense that he would want a younger, inexperienced boyfriend, as he seemed to enjoy feeling unquestionably superior and in control.

I think part of me knew he didn't really care about me, and I also think I knew that my feelings for him derived from his status relative to mine— the way he made me feel socially—more than from a genuine appreciation of him. This mismatch eventually came to a head during our breakup, which I remember vividly for how physical it was. During our relationship, sometimes he would raise his voice, as would I. But we had never fought like this before. Things got out of hand quickly.

The next thing I knew, he had me by the shirt collar and was throwing me over the side of the couch. He took my stuff, threw it in the hallway, and then, with his hand on my shirt, tossed me out, too. The door slammed. I stared at it. Why was I always on the outside?

Standing in the wide-open hallway, I had no idea what to do. Every path forward seemed blocked. I hadn't been out to my parents for very long, and I hadn't talked to them about my dating life at all, and I especially didn't want to tell them that my boyfriend had just literally thrown me out of his apartment because I'd said I was insecure around him. It seemed like another one of those things that would prove them right—if I hadn't "decided" to be gay, this never would have happened.

But I also didn't know what to do. The obvious solution was to go back to my apartment, since Brad and I hadn't been living together, but mentally I couldn't even get that far. I went downstairs, where I saw that it was raining, and did the only thing that came to mind: called my dad. I didn't say very much—just that I felt like I knew Brad had gone too far and that I was now standing outside his apartment in the rain feeling lost and trapped.

This moment was one of many when I knew I was lucky to have my family. Although things had been shaky between us in the past, I knew I could count on them. Domestic violence is a pervasive problem in the gay community that doesn't get discussed often, and many gay kids don't have the option to call their parents for support when something like this—or much worse—happens to them. I was grateful to learn that the fear that my parents wouldn't be supportive was, of course, unfounded. Dad was really mad that I was in that position; he made sure I knew how to get home. It was simple advice, but it was what I needed to snap out of it and catch the late bus from downtown to my apartment.

But things did not improve for me; to be clear, this is not a story about a breakup that turns out to be a blessing in disguise. Sometimes the story is just sad, and the main character doesn't ride off into the sunset in a motorboat with the love of his life. Soon after that, I flunked out of UW-Milwaukee and moved back home, where I re-enrolled in the community college. I knew, in the eyes of my parents, of Brad, and of my friends, that I had failed.

....

Returning home got me back on my feet long enough to find Eau Claire. Once I was ready, I packed up the Saturn, yet again, made the twelve-hour drive to the Northwoods of Wisconsin, and settled in to finish my college career.

Once I moved to Milwaukee to work at First Stage, I began investing in "putting myself out there." This being my first real go at dating, it was not a twenty-first-century love story worthy of mention in a *New York Times* wedding announcement. (And I would know. But we'll get to that soon.) I failed to meet anyone. And by anyone, I mean anyone interested in *me*. Everyone was looking for everything but a relationship. If I'd been more secure in my finances and lifestyle, maybe I would have felt differently, but I was failing to make ends meet and so emotionally drained from working seventy hours a week at the theater and at Starbucks that the anxiety of impressing anyone wasn't exhilarating. Instead, it just felt like another precarious uncertainty to worry about. I would start teaching at eight in the morning, close Starbucks at 10 p.m., and then fall into bed in my musty basement bedroom to sleep for a few hours, only to get up and do it all over again. Because I was barely seeing friends or going out to bars or parties, scheduling bespoke drinks dates on apps was the only way I could squeeze in time to meet new people. But it quickly became clear that these dates were unlikely to get me what I wanted: the possibility of building something. On date after date, I felt uninteresting, unattractive, and out of touch. It seemed impossible to connect with anyone, not least because my dream of becoming, essentially, a homebody was unfathomable to most people who used apps for hooking up. Every date I went on, and relationship I started, seemed wrong and would only get more wrong from there. Even though the process was repetitive, it was always so heartbreaking: I would hang out with a guy for two or three weeks, with our never talking about anything more than what we'd seen on TV, what we should have for dinner, or lighthearted stories from our lives. Everything remained on the level of small talk at a party. Then, one day, he would tell me (probably via text) (if he bothered to tell me at all): "Yeah . . . I'm bored. We don't need to hang out anymore." Oh. OK.

I persevered. I realize that this is just how online dating goes: it doesn't work until it does. But in the meantime, it's *so* frustrating. Somewhat pathetically, I always told myself what a mother would tell me: *He just needs to get to know me better!* Until then, I'd thought I was a catch, or at the very least an interesting person to be around. Even though I hadn't fit in when I was in high school, I'd never had particularly low self-esteem—I thought I didn't belong, but I didn't think that I was undatable. As my time in college straightened out, I'd begun to think more highly of myself. I was funny, I had interesting stories, I was great with kids, I had my own bowling shoes, and I knew how to drive a four-wheeler—why wouldn't anyone like that? Yet the qualities people wanted in Milwaukee were not what I had to offer. At least, the men I was meeting weren't interested. I know that sounds a little dramatic—Milwaukee is not exactly New York or London—but status obsession dominates in every city. I was always very forthright about what I wanted—partnership—and while the guys would never reject me outright because of it, it would soon become clear that they wanted the opposite: something easy and breezy, from which they could opt out at any time, and that started to get old.

I didn't really get it: they wanted to get coffee, browse bookstores, go to brunch, and introduce me to their friends, but they just didn't want to call it a relationship. They wanted something that was convenient on a day-to-day basis, but I had more than enough instability in my working life, and I could browse bookstores and go to brunch with my friends. I didn't resent them for it, but anytime I'd ask if they were interested in taking things a bit further, soon enough my text messages would start going unanswered.

As time went on and I became more and more frustrated, people would try to set me up with their friends—I think because they felt sorry for me. I'd grab Thai food with a nurse practitioner or law student, but none of them would have any interest in dating a teacher/barista except as a fleeting novelty. "Oh, one time I dated this guy who worked at Starbucks—isn't that funny? His family has a *farm*." Free Frappuccinos weren't enough of a perk for them. The idea of bringing some of these guys back to my basement was so unappealing as to be unimaginable; it would only emphasize that I was making $19,000 a year with $70,000 in loans to back it up. One look at the basement would remind any potential suitors that there were lots of rich guys with condos waiting for them downtown.

Finally, after mostly giving up on dating, I went to a house party, where I met Ethan. Ethan was another theater type who, amazingly, wanted to talk about books and feelings. He was adorable, charming, and easy to talk to. We hit it off right away. We were both teaching theater, and he worked at Caribou Coffee—it was almost too perfect. We made ourselves officially boyfriends within a few months. After so many bad dates and quarter-relationships, Ethan seemed like a miracle and the most natural, obvious person in the world; talking to him was almost a relief. Life with Ethan was fun, secure, and for once, stable.

We spent every day together, showing up at each other's work to say hello, checking in on his family, and spending practically every night with them, too. He traveled to Michigan to meet my family. We all liked one another. When I didn't get the full-time teaching position at First Stage, we moved to Chicago together, in search of better opportunities. We both wanted to find jobs in the arts scene, and Chicago seemed like an easy answer. I transferred to a Starbucks downtown and off we went.

Once again, things did not go as planned. We were regrettably asked to leave our first apartment, a garden sublet. We should have known something weird was going on when we were asked to pay $3,000 up front by the current tenant. Neither of us knew how to tell the difference between a shady sublease and a real one. We'd been living there a few months when one day the property manager showed up and had no idea who we were or why we were there; we showed him the forms we'd filled out and the letters we'd signed, but the property manager was unimpressed. We had to leave at the end of the month.

Meanwhile, I was having a "we're not in Kansas anymore" moment at my Chicago Starbucks. Late one night, a man who seemed unwell pulled a knife on me at the register. Well, *knife* isn't quite right; it was more like a machete. He casually opened his coat to show it to me when I explained that Starbucks didn't give out free water for customers who wanted to make their own tea. He opened the coat, I prepared the tea, and a coworker called 911. The cops showed up, escorted the man out, and I closed up shop. By the time my stop was called on the Red Line, I was ready to toss in the green apron as soon as I could.

I found an office job and then, to supplement our income, I took to Airbnb, often renting our living room couch and air mattress to travelers who couldn't afford the steep price of hotel accommodations in Chicago. Sometimes, when the rates were right, we'd let out the entire apartment and leave the city, spending weekends with our parents in order to make enough to cover rent for the place we weren't even staying in full-time. We hosted travelers from all over the world and would often spend evenings showing guests the neighborhood.

Ethan and I had been in Chicago for about a year, and things really started to feel like they were lining up and making sense. But then, one day, a text message came through while I was at work that shocked me: "Don't come home for Thanksgiving. I'm going back to Milwaukee." Cue the record-scratch sound effect. Yup, after two good years together, Ethan was dumping me via text message. Once again, I found myself in total crisis mode.

I came home, and he was gone, along with all his stuff. The self-pity and insecurity rushed in as I looked around my suddenly empty apartment. With a pint of ice cream and *Steel Magnolias* on repeat, I started to doubt all the decisions that led me to where I was. How had I managed to get to this point? This was not where I imagined it all leading just a few years ago. I was in serious need of a Julia Roberts *Eat, Pray, Love* intervention. Why would someone abandon me like that? If I wasn't worthy of love, was I worthy of seeing my other dreams come true?

I felt like I'd wasted my bachelor's degree by abandoning nursing and set myself up for failure. I wasn't good at much except being loud and silly and dramatic (turns out those are great ingredients for an amazing teacher), but I knew getting into acting wasn't a smart choice to pursue any further. After undergrad, a few close friends moved to New York to try to make it, but I never even really fantasized about following them, doubting my ability to actually land anything. Some of them are still there, but years ago, I knew I would have failed immediately if I'd tried to do what they had done. I didn't have the confidence to go. I couldn't shake the feeling that I seemed to fail at making the little pieces of what I had accomplished add up to anything. And my heart hurt knowing I doubted myself so much, and that I didn't seem to be enough for others to love, either.

With Ethan no longer paying his share of the rent, I picked up more gigs. I started bartending at a comedy club, which came with the benefit of free improv classes. I tried my hand at stand-up, but the few times I did, I was usually at the bottom of the list. By the time I took the microphone, there was one person left in the room, my friend Caroline. She still laughed at my jokes. A group of comedians and regular late-night pancakes at IHOP started to make the breakup just a little more bearable.

I'd started to think about applying to graduate school to become a full-time teacher, but I thought it was a good idea to get more experience to see if I actually liked it first. It turned out, I did. I'd worked in the classroom at First Stage, but those were one-off acting workshops. So I got my substitute teaching license in Chicago Public Schools. As a substitute teacher I went everywhere and tried everything: all age groups, all subjects. Substitute teaching in Chicago Public Schools was like drinking from a firehose: sometimes I'd show up to a school and the administration would give me one look and say, "You're going to get eaten alive." Sometimes they weren't wrong. But I found I really connected with middle school students the most—they can be super difficult (ask any parent of a young teenager), but when you have a breakthrough and can build a rapport with them, it feels like such a win. I had a few tricks up my sleeve, and the improv training came in handy; I loved figuring out how to engage the students and how to earn their trust. I remembered my mentor in Milwaukee, Ms. Sheri, recommended welcoming students and introducing yourself at the door. This was mostly a fail, though there was always that one student who was happy to see anyone with a smile. (I remember that feeling myself in middle school.) Substitute teachers are like red meat in shark-infested waters. Nevertheless, I did my best to balance "Hey, what's up, I'm a nice guy! Let's do these worksheets!" and "Please put your phone away. Yes, I see your phone. No seriously, I see your iPhone right there. Oh my gosh—stop putting me on Snapchat." This was, of course, a great trial by fire in classroom and behavior management. I know there are many people who would run the opposite way after a few months of eight-hour days with teenagers, but the more time I spent in the classroom, especially with students navigating trauma, or just the ins and outs of middle school, the more I wanted to stick around and help. One day, a student was so worked up, he got out of his chair, picked it up, and tried to throw it across the room at me. He wasn't strong enough, so it went up in the air, landed, and skidded to the front of the room, where I stopped it with my foot. Standing in front of all his peers, attempting to show his strength and dominance, he had failed, and he immediately burst into tears. Deescalating the situation in such a dramatic way could make a teacher feel like a badass, especially when it feels like the room wants you to fail, but I looked at this teenager in front of me, hurting, and I knew I wanted to do everything I could to understand why he hurt the way he did. I had hurt so much in school, and I started to wonder if this was where I was meant to be. Eventually I found a school in Lakeview that gave me a regular offer, asking me if I'd like to come back the next day every time I finished a class.

The long days full of drama in the classroom, mixed with the long nights at the comedy club, as well as the rotating cast of tourists sleeping on my couch, kept life pretty interesting. Sometimes I would teach, take a class, work a shift at the bar, and then come home to find a group of French college students sitting around my dining room table, completely forgetting I had rented the apartment out. A part of me fantasized about dropping off the grid, traveling the world, and spending more time finding myself.

But I couldn't have afforded to drop off the grid and find myself, so I did the next best thing: I applied to become an American Airlines flight attendant. I went through the entire interview process, which included traveling to Dallas twice, and was eventually offered a job. The next step would be six weeks of unpaid training in Dallas. I was advised that everyone had to purchase their own uniform and pay their own way through training. They told me I could start on January 15.

And then . . . I got cold feet. I was allowed to postpone the training, so I did. Every couple of weeks from then on, I'd get another call from American: Was I ready to participate in the upcoming training session? My answer was always "Um . . . I don't know!" I'd thought it would be fun, but once I actually had the chance of taking the leap I could only think, *Whoa, whoa, whoa—calm down. Who said anything about a* job? The prospect of such a dramatic and unusual change was daunting. Also, it would have been yet another random, weird thing for me to do.

My gut was telling me it was wrong, so by the summer I had started looking into grad school instead. I knew my home was in the classroom.

8

Meet Pete

I enrolled in a master's of education program at DePaul University in Chicago, which allowed me to continue substitute teaching and renting my place on Airbnb. After leaving just one information session for incoming students at DePaul, I felt more confident in the path I'd chosen. Moreover, my cohort was filled with other professionals switching to education from fields like medicine or the military. I was making a change that would allow me to work toward a career as a full-time teacher, giving me a path to health insurance, a regular paycheck, and stability.

After some time, and much to my dismay, I returned to the exhausting world of dating. Ethan broke my heart—with him things had finally started to make sense—but I knew I was ready to start again. Everything progressed much in the same way that it had before I'd met Ethan— guys were willing to go on a series of "dates" so long as I never expected anything beyond a cursory discussion of their favorite television shows or overpriced avocado toast. A few weeks into seeing someone, he invited me over for a few *Will & Grace* sessions. We drank wine, he was charming, but that's all it was. Wine and *Will & Grace*. No touching! Finally, after a few weekends of laughing and watching Jack-and-Karen hijinks while sipping chardonnay, I asked, "So, uh, what's going on here?" He then proceeded to tell me—are you ready for this?—that he was *just trying to figure out if he still loved his husband while they were on a break*. I have never left an apartment faster. I may have left a shoe behind.

MEN!

I remembered that, in middle school, there was a man who ran a student leadership program who was single and had adopted a kid on his own. He never said he was gay, but later I realized he might have been. He was a really nice, caring guy who must have just never found his match. I began to wonder if that was going to be me.

I don't want to suggest that that man's life was a terrible fate—I'm sure that his life had been fulfilling. (And actually I have no idea if he was really single—it's not like gay men were open about their love lives in Traverse City in the year 2000.) But at the time I could think of nothing but the apparent impossibility of ever living a happy life, and this was especially painful given that my vision of a happy life didn't seem like so much to ask for. I just wanted someone to eat my casseroles!

I know that thinking my romantic prospects were doomed because of a failed relationship at age twenty-four seems melodramatic. Nevertheless, I *felt* melodramatic. In the Midwest, people tend to settle down earlier than on the coasts, where it's much more common for people to marry in their thirties, or not marry at all. (The ban on same-sex marriage would not be overturned in Michigan and in the rest of the country until 2015, so it's not like I could have gotten married anyway, but barring that, I wanted a long-term, marriage-like relationship.) Most of the couples I knew were straight, and they were settling down by this time. Most of the gay people I knew or met were more interested in doing anything but that. Once again, I found myself not fitting in, and I didn't really understand why. I was not a weird person! I think! Not that there's anything wrong with being a weird person!

After another series of boring and profoundly disappointing encounters, I was ready to call off dating for a while. I kept Hinge, a dating app that links to your Facebook profile so that it can pair you with friends of friends or people in your "social network," on my phone. Nothing much came of it, but the conversations were genuine.

In the summer, when I wasn't substitute teaching, I worked for the exchange program that I'd participated in as a chaperone at Chicago O'Hare. I'd hang out in terminal five, waiting for the flight from Germany to arrive, and then scoop up a hundred Germans and lead them to terminals one and two—going through security sometimes ten times a day—so they could get on domestic flights to meet their host families. One evening, the last student of the day had a flight that was delayed for hours, so I agreed to stay late. While hanging out at the gate late into the evening, I opened up Hinge and saw a message waiting for me from someone named Pete. A cute guy in a suit. A veteran?! The essential beach picture. In one of his pictures, he was standing at a podium with his name on it—bingo, a clue! At the time, there wasn't much information about him available online—just the beautiful coming-out essay he'd written for the *South Bend Tribune* after returning from a deployment in Afghanistan, and mayoral stuff about South Bend. From this, I deduced that he was the mayor of South Bend. I'm sure our first conversation was extremely exciting. It probably went something like this:

"Hey there."

"Hi!"

"How're you?"

"Great—what're you up to?"

But we hit it off immediately.

Virtually, at least. He'd just had surgery and was spending a lot of time on the couch. I quickly went from being the substitute teacher telling kids to put their phones away to giddily checking mine every five minutes. I didn't have a car to go to South Bend whenever I wanted, and he was busy being the mayor, so we spent a while texting before we actually met up. Despite the contemporary mode of communication, our flirtation seemed sort of old-fashioned—our distance forced us to get to know each other first. I proposed a FaceTime date, joking (but seriously) that I wanted to see him face-to-face to confirm he wasn't an axe murderer, and we "hung out" that way: me in my Chicago living room with a glass of wine, him at his desk in South Bend with a beer. It was sweet.

I'd been talking to Peter for about a month when my friend Aubrey invited me to come visit her in Michigan. I figured seeing two people was a great reason to splurge and rent a car: I messaged Peter and said I'd be passing South Bend on I-94—maybe we could have a date? He agreed to meet for coffee.

I was beyond nervous. Those FaceTime dates had gone so well, but I was just so tired of being let down. When the day finally arrived, I got stuck in traffic leaving Chicago, and, apologetic, I had to call him and say that we might have to cancel. I assumed that because he was mayor, he would really only have time for the afternoon coffee, but he was chipper and gladly told me he could wait to have dinner with me. (Later, his staff told me he'd been giddy the entire day, and he'd suspiciously canceled evening meetings.)

When I finally made it to South Bend, I (chivalrously) picked him up in front of his house. I rounded the corner and saw him standing on the steps waiting for me. My stomach was already in knots. When he opened the door, we both said, "Howdy" at the same time. Because of all the texting and FaceTime dates, it felt as if we already knew each other. He directed me to the Irish pub Fiddler's Hearth in downtown South Bend, where he enthusiastically introduced me to Scotch eggs, which are soft-boiled eggs wrapped in sausage and then deep-fried. (Be still my Midwestern heart.) I intuited that my appreciation of Scotch eggs could be a make-or-break moment for him. Luckily, they're delicious (yes, I realize in a gross way), so I passed that test.

Then, it was my turn to administer some tests of my own. So . . . I put it all out there. Although I was used to being forthright on first dates, I was sick of going on them, so this was a little extreme, maybe even counterintuitive. I described some of my bad dates, I said I wanted kids and marriage (Chasten, what were you thinking!), and I said I had just started grad school so I was broke most of the time. (I left out the mountain of student loans.) He kept smiling, laughing, and asking me to tell him more.

The meal had ended, but the conversation was just getting started. I was about to feel sad that our date was over when he pulled a pair of tickets out of his pocket and asked if I'd like to go to the baseball game down the street. I would. As we approached the stadium, I was quickly reminded that he was *the mayor*—a local celebrity, a guy everyone in town had an opinion about. He started getting approached for photos and chitchat; I had no idea what to do with myself. Sure, he was out now, but it didn't seem appropriate to introduce your constituents to some guy you had met on a dating app and had seen in person one single time. I settled on awkwardly hovering too far away to have a conversation with anyone but close enough that it was kind of creepy. Once we made it to the concession stand, we both ordered drinks. When Peter's arrived, the bartender told him, "It's on the house tonight, Mayor." Then, she gave me mine. "That'll be eight bucks." Before I could reach for my wallet, he paid, which was both a relief ($8 is a lot for a beer!) and a sign: he wasn't ashamed to be on a date or trying to hide it.

We watched the game for a while, until he mentioned that every night there was a light show on the river, a marquee achievement of the revitalized South Bend. A walk by the river. Nighttime. Intrigue. Suspense. Romance.

As we were strolling along the river blanketed in a beautiful light display, I brushed my hand against his, and he took it. As we walked back to the car along the river, still holding hands, he told me about his city and why he had moved back.

When we finally made it back to my rental car, I realized I was super-late to meet up with Aubrey. Initially, I'd told her I was stopping to have one drink and then I'd be on my way, but as that plan derailed, I kept texting her feverish updates.

Just as we made it back to the car, there were fireworks going off at the baseball stadium, lighting up the entire downtown sky.

I was soaring. It was like a made-for-TV movie. Once I finally got to Aubrey's house in Michigan—sorry, Aubrey—she could not get me to shut up. But the next day I was apprehensive. I could tell Peter had put a lot of thought and strategy into the evening, which I admittedly loved (especially because it was after a last-minute change of plans!), but it also made me think: *politician*. I had grown up disliking politics, and even after my liberal awakening, I still wasn't keen on politicians. I knew they were necessary, but they seemed more like a necessary evil than a necessary good. I assumed the kind of people who went into politics were distant, slimy, ladder-climbing egotists who make life harder for people who live, literally and spiritually, very far away from them. That it was more about status and favors than goodwill and change.

Good politicians are very few and far between. Peter seemed sweet, but even more than the other guys I'd been going out with, I wondered if his interest and curiosity were just lip service, and his amazing first date a strategy for making him seem like a nice guy. I didn't want to be tricked, so I resolved to stay reserved. He'd also just come out, and the idea of eventually moving to *Indiana* for this guy—which, since he was the mayor of South Bend, was the only way it would work; he couldn't pick up and move to Chicago—seemed way out of bounds. I mean, OK, I'm from Michigan, not exactly a hotbed of progressive politics and culture, but Indiana is something else. And even if I did like him, I assumed he'd want to play the field.

But we kept talking. And talking. And talking. Like it or not, I was getting really attached. I started spending long weekends in South Bend, and a few months in, Peter invited me to his regular Sunday evening dinners with his parents, Anne and Joe, who lived just around the block from him. Anne was gracious and welcoming from the get-go; I think she was just as excited that Peter had fallen in love as he was. Around their small table for four, Anne seated across from me, Peter across from his father, I watched as Joe overwhelmed Peter with a deluge of questions about the daily news or what was happening downtown at City Hall. Peter would ask him about his courses at Notre Dame. Anne and I would swap glances, and she'd raise her trademark single eyebrow that seemed to ask, "Don't they know we're here, too?" We couldn't get a word in edgewise when Peter and Joe got to talking.

Once Joe would turn the conversation to me, however, the nerves arrived; Peter's father was a professor, and I wanted to impress him. "Chasten!" he'd say. "What are you reading? Did you see that article about [insert topic] in the *Times* last Sunday? How are your parents?" "FAN-tas-TIC!" he would remark about just about anything, in his unique, not-quite-British accent. (Joe immigrated to the States from Malta in the '70s.) Even though I was intimidated by his intellect and his curiosity at first, it didn't take long for Joe to make me feel welcome.

South Bend was quickly starting to feel like home. So less than six months after we had started dating, I moved in with Peter.

9

Moving In with the Mayor

It was very soon, and it wasn't like I had a very good track record, but I just knew it was right. When I had moved in with Ethan, I knew we were taking a huge leap. But that was OK. I loved sharing the big city experience with someone—moving to a new place, picking out an apartment, and "surviving" the daily grind with him. I hadn't thought much about living with a boyfriend before, though I was aware of all the stereotypes about interior decorating. Things were never perfect—I always felt I was more focused on work because Ethan could write home for money and I couldn't, and that dynamic often made me feel insecure—but I liked having someone to come home to. It was nice to share a space with someone I loved (and liked). Even when I was rushing around trying to find a job and worrying about making it all add up, I loved watching Ethan make music and fill his time with his passions.

Somewhere deep down, though, I always knew that Ethan and I had probably rushed into it. With Peter, I had no misgivings. I felt like we were both at a "no bullshit" point in our lives. Somehow my head wasn't telling my heart to slow down. It felt safe.

Or maybe intuition had nothing to do with it, and I had just gotten lucky. If it hadn't worked out, I wouldn't have been the first person to have declared "He's the one!" only to have to revise the statement a year later. There is a "true love" component to our story, but much of the decision was practical. I was traveling to South Bend every weekend to see him, and the relationship was going so well that splitting the time between both places started to seem a little ridiculous and inconvenient. Every time I boarded the South Shore train back to Chicago, or drove the rental car away from exit 77 on I-94, the feeling of leaving Peter behind stuck with me long after I plopped my bags down in my apartment on Winthrop Avenue. I got a substitute-teaching license in South Bend, which didn't take much more than a background check and a bachelor's degree, while maintaining my work in Chicago, and I was also still a full-time master's student at DePaul. In South Bend, substitute teachers made around $60 a day, while in Chicago the rate was around $150, so it was worth it to teach three or four days there. I'd travel to South Bend on a Thursday, teach on Friday, and have the weekend with Peter (barring emergency mayoral duties, which required developing a stronger sense of patience than I had when we first met) before returning to Chicago on Sunday or Monday morning. I still didn't have a car at the time, so any arrangement often involved Peter driving me to school in South Bend to teach, or having a staffer pick him up or drop him off at work so I could borrow his car for the day. Luckily, this small portion of the Midwest is one of the few places in the United States with a reliable train system; some days I'd take the 6 a.m. express train from South Bend to Chicago, where I'd hang out at Millennium Station until it was time for class, teach at a school close to a train line, head to DePaul that evening, and take the late Amtrak train back to South Bend, arriving after midnight. Sometimes I could stay at my apartment in Chicago, but I was still renting it out through Airbnb, and that was too lucrative to pass up.

This was a difficult schedule, but for the first time, it felt productive, like I was getting somewhere. I was actually good at grad school, I loved teaching, and by the time I moved in with Peter, I was madly in love with him.

There were challenges, but they felt surmountable. It might be because Peter is so easygoing, which is odd for someone known as a high-achiever, but whatever the reason, the should-we-move-in-together discussion was maybe the first major decision I've ever made in my life that didn't come with a draining series of increasingly fraught considerations. My lease was set to renew on January 1, and that gave us an excuse. If it doesn't work out, we agreed, I could just move back to Chicago. So I had a Craigslist yard sale—by which I mean I invited a bunch of strangers from the internet to come to my apartment and buy my stuff—packed the rest of my clothes and books into Peter's Jeep Patriot, and moved in with the mayor.

....

When I officially moved in with Peter, I had no reason to worry about clashing design sensibilities or Peter's unwillingness to contribute to household chores. (Though he will fight me on this.) The house was built in 1905 and had been left to foreclosure; Peter bought it in the late 2000s, when the price was dropping dramatically every few weeks. The house had sat vacant for quite some time before he moved in. The basement flooded, and a family of raccoons had taken shelter in the attic. He renovated it with his savings account, which made it habitable if not exactly appealing to the eye in every corner.

The house has a lot of character, by which I mean many living, breathing characters have made their homes in it. When I decided to host Thanksgiving for Peter's parents and my cousins who had driven in from Chicago one year, our stove gave out two days before the big event. Because the house is so old, and doorways aren't always standard, we had to take the doors off their hinges in order to fit the new stove. I was determined to have a big to-do, with everyone sitting around the table, and I succeeded: during the meal, the chandelier started shaking and flickering as rumbling and scratching echoed throughout the dining room; a family of squirrels had moved into the soffits of our ceiling. Another time, plaster fell off the wall in our closet, exposing the brick chimney. For months the hole sat unattended, filling our closet with the songs of birds that had made a home in the chimney. Yet another time, raccoons got in through a hole in the garage. We didn't realize it until one day when we opened the garage to find that our furry dumpster-diving friends had fallen through the drywall in the ceiling, scattering their poop everywhere and wreaking havoc on everything from the car to the bicycles on their way out.

With the mayor always away at work, I quickly began to feel like Snow White wrangling woodland creatures in our home. But the difficulties of our relationship have never come from that. The only thing that's annoying about Peter's lifestyle is how reasonable and laid back he is about, well, everything. This can have its advantages; for example, when Peter bought the house, he painted the kitchen the most awful shade of yellow—a yellow so neon I had wondered if it was a mistake he hadn't had time to fix. When he went on a trip during the presidential campaign, I hired a handyman to paint it white. He came home and didn't even notice. When I told him what I'd done, with a dramatic reveal, he didn't care. "Oh, that is nice. Yeah," he said. "Well done." I regretted that I'd spent years hating that yellow when a solution had been a short drive to Home Depot away. He was grateful for the update, and I was relieved the kitchen was appropriate for outside eyes again. If you squint watching his ads running for DNC chair or president, you'll still be able to glimpse this most awful affront to modern decor in the background.

Though of course it was a novelty to be dating a mayor, I hadn't really expected Peter's status would affect me, as his new boyfriend, that much. This was likely because I'd never really thought about mayors or how much they have to do before. If I thought of them at all, it was as wholesome, hand-shaking men who cut ribbons at ceremonies. In my mind, they all seemed to be from the 1950s.

As soon as Peter and I became official, I often felt conspicuous in South Bend. People would see us together and start whispering about who the mayor was with. Or at least I imagined they did that. And then I imagined they rushed this gossip to a gathering of their closest friends, where they sat around the coffee table and speculated about the new hunk the mayor was dating, like a scene from *Big Little Lies*. (What? It's my book and I'll *Lie* if I want to.)

In reality, they were probably just whispering because they'd seen the mayor at the gas station. But while being a local celebrity's plus-one occasionally made day-to-day living awkward, the real difficulty came when I got to accompany him to the more glamorous stuff, and it was clear that I had no idea what was going on or what the hell I was doing. (This is quickly becoming a *Princess Diaries* kind of story, I know.)

A couple of months into our relationship, Peter invited me to be his date to (what felt to me like) a very fancy political affair in Chicago. I was really happy to be invited: Peter's willingness to bring me to events so early on made me feel secure in the relationship, and it helped me feel less catastrophically intimidated by the events themselves, too. But this particular event was a harsh introduction to the kind of social climbing, and occasionally, brazen rudeness, that go unchecked in these spaces. While hugging the wall as Peter mingled with other attendees, I'd occasionally be approached by the sort of overly judgmental political types who only wanted to talk in order to figure out whether it was good to be seen talking to me. (At that time, it was decidedly not good to be seen talking to me.) I had never been good at schmoozing with people with status, people who had what I referred to then as "real jobs." Yes, a teacher is a real job, but some in these circles didn't seem to think so. I had never been around people who were this important, or who wanted to be this important. It seemed most everyone there had something to prove.

I tried not to take anything personally in these spaces, but I felt like such an imposter. I'd stay on the periphery and try to discreetly tug at the sleeves of my blazer, which were just a tad too short. (I had purchased it on clearance for these occasions.) Peter would work the room, and I would smile as I listened to other people's stories, and the occasional political grandstanding. My mind was racing as we moved around the room, saying hello to mayors, journalists, and well-known figures. I told myself I had no business trying to make small talk with anyone in this world. Though there were many kind people to be found at these events, I imagined some were silently pitying the weird substitute teacher who seemed *very* out of his element.

It's funny to think back to just a few years ago, when Peter and I would attend events where hardly anyone knew who I was. I could navigate the room with a breeze. Not many people wanted to talk to the boyfriend (and, later, husband) of Mayor Pete. I could go to the bathroom whenever I wanted. I could visit the bar without fear of being photographed with alcohol in my hand. Most importantly, I could enjoy the cheese spread. It was easy to blend in then; I had no idea what sort of future I was in for, especially when it came to losing all that anonymity.

....

A few weeks after that gathering in Chicago, Peter asked me if I owned a suit. I did not—I had the blazer I'd bought at H&M for $50 when he asked me to join him at what became my crash course in political schmoozing. At the time, that was the most I had ever spent on an article of clothing. Fifty dollars was a lot of money for me, so the question induced a momentary panic. But we hadn't been together that long, so I just kept it cool and said no, I didn't have one. The next weekend, he took me to the mall, led me into Banana Republic, and bought me the first suit I'd ever owned. "You're going to need that," he said, and then vanished into the mist. (He just went to get a pretzel.)

A few days later, he gave me a Christmas card, and inside, there was an invitation to the annual White House Christmas party. Thank goodness I had something to wear.

There was no one I could consult to ask what it meant when your boy-friend invited you to the White House for Christmas, but it didn't matter—how romantic, how exciting, how *embarrassing* to have had my boyfriend buy me a suit so he could take me to meet the president. (In photos of us from the night, I look ridiculously skinny. I can't even fit in that suit anymore, which is rude. But maybe also a sign of true love?) Nevertheless, I went to DC.

I'd never been to the White House before, and the tour we got was great. But the cursed highlight was meeting Barack and Michelle Obama. At one point in the revelry, it was announced that the Obamas were arriving from the residence to greet any visitors who wanted to meet them. Peter—who, in addition to his other accomplishments, had been identified by Obama as a young Democrat to watch—told me to wiggle my way up to the front and say hi. "*No way*," I replied. How could someone as awkward as Chasten say hi to the president without embarrassing his rising-star mayor boyfriend?

But soon I found myself maneuvering through the tight crowd that had gathered to shake hands with or get a picture of the president. I was almost to the front of the line, things were a little chaotic, and I was reaching my hand over the person in front of me to shake hands with Obama when a random guy barreled into me from behind. I turned to look at what had happened, and in the meantime, I felt a hand on my hand. I turned back around, saw Barack Obama was holding my hand, and immediately recoiled. About halfway into this maneuver, I realized what I was doing, so I tried to recover by grabbing his pointer finger and shaking it. Like an infant! But not in a cute way! "Merry Christmas, Mr. President!" I exclaimed, red-faced. "Yes," he replied, staring at my hand shaking *his finger*. By the time Michelle made her way to me, I was on the verge of tears for feeling like an absolute dimwit. Looking back in retrospect, after meeting thousands of people on the campaign trail, I now know that there is goofiness and memorably uncomfortable hilarity every day when you have to meet so many people. Last year, this innocent episode of finger-pulling wouldn't have even registered on my scale of "bizarre things we're *definitely* going to reflect on when we get back to the car." But at the time, I was *very* worried that when the Obamas retired to bed that night, Michelle would say something like, "Hey, did Mayor Pete's boyfriend pull your finger?" And then President Obama would laugh and reply, "Yeah. What a weirdo. Let's never invite them back."

I returned to Peter horrified. "What's wrong?" he asked, and I could only reply, "I think I just pulled Barack Obama's finger." Peter laughed. I enjoyed my share of White House eggnog, and the rest is history.

As time went on, navigating these spaces got easier for me, in part because of the way Peter handled them. He quickly proved he was the same guy everywhere he went; he never pretends to be something he's not, but he still accommodates different types of people, without making the situation awkward or contentious. And he was never shy about introducing me as his boyfriend—even with Mike Pence. One evening, Peter and I attended the Indiana Society of Chicago dinner. (Yes, that's a thing.) Mike Pence was making his way around the room, greeting mayors and elected officials from different cities. Then, when he saw the South Bend table—and saw Peter and me approach him for a handshake—for some reason he didn't have time to stop and say hello. Peter swears it wasn't an offense, just an accident, but I knew that look in the governor's eyes—I'd seen it all my life from hateful passersby. I didn't need the handshake, but if I've learned anything about my husband in the last five years, it's that he always takes the high road and never returns nastiness with nastiness.

When Peter says Mike Pence is a decent guy, he doesn't mean everything he does is acceptable. He just means that he's quiet and capable of exchanging pleasantries with an openly gay man despite being on the record all over the place as despising, ahem, our kind, and actively campaigning against us. (See: the Religious Freedom Restoration Act.) Whenever Peter would have a sidebar with Pence at an event, I would look over at the two of them chatting like nothing was odd and marvel. I know that this is a hor-rifying proposition for many liberals and progressives, who would like to say that if given the chance they would loudly protest Pence's presence and leave the room in a dramatic and meaningful huff. Watching Peter work with someone who was on the record against our own rights with a knot in my stomach, feeling as if I wasn't supposed to speak up on behalf of the countless Hoosiers he'd harmed, I always thought something similar. How could my partner work with someone so awful?

Because South Bend was more important.

That is, as I would come to learn, leadership: the ability to put aside (huge) misgivings for the good of the people who elected you into office.

But I'd still wonder, *How does Peter do it?* Eventually I learned that there's a time and place to voice my opinion, and I knew that Mike Pence didn't care about me or what I have to say at all. If I walked away from him in a dramatic and meaningful huff, it would only serve his narrative about us troublemaking gays. He wasn't worth my pleasantries, but our city also wasn't deserving of the consequences of my potential disrespect. I held my tongue, and I held Peter's hand. As a political spouse, I would come to learn that there are many times it's best to let go of what you can't control. Besides, I always trust that Peter knows what he's doing.

At less contentious or awkward gatherings, Peter would pair me up with someone to hang out with so that I always had a backup conversation partner while he got down to business. If he wanted to be able to quickly exit the situation, he'd purposefully leave me out of a conversation so that I could come up and pull him away for some private reason—namely, that he was just as excited to get to date night as I was. I got very good at determin-ing when he wanted my backup. Otherwise, he made a note of introducing me to everyone worth being introduced to, and he would take opportunities to center the conversations on me—"Oh, Chasten grew up in Michigan," or "Chasten's a teacher—he can tell you all about the substitute program."

Still, there was much to figure out as we became more well-known as a couple. It was awkward to be introduced as Peter's "boyfriend." For one thing, you can't go around saying "boyfriend" in a political context for very long. The word suggests a high-school-ish lack of seriousness. "Oh, this old thing? Just a boyfriend I found lying around." (For that we can blame the patriarchy, with a dash of homophobia. While "girlfriends" can ground the stereotypical "bachelor" to the real world—or the word can also just mean "friends who are girls"—a "boyfriend" is seen as suspicious until he puts a ring on it.) Once we started calling each other "partner," people took us a little more seriously, but it's still rare to show up at a political event where everyone knows why I'm there. On the flip side, there were, comically, some people who didn't realize Peter was gay until he introduced me, very pointedly, as his significant other. When we were still dating, he took me to a wedding in South Bend where an older couple from our church came up to us and started telling Peter all about how he should *really* meet their daughter, wink wink. "She's a *doctor*, you two would really get along," they gushed. "You should have coffee! Or maybe dinner! You could come to the house!" As I stood by silently enjoying the dramatic irony, Peter was super-gracious. "Oh, yes, I'd love to meet her," he replied without missing a beat. "Do you think she'd mind if I brought Chasten, my partner?" A chorus of "Oh! Um! Oh! Goodness!" followed.

The more public and serious our relationship got, the less intimidated I felt, but constituents and voters still frequently mistake me for a staffer, and sometimes I'm not sure I'm not one myself. It was quite common, early on in South Bend, that someone would slickly hand me a card and say, "I know Pete's probably really busy, but let's get our offices to connect on this." I'd look at their card and smile. "Would you like for me to get this to Pete's office?" Landing a comeback that lets someone know you're the husband, not the body man, is a feat in conversational agility. It was never my intention to be unkind, but it was also important for me to establish that I was an independent human being, and that I did not work for the mayor.

And it can be hard sometimes, even now, to remember that I'm just that—a person separate from my husband. After all, next to Peter, who am I? As our relationship approached common knowledge in South Bend, I felt I'd become the sounding board for the entire city—people might be nervous or awkward approaching Peter, but they were very comfortable telling me what was wrong with the town, or oftentimes, him. Of course, often it was all pleasantries. Peter was well liked in South Bend, and usually most folks just wanted to stop me in the grocery aisle or coffee shop to say how appreciative or proud they were of him. I always wanted to help, but I also found some folks—and I say this with the utmost respect for our community—less than fully respectful of my time, my relationship, and my personhood. Without ever really being told, I understood that I represented Peter and his administration, so I had to be on my best behavior (and wear a presentable outfit) every time I stepped outside my front door. Even when someone would say something homophobic or otherwise deeply hurtful, I couldn't just tell them to you know . . . even if they deserved it. I had to learn very polite, political ways to quickly separate myself from the offender and Peter from the negative claim.

The first step is to assess the situation: Am I safe, or is this person a "volcano," ready to blow up at me? What do I have to gain from engaging with this person? If a guy is calling me a name in the produce section at the grocery store, nothing good can come from any conversation I have with him. He thinks he knows who I am and has responded to that false image.

However, there are other situations in which I've been able to have a little fun. If some lady snarls something rude to me in passing at Target, it's easy to disarm her with openness. "I'm sorry? Did you have a comment you'd like me to submit to the administration?" Typically, these sorts of people always get embarrassed and shuffle away; they don't expect you to respond to their rude commentary. It's sort of like Twitter in that respect. (On the other hand, when someone at a rally is shouting at me that I'm Satan here to suck the blood of children, my first thought is *Well . . . they're clearly never going to have a conversation about equality.*

I don't consider that kind of aggressive, vitriolic person a lost cause, exactly, but I don't consider them worth my time in the moment, either. Which is also sort of like Twitter.) Ultimately, the advice I'd give for dealing with these situations resembles what I'd tell a student who was being bullied: remember that person's comments say more about them than they do about you.

....

Peter was showing me a world I hadn't known existed. I wasn't sure if I immediately liked it, mostly because I didn't feel like I was supposed to be in it, but I reckoned it didn't matter anyway because I wouldn't be part of it for long. Peter wasn't necessarily comfortable in all these spaces, either (in fact I'm sure he found them exhausting at times—he's an introvert), but he seemed to approach them with a confidence that I admired and lacked. Though our relationship was going really well, it seemed too good to be true. I'd never had an experience that suggested the nice thing would work out in the end. Everything had always felt especially difficult for me to figure out on my own, and I had never been around anyone like Peter, who made me feel like it all added up to something and that I was worthy of good things.

If it were just about public appearances and acting gracious as the mayor's partner, that would have been an easy enough emotional endeavor to pull off. But it wasn't only on special occasions, with voters and constituents, that I felt the need to be more buttoned-up and presentable. Most of Peter's college friends come from Harvard, Oxford, and other more formal institutions—I'd always been led to believe that this made them better than me and my experiences. Their skills and accomplishments are easy to describe: they've traveled the world on scholarships, taught at Ivy League schools, won awards, and been in the news for the right reasons. They're also about seven years older than I am, so the success disparity makes some sense, but at first, it felt like they all came from Planet Genius. I would be at these events with Peter in New York or DC, and whenever any of his friends asked me what I did for a living, I had to reply that I was a substitute teacher and graduate student. Their response was very different from what snarky people at parties said: they never made me feel like they were looking down on me; they welcomed me into their lives because Peter meant so much to them, and I was struck by their sincere interest in my studies and experience in the classroom. Nevertheless, being surrounded by so many people who had achieved so much still made me look down on myself. In graduate school, I would get frustrated doing my readings, which often took me an entire day to finish, and sometimes my thoughts would start to spiral. Why can't I understand this article? Why didn't anyone tell me this stuff before? If Peter helped me, I would start to focus on him: Why does Peter know all these words I don't know? Everything seemed to come so much easier to him. It seemed as if Peter had never struggled to do his homework in his life, and what's more, he wouldn't have still been doing homework at age twenty-eight. (At age twenty-eight, he was running for mayor.)

Within these new social circles, I found myself surrounded by editors and DC types, and I was even more out of my depth. Everyone was introducing themselves with a business card, which I didn't have, so I simply had business cards made up. "Chasten Glezman, Teacher," plus my email, of course. I never expected to get a job out of it, but when it came to navigating the DC handshake-card handoff, I started to feel like I could blend in just a little bit more. Upon inspecting my interlocutor's card, I'd most likely read something like "Executive Assistant to the Ambassador." I would hand mine over and reply, "Well if you ever need any tips on managing middle-school students! Ha ha." Usually they would offer some deadpan response to my card and return to working the room, probably looking for another executive assistant to an ambassador to talk to.

Looking back, I'm really proud that I somehow managed to figure it out. I may have left school with a mountain of student debt and issues that are best left to a therapist, but I got my bachelor's degree, something

I thought so often about giving up and walking away from. Not only am I alive, but I found something I was good at, went to grad school, and finished at the top of my class. I often tease Peter because I have a master's and he doesn't—his Rhodes Scholarship covered a second bachelor's. Nevertheless, I still have to listen to his introduction five times a day: "Harvard-educated Rhodes Scholar who was elected the youngest mayor of a town over one hundred thousand, who took a seven-month leave of absence to serve his country in Afghanistan." There's no animosity here, because he always builds me up, especially when it comes to areas I excel in. If anyone in this relationship is bragging too much about the other at dinner parties, it's him. He never makes me feel like the dumber one in the relationship, even though I totally am the dumber one in the relationship. Not to be self-deprecating—I just married a polyglot superhuman.

I understand that part of what feels like his super-humanity comes from circumstance and luck, but I also believe that some of the ways Peter sees the world, and approaches service, come from the horrible years of repression he imposed on himself. I couldn't bear to stay in the closet when I was a teenager, and I spent years after I busted down the door battling depression and suicidal thoughts and coming to terms with the internalized homophobia that made me feel worthless. Peter, on the other hand, felt he had to stay in the closet if he wanted to make it, and he carried many of these same feelings with him in secret. I can only imagine how dark and isolating it must have felt for him. There's no right or wrong choice here, because there is no right or wrong way to come out. When you're ready, you're ready. I think Peter knew he was destined for great things, but he also knew that his potential wasn't set in stone: he felt the secret he was keeping could set him back, or stall him forever. I felt like it was eating me alive from the inside, and if I didn't let it out, it would destroy me. For many queer kids, it's not as simple as saying, "Let's see what happens!"

Not everyone gets a coming-out party. Even though I endured a lot of pain after I came out, I was able to be fully myself while living through it.

Although Peter didn't come out until he was in his thirties, he was able to come into his own in ways that continue, really, to elude me. Most of the country knows how impressive his résumé is. He'd become an expert on national security when I still probably couldn't use the phrase *national security* in a sentence. (Now I can, and on live TV!) I don't feel jealous of what he has—the only thing I find myself envying, in darker moments, is his assurance that things will always work out, and up. If coming out hadn't been what it was for me (including the mental health journey it sent me on), then perhaps figuring out the other parts of life could have continued getting easier for me as well. I could have applied myself to my undergraduate degree, gotten a job right out of the gate, and worked my way up. Who knows what job it would have been? I could have had a steadier life. Just by living in one place, and studying at one university, for four years, Peter developed a stronger connection to his studies, his friendships, and his community. I was always moving around, which made it harder to develop strong ties and focus on learning. Peter remained focused on the possible, not the personal, while I was mostly running from myself. I thank God our two paths eventually crossed.

This tension from our differences came to a head after we'd been living together for about a year. I'd finally done the responsible thing of officially changing my address, which meant that bills and collections notices were showing up at the house with increasing frequency. For the most part, I was fastidious about intercepting the mail because I was so anxious about Peter seeing one of the letters and asking questions about what I owed. I often got home before he did, so the mail was easier to collect, sort, and hide. I was always spiriting the mail away to my desk drawer. It was like I was conducting a doomed affair in a pre-telephone era, except that I dreaded opening the suspicious letters I received, and the weakness in my knees I felt when thinking about who sent them was not romantic at all.

I must have been acting weird, because one day Peter came into the living room holding an opened bill and said, "Chasten, you need to tell me what's going on." I'd missed a letter and he had opened it. I know many people will feel shock at this—and that many publications will be tempted to run "Mayor Pete Snoops Through His Husband's Mail—and He's Not Sorry!" headlines. He may have just assumed the official-looking letter was for him, but needless to say, he knew I needed a hand. Before I could answer, he added, "You need to let me help you."

Hearing someone I loved tell me I needed help made me burst into tears. In addition to my student loans—which I was able to avoid for the time being, since I was in school—I'd also been dodging medical debt for years. While living in Chicago and being in-between jobs, I didn't have health insurance. One day, I developed an excruciating stomachache, like nothing I had ever felt before. There was a lot of blood involved—I'll spare you the other details. After a few hours of hoping it would subside, I knew I couldn't stay home. I had to go to the ER. I took an Uber to the nearest hospital and wound up having to stay overnight. The next morning, while the nurse was administering my medications, I asked, "Am I being charged for those?" She laughed. "Well, of course."

"It's OK," I said, trying to get her to stop what she was doing. "I'll have my boyfriend bring Tylenol from home. Am I charged every time something is scanned?" Again, she chuckled. "That's how it works." For all my experience working as a nursing assistant, medical billing was not something I was familiar with. I asked to speak to the doctor for a discharge, fearful that the bill was going to be too much. He suggested a week of bedrest. I asked if I could do that from home, since I didn't have insurance. He eventually obliged. I took an Uber back home.

A few weeks later, one bill came in from the hospital, one from the radiologist, one from the lab, and several others from different sources. After one night in the hospital, I'd come away with $12,000 in bills. (I didn't even have a lake-view room!) I could never seem to get a handle on them—it was all too much. I'd call, explain my situation, and say I had no insurance, and a passive collections agent would respond, "I'm sorry to hear that, Mr. Glezman. Will you be making a payment of $12,000 today?" Within a few months, my credit was trashed, and it seemed I would never get out from under the constant stream of bills. I was angry at myself for going to the hospital, but what are you supposed to do when you're in that much pain, and you're afraid? On top of the reminder of the debt's impenetrability, it was so embarrassing. I hated what I thought it said about me: that I was foolish, that I had failed from the get-go by taking out so many student loans, not having health insurance, and paying for stuff with credit cards when I didn't have any money in the bank.

Why would someone like Peter want to be with someone like me? I was constantly admitting my faults and fears to him while he listened patiently and responded with reassurances and actionable suggestions for managing the problem (he loves an actionable suggestion), as well as reminders of all the things that made him love me. I was totally depleted of any feeling except fear. How many issues was I going to reveal to him before he decided it was too much? We'd already talked about my trust issues, the sexual assault, my sense that it was impossible to get my life going. He knew I had a lot of student loans, but he had no idea how bad they were; I'd made it seem like I'd pulled myself up by the bootstraps to make my life in Chicago work. He covered most of our expenses. Sometimes I'd cover groceries, insisting on paying at the checkout while praying my credit card wouldn't get declined.

He'd never seemed to care about any of this before. We didn't really talk about dividing up our budget, and I felt like a grifter, dreading the day Peter would come to his senses and realize he'd been subsidizing the life of an indigent. It was like we'd each been approaching a brick wall from opposite sides, and with this new revelation we'd gotten as close as we could to each other, but we were going to have to admit there was no way I could get around it to reach him on the other side.

As I sobbed, I knew our relationship was over. Maybe he wouldn't break up with me right then—that would be insensitive—but he would slowly pull away, spend more nights "working late," until it became clear there was no more "us." I could see the whole sad story unfolding right there, and then I would be back where I started, except I would also be in South Bend, so I would have to move again, because I was not about to endure a devastating breakup only to continue living in the town that was *literally run by my ex*. I would never be able to show my face at Fiddler's Hearth again!

No, Chasten—wrong again. Peter sprang into action, or his version of action, which is to say he went to his computer and opened a blank spreadsheet. "Let's figure this out." He was so reassuring in that moment, it was almost overwhelming. (He never panics, and it's easy for his calm affect to wear off on you.) We spent the next few days figuring out who I owed, what I owed, and if it was negotiable; he helped me make calls to the collections agencies and hospital billing departments. He also helped me come up with a budget so that I could manage my finances while still paying off the debt. Until I met Peter, no one had ever explained finances to me. Balancing a budget seems like it should be straightforward—just, like, add and subtract, right?—but it turns out: it's not! Watching Peter look at all my different interest rates and figure out the smartest way to work through my debt was like watching one of those champion Rubik's Cube solvers: the concentration, the expertise, the elegant maneuvering, the speed, the color coding!

Initially, if briefly, I felt relief—for the first time ever, someone confident, capable, and assured was not only telling me everything was going to be OK, but also demonstrating to me how that would come to be the case. But guilt and shame rushed in soon after. I had burdened someone else with my burden. Not just someone else—someone I loved. I don't think there's a single person in the entire world who enjoys borrowing money, especially from their partner. The feeling that I was a deadbeat and a moocher had been around from the beginning. I'd been borrowing things from him and accepting his help since we met. Now this element of our relationship consumed me. It felt so uneven. What did I have to offer him in return?

I really believed that having money meant you were successful, and my inability to pay for the ER was yet another example of what a failure I was. I didn't want to be in debt to someone I loved; it was bad enough being in debt to people I hated. But when I expressed all this to him, he convinced me that accepting his help wouldn't hurt our relationship. "Seeing the person you love walking a little lighter, knowing they're cared for and going to be OK, is a far better feeling than having money," he said.

Before my first full-time teaching position, I never had any disposable income, so I didn't know how to save it. I still don't quite understand the ins and outs of retirement funds or the majority of lines on our tax returns, mostly because I still can't wrap my mind around the fact that any of that stuff really exists. I was always horrible at prioritizing and strategizing; I just panicked and bought whatever I needed and didn't think about the future, because the future was almost certainly going to be bad.

It turned out, though, the future wasn't so bad, because I found a loving partner who was willing to hold my hand and help me figure it out. Someone who was willing to have tough conversations, and someone who was willing to let me cry on his shoulder when I needed to. I don't think I truly began to believe in myself until someone like Peter came along, looked me in the eye, and said, "You know I believe in you, right?" I was so wrapped up in the ways I felt broken, and he was so wrapped up in the ways I made him feel whole. He wasn't just helping me manage and surmount my medical and student debt—he was helping me manage and surmount my doubt. That is partnership, and that is love.

In return I believe I did the same for him. He'd always been so driven by success and achievement that he believed having anything else in his life was incompatible. When the opportunity for advancement appeared, he took it. When the opportunity for love appeared, he ran. By the time we met, he, too, was ready to ask for help.

For all the blubbering I did on the couch, I'd like to think I did a great deal of listening as well. Peter is known for daydreaming, or at least getting lost in thought. I usually poke at him when it seems he's gone off somewhere else in his head. "Hey," I'd say. "Where'd you go?" At first, he'd just say sorry and come right back to me with a smile. But with encouragement, ("Peter, tell me what's going on in that head of yours"), his "Sorry" slowly evolved into "I don't know how to put it into words," which, over time, became "Chasten, can I tell you something?"

I believe those exchanges prepared us for what came next. Though we're very different people in some ways, we both have the same approach to each other's problems: "I love you. How can I help?"

10

Vows

Peter likes to poke fun at me for how up front I was about marriage on our first date, but he's quick to tell that part of the story when journalists or friends pry, which vindicates me. I know I was a little too forward, but I was just done with the bullshit and needed to start focusing on the good shit. But the gamble that is TMI paid off—it didn't take us very long to realize how in love we were. Peter is surprisingly romantic for a know-it-all. He has an eye for special details that probably comes from how much he reads. In our early years of dating, when I was traveling between Chicago and South Bend for graduate school, he would leave me little notes to find when I came in at midnight. Sometimes they'd even show up in my lunchbox—tiny gestures of motivation and encouragement, and a reminder that I for once had someone in my corner cheering me on. He's also a great, sensitive photographer; he always captures things I'd immediately forget about otherwise. When we're lying on the couch thumbing through old photos—friends' weddings, trips up north for Christmas, dancing with friends, sunsets in the backyard—I'm always taken by how he captures me and how he seems taken with my presence in his. Whether I'm laughing, napping, or playing with the dogs, being truly noticed can feel like a huge gesture.

I'd long known Peter was the one, but I didn't have plans to propose to him. For one thing, he'd only just come out right before we got together, and I wanted to make sure he was ready. For another, cultural understandings of marriage proposals are 100 percent heterosexual, with the man getting down on one knee and I don't even need to finish the rest of that sentence. Lately, there have been subversions of the theme, with women proposing, or the couple discussing their plans to marry beforehand without either one of them arranging an embarrassing surprise on the Jumbotron. But gay proposals are rarely discussed, and at the time I'd certainly not heard about any. I'd thought so much about marriage, but I hadn't given much consideration to what happens between being not married and married. I'd always imagined the "Yes, yes, of course, yes!" excitement, but I'd never imagined who was asking. Or where. Or how.

I was still not thinking about proposing when the race for the Democratic National Committee chair was approaching, and Peter had to decide over Christmas 2016 if he was going to run for the position. We had planned to take a trip to Europe together. (By this time, we discovered we both shared an affinity for loyalty programs. We were always finding creative and elaborate ways to acquire airline miles in order to save them up for a big trip.) But now that Peter was a potential contender, he needed to stay behind to work out the details with his team. We decided that I, always up for an adventure, would do the first part of the trip—Turkey—alone, and he would meet up with me in Berlin a few days later.

Turkey was wonderful, but I was really looking forward to meeting Peter in Berlin and, among other things, showing off my German to the infamous speaker of eight languages. (Thankfully, German is not one of them.) On the late-night flight from Istanbul to Berlin, I settled into my seat, put my headphones on, and embarked on a nap. Then, too soon into the voyage, a flight attendant was speaking over the intercom in a rushed, urgent tone. She didn't speak English, and I couldn't make out all her German—all I knew was that we were making an emergency landing for what the pilot later called "secret reasons." A woman in the back of the plane, who must have heard the flight attendants talking in the galley, promptly asked/shouted if there was a bomb in the bathroom. The situation was so abruptly absurd and terrifying that I could hardly bring myself to believe that it was anything more than a dream. It was far too surreal. As passengers panicked around me, standing up and demanding the flight attendant tell them what was going on, I attempted to text Peter as the plane descended faster than I had ever felt a plane descend before. The man next to me was crying and texting his wife back in the States. We looked at each other; his eyes seemed to express "Surely, we're not dying like this." He and I frantically texted our respective partners while other passengers shouted and demanded answers as they moved around the cabin. The plane quickly approached some distant lights in the darkness. The texts I sent to Peter went something like "something happening on plane, love you love you love you." I'm extremely dramatic in day-to-day life, but when things are actually dramatic, it's hard to match expression to reality.

When we finally touched down in what turned out to be Bucharest, we weren't allowed to taxi to the terminal, and police met the plane on the tarmac. Passengers were moving around the cabin—as much as that was possible—and demanding to get off the plane. I sat still in my seat, waiting for answers. And, I guess, in the back of my mind, for terror. Eventually, we learned that there wasn't a bomb in the bathroom. They'd just thought there *might* be! I had never breathed such a sigh of relief.

By the time I made my way to Berlin, I was having the kind of thoughts you expect to follow a near-death experience: *Life is so fragile! Live every day like it's your last! Leave it all on the field!* So I decided, the moment that plane took off, that when he got to Germany, I would propose to Peter.

We'd been together for a little over a year at this point, and living together for several months. It was fast, but it wasn't Elvis-officiating-in-Vegas fast. Still, I knew Peter wasn't ready. Not that he had told me he wasn't, but I just knew he wasn't. We loved each other, but there was no rush on either of our parts. I just needed to express what I felt, that when he was ready to move forward, I would be, too.

I decided to do it with a watch, because, you know, time. I thought this could be a nice combination of the two types of marriage proposal. I would be initiating a pragmatic discussion about marriage with my partner—the modern way—but I would also be able to maintain some element of the romantic ambush, which still had its appeal because, well, it was romantic. I'd never heard of a proposal being done this way, but once I saw the watch in the store, I knew it was the right move. Besides, the watch was much, much more affordable than the rings in the next display case over.

When Peter arrived, I was all emotion. He was so excited, and relieved, to see me; I was so reassured by his presence but also extremely antsy about the surprise. He arrived at the hotel, and before he had a chance to settle in, I asked him to join me on a walk. It was freezing outside, but he agreed. We walked down Unter den Linden to the Brandenburg Gate, where I explained I used to walk this street when I was studying in Germany. I'd take the train from Loburg, get off at the Hauptbahnhof, and walk my way around the city. I loved taking a break at the Brandenburg Gate to people-watch. My visits to Berlin had been some of my favorite times during that period—they made me feel truly independent, like I could be whoever I wanted to be. I told Peter that I didn't want to watch the rest of the world go by without him. I didn't ask if he would marry me, but as I reached into my bag, leaning against the Pariser Platz sign, just outside the American Embassy, I told him that I wanted him to know I was a sure thing if and when he was ready.

His eyes widened, and we both began to cry. It was such a happy moment that I thought no traditional proposal could have been better—not least because this was entirely ours.

Time passed. 2017 was 2017—terrible in new and surprising ways. Peter didn't win the DNC chair election, so we went home and stayed focused on South Bend.

Then, about a year after I proposed, we were in O'Hare, about to take another short winter vacation. Every time we made our way through ORD, we'd make a point of passing the gate where I had first "met" Peter, chatting on Hinge as I waited for exchange students to show up. Sentimental, but it was nice. Everything seemed normal, except that that morning, Peter had been really adamant that we get to the airport on time. (Despite his on-top-of-it-all reputation, this was very unlike him.) Once we were in the terminal, he casually suggested we swing by B5, as was tradition. Not too weird. When we got to the gate, it was packed—a flight was about to board. (Or maybe the flight wasn't scheduled to board for fifteen more minutes, but everyone couldn't help themselves and had to line up anyway.) That was when things started to get a bit strange. "Oh, let's sit down for a second," Peter said, but two minutes later he was standing again. "What if we stood behind the gate agent's desk by the windows? To look at the planes?" OK . . .

We found ourselves in a little private area among all the angry people irritated that they still had several hours to wait before they could arrive, tired and probably smelly, to where they were going. We stood there watching the planes for a moment, and then he began his monologue. Life with him would always be this way, if I were OK with it—sneaking moments away, an adventure both coming and going. Then, he reached into his backpack, got down on one knee, and presented, with the typical proposing-man flourish, a ring.

I really, really hadn't seen it coming, but of course I said yes. Then we got some coffee and went on our trip. I spent the whole flight looking over at Peter. How did I get so lucky?

....

The best part about planning our wedding was that Peter didn't care about the little details [cackles evilly]. He just wanted to get married in his church. He came to our initial "get to know you" meeting with the wedding planner and was so out of his element that he helped pick the colors (blue and purple) and then gracefully bowed out. (Later, he contributed the Wedding and Budget Planning 2018 spreadsheet.) He does not care about chair shapes or flowers or linens, a viewpoint I respect but do not understand.

I'd like to think I was not a groomzilla, but I came to understand why wedding planning makes everyone turn into the worst version of themselves. Because the finer details of wedding ceremonies aren't actually *that* important, they're the perfect outlet for melodrama. Everyone involved feels comfortable projecting their deepest insecurities and desires onto napkin shape and seating arrangements because, in most cases, the wedding only lasts a day. Then you have to go back to your life. Or your glamorous Instagrammable honeymoon on a Greek island. But after that you definitely have to go back to your life.

We were ready to get married and weren't really interested in a long engagement. This was for the best, as the conversations that started with "Maybe let's get married in the summer with just our families up in Traverse City" quickly turned into "How do we get the guest list down from six hundred?!" We were engaged in December, and by April invites were going out for a June wedding. I had no interest in dragging out plans for a year, and hindsight being 20/20, can you imagine planning a wedding while one partner is running for president? Neither of us saw that one coming until months later, fresh off a honeymoon, when we started throwing the idea around.

As they do, normal wedding pressures crept in. Dueling maternal opinions gave way to "Well, it would be rude not to invite so-and-so." "Oh, if we invite her then we have to invite him." "She would be so fun on the dance floor!" Peter's list of people who fit into the "It would be rude not to" category was much longer than mine, and somehow we went from "We'll only invite our parents and close friends" to a list of five hundred people.

We agreed we wanted to have a fun, low-key wedding, not just because we're fun and low-key people—*puts hands on hips* we ARE—but also because we had an eye on the budget. Still, the pressure to put on a fancy, elaborate party remained, and it grew as the date approached. There were going to be some high-profile guests, and once we announced the engagement, we learned that the *New York Times* wanted to write a Vows article about the day. I knew they'd focus on all the little details we were planning on omitting from the budget. (Not the last time the *Times* would scrutinize every little detail.)

We wanted to hold our ground, but people kept telling us: this is the most high-profile gay wedding in the United States this year! Plus, it had been a long time since the mayor had gotten married in office, and in a town the size of South Bend, that was kind of a big deal. *It's the mayor's wedding! It's the mayor's gay wedding! You have to do it right!* Maybe the idea that our union was really important to the *very history of this nation* went to our heads a little bit, but soon we were calling wedding planners and figuring out how to make our special day as "South Bend" as possible. I didn't want to forfeit our personalities just because people were paying attention to it, but it felt at the time that the wedding had to be a *thing*.

One thing led to another, and expenses just kept adding up. The wedding planners had their own ideas, our parents had their own ideas, and the second cousin who got married in Florida had an *absolute must* idea. "You should do a fireworks display!" Yeah, no. "Oh, Chasten. I hear you on the small arrangements, but a slightly larger flower display would be so beautiful in June! It's just $1,000 more!" (Just?! No thank you.) "Mono-grammed cocktail napkins are an essential touch!"

Can I just stop here and offer a piece of wedding advice?

NOBODY NEEDS MONOGRAMMED COCKTAIL NAPKINS.

We'd move on to more elaborate ideas, like adding seventeen special details to each guest's place setting so they'd have no space to actually eat! (Besides a small table for Grandma and Peter's aunts from Malta, we decided to skip a seated dinner altogether.) There are so many little things that no one cares about or notices, but the people selling them assure you they're vitally important.

We didn't go wild over monogrammed napkins, but we ended up paying more than we wanted to. (Of course.) We decided to have the ceremony itself at the Saint James cathedral. As for the fun stuff: Peter and I set aside time to drive over to Chicago for what we assumed would be a long day of choosing suits and outlining wedding registries. As you might have guessed, he's not picky, but I am, and I just knew that I wouldn't find anything I liked—that I was in for a hard day of frustrations and disappointments. I steeled myself for this. What happened instead was that we walked into a department store and told an employee that our colors were blues and purples, and he brought back two Ted Baker suits in different blues, both with purplish undertones. We tried them on, loved them, and were out of there in less than half an hour.

I'd been shopping with girlfriends for their wedding dresses, and so I was sort of disappointed that I didn't get to have a big day out choosing a suit, getting a little tipsy on champagne as I modeled and fretted about options for an adoring group of friends. But we did have a nice time. By the time we made it to Pottery Barn for the registry, however, both of us were crashing and began scanning things the clerk told us we *absolutely must have* just so she would leave us alone. After the wedding, we ended up with four forks and thirty plates.

As the wedding approached, there was minor chaos. The parking lot was more potholes than gravel, and the venue had said they'd level it before we came in with our tents. But that didn't happen. My dad, being the magnificent *fixer of all things* guy he is, took his truck, borrowed a wheelbarrow and some shovels from a neighbor, picked up a load of gravel, and did it himself the day before the party. The same day, the taco truck came to set up and discovered the power outlet they needed wasn't available, so an electrician had to come and install one. (Inevitably, during the reception, the power kept going out because the taco truck was sucking so much energy. The guests salvaged the situation by singing until electricity was restored. No one could be too upset about it—at least there were tacos.)

On the day of, it was miserably hot, pushing one hundred degrees and humid. (Someone tell Alanis that rain isn't nearly as bad as projected thunderstorms that never arrive.) All our flowers wilted within an hour of being delivered; Mom, being a problem solver, procured a cooler and ice and those little, battery-operated misty fans for the wedding party. It was less than half an hour before we all gave up and ditched the whole photoshoot idea, retreating to the air-conditioned basement of Saint James until it was showtime.

Even with all the near catastrophes, the day was wonderful. June 16 was the same day as South Bend's first-ever downtown Pride celebration, so on our way from the church to the reception, we joined in the revelry, arriving in a red 1961 Studebaker Lark (manufactured in South Bend) loaned by a fellow parishioner as the crowd whistled and cheered. But my favorite part was sneaking away with Peter and watching everyone from the staircase, seeing our friends meet, enjoy one another's company, and get competitive with one another on the claw machines and Skee-Ball alleys we had rented for the reception. (Those are our favorite arcade games.) And then we took to the dance floor, of course.

Before I met Peter, my ideas about marriage were, naturally, very abstract and very limited. When I thought it would never be available to me, I wanted it desperately, but I didn't know much about what I was so eager to have. Marriage equality passed three days after my birthday in 2015, and though I read the headlines with a sense of victory, the decision still felt precariously abstract. I never assumed it would pass, and when it did I couldn't believe it wouldn't be overturned. The news didn't compute; I knew too many people who hated gay people for it to make sense.

Once marriage began to feel like a real possibility, it was still overwhelming to think about. My student and medical debt had always been a strain I thought I'd have to deal with alone, and although I worried they would feel like a burden to Peter, his ability to take it all on board, as well as his help managing my anxieties, meant more to me than any material help he's given me. The deep, almost spiritual commitment to take care of someone and remain on their side through everything, from squirrels in the ceiling to ad hominem attacks on the debate stage, is something I'm so grateful I get to experience in my lifetime. It infuses disagreements—about the mundane and about slightly weightier matters—with purpose and security. And it makes all the good times better, too.

Three
·····················

11

Running: Part Two

Marriage didn't change much between me and Peter. I'd already been the mayor's partner; being the mayor's *husband* had a nice ring to it, but the expectations were the same. I was representing his administration in a tricky capacity: I had no official title and no real guidelines to follow, but if I messed up, it would reflect poorly on him, or even on the larger idea of who we were or could be. I had been building my own model for what the mayor's spouse did, and I thought I was doing a pretty good job.

Because Peter and I met during his reelection campaign for mayor, I had gotten a thorough introduction to campaigning early on. Although we'd only just started seeing each other, I'd often stop by the campaign headquarters in the back of the local county Dems' office, and he'd introduce me to his small staff. They must have known I wasn't just "a friend," but they never said anything about it.

We didn't have a ton of time to spend together, so I often went out canvassing with him, too. What better way to get to know your new boyfriend than by spending a few hours every weekend telling strangers why he was a good mayor? (And hearing what they thought of him.) On weekends, we'd pick up coffee at Chicory Cafe, go to the campaign office to collect materials, spend a few hours knocking on doors, and then head back to the office, where he'd make phone calls and have meetings and I'd hang out getting to know his campaign manager and volunteers.

This was my first time being involved in a political campaign, and it showed me how fast they could move. Even though there wasn't nearly the same level of media scrutiny as during a presidential race, and even though he already had the Democratic nomination and was likely to win reelection, Peter was always checking his phone; he had to be on call for any and all questions or near disasters.

As our relationship got more serious, I helped out more and more. Constituents knew education was my thing, but I didn't have a specific role or initiative. Peter and I would talk about the importance of spending more time in public schools and hosting more education events. He likes children and values teachers, but before he started dating someone with experience in the classroom, he hadn't realized how truly helpful it could be to stop and talk to families and children at length. I taught him the importance of getting down to eye level with kids and how to actively listen to them.

Once we were engaged, and then married, it became clearer to the community that I was there to stay. Technically, I became the First Gentleman. But what did that mean? I tried to start a teachers' support group called Recess, which met at a local coffee shop, the aim of which was to brainstorm ways to improve the public schools and work through problems together, but I felt so anxious about the appearance of a conflict of interest that it didn't end up going anywhere. Although the mayor's office and the school board were separate entities, I felt people would take my words on public education to be weightier than they were, or they would always be comparing me to Peter, thinking I was a lesser version of him. One time when I was subbing in South Bend, I went to a staff meeting at a school where I worked, and I raised my hand during a discussion about student behavior and classroom management problems. There was no recess in middle school, I pointed out. Why didn't we add it? What if, instead of always getting frustrated with students in the cafeteria, we let them run around in the gym or out on the football field when they finished their lunch? Teenagers also needed time to socialize freely and expend some of the excess energy they used to get into trouble; there was no time built into their daily schedule for just *being*. Couldn't we have teachers rotating on recess duty?

"Is that your idea, or is that the mayor's idea?" came the response from a teacher in the back. I was so shocked. Of course, it was my idea; I was in graduate school to become a teacher and had recently been discussing this very idea with other teachers. But even if it *was* Peter's idea—who cared? It was a great idea.

While I felt nervous that I was always being watched and scrutinized, South Bend had become very . . . comfortable? with me. I'd be half-asleep in line at the coffee shop when a sharp voice would come from behind me: "Hey. Your husband's really messing up this streets initiative." I'd turn around, they'd look down at their phone. They weren't so much inviting a conversation as they were treating me like a living, breathing suggestion box. More explicit refrains weren't uncommon. And then there were the awkward moments when I would be picking up toilet paper and a neighbor would stop to gush about my husband, whom they'd watched on the news that morning and thought was "just so darn cute." I'd try to slip the TP into my cart without breaking eye contact. At first, I didn't always know how to respond to some of the negativity or political commentary, which I didn't entirely understand; I can't imagine ever approaching a stranger and immediately offering advice or feedback about their spouse. I usually had no idea what some of these people wanted to hear or what they thought they'd get out of these confrontations. For the most part, the interactions were positive and courteous, usually resulting in a selfie or an invitation to some sort of community event. But when it came to meeting frustrated citizens, I knew the listening part, even on my end, was extremely important. Being mayor is a difficult, hands-on job that requires officials to take on some of the most important challenges, and confront some of the hardest political issues, of everyday lives. I couldn't just scowl at constituents and tell them to get lost when it was uncomfortable. In some sense, they felt I was responsible for the city's problems—whether they were right or not, that was what I had signed up for by marrying Peter.

Eventually, I learned to keep my responses short and sweet if I didn't have the answer they were looking for: "If you have an issue, you can call 311 or the mayor's office. Right now I'm trying to get a cup of coffee." If someone was being truly hateful, bigoted, or otherwise crossing the line, I would add, "The city is committed to helping all the human beings who live here." Although I always felt bad that some constituents were so dissatisfied, and I wanted to help, I knew there was little I could do to assuage their anger in the moment, but I would silently remember to relay any legitimate concerns to Peter and then go about my day.

Even though I'd started experiencing my fair share of political drama, I hadn't realized—or ever thought much about—how stable this lifestyle was. It seemed new and strange to me. For a time it was surprising, almost exciting, to be recognized out in public, while at the grocery store or walking the dog. (The majority of people were friendly and supportive. Often, someone just wanted to "pick my brain.") I was going to interesting events and learning so much about politics, government, cities, and schmoozing, even if the lessons weren't always happy ones. Peter's schedule was hectic, but although there was no nine to five, we adapted and had a regular-ish life. On weekends he'd always have a couple of obligations, but we could usually enjoy some free time, even traveling for weddings or going to Michigan to see my family. And his staff respected our date nights—not least because I insisted on it. Repeatedly. Wednesdays, 6 p.m. sharp. If he was going to be more than fifteen minutes late, his chief of staff had to let me know. Having to ask Peter to help us establish this very firm expectation made me feel overbearing and like a nuisance at first, but his time was a hot commodity and everybody wanted "just five minutes." If there wasn't a hard no, six o'clock turned to six-fifteen, which turned into "just one more call," which eventually delayed us an hour or two. If he was doing morning media the next day, and had to get up very early, then he typically wanted to be in bed by 10 p.m., so we didn't have much time to waste. Gym, dinner, walk the dogs, one episode of *Game of Thrones*. Every minute was precious.

I'm sure you can guess where this story is going. When Peter and I went on our first date, in the middle of 2015, the future seemed a ways away, but I still had to ask what was "next" for him. This wasn't exactly a euphemism for "Are you planning on ever running for president?" because it would never have occurred to me in a million years that anyone I spoke to might one day run for president. I just meant, like, well, "You're young, you're clearly ambitious, and you can't be the mayor forever." (Though if he had been planning on being mayor forever, that would have also been good to know, because it would have been a major red flag and this book would be called *My Date with a Dictator*.) Plus, as I've already said, I was shamelessly focused on my romantic future when I met Peter. I wanted to know if he had time for a serious relationship.

Initially, he was equivocal. "I don't run for office to run for another office," he said. This seemed a little too coy, so I pressed. "Come on," I replied. "You don't have *any* idea what you're going to do after this? Governor? House? Senate? Very important position that I haven't heard of but is actually very important?" But he was firm. He maintained that he was really focused on doing a good job for South Bend.

As our relationship progressed, I was really impressed with the way he thought about politics. He was ambitious without being ruthless, pragmatic without being insensitive. He understood that politics could be dirty and craven—all politicians understand this. But it's also the system we have to work with. If you do a good job as mayor, he said, you have options; if you do a bad job, then nothing else matters. He understood that doing good for the community came first, and that is one of his defining characteristics as a public servant. I had watched others in politics focus solely on the ladder, climbing it fast and doing whatever it took to reach the top first. But with Peter, I was struck by his investment in the *job*—in the people he was elected to serve and his ability to make their lives better. Even when it was hard, and he was asked to solve for factors beyond his control, the grace with which he approached service, and the office, astounded me. Even in the comfort of our own home, when I'd ask him what he *really* thought, he rarely had a harsh word for anyone. Once, I asked him how he felt about a figure in town who was known for showboating and holding up progress for the sake of a few likes or shares on Facebook, or maybe even a headline. "Holding grudges is exhausting," he replied. If it was Mayor's Night Out, the city's regular town hall, you would think whoever was seated in front of him was the most important person in the room, and that's because, to him, they were. I had a lot of ideas about who politicians were, but living up close to one, especially one so deep and active in the arena, showed me just how brave, empathetic, and impactful truly good servants could be.

We'd only been together a few months when the 2016 presidential campaign started heating up. As he and I got closer, Peter was doing a lot of work for Hillary Clinton in Indiana, supporting her around the region and facilitating an event at a United Auto Workers plant. We discussed the slim possibility that he might be appointed to some kind of junior position in her administration one day, but he mostly just wanted to do his part on the campaign as one of the more prominent Democrats in Indiana.

We all know how that whole thing turned out. On the day of the presidential election, I had class in Chicago, and I was nervously refreshing the news on my computer all day. By the time I was on the Amtrak back to South Bend at 9 p.m., things didn't look so good, but I continued desperately refreshing the news on my laptop. When the election was called, a group of men at the front of the train car started cheering, and I called Peter. *Did that really just happen?* He was just as dumbfounded as I was. We barely spoke in the car when he picked me up. Only when we got into bed and had the lights off could we broach the subject: this was terrifying. So many people were going to be empowered through the president-elect's xenophobia, racism, homophobia, and misogyny. How could the US survive four years of this man?

Meanwhile, the future of the Democratic Party was uncertain. If the world didn't end, a new guard was going to have to step in.

Nevertheless, I really didn't sense that Peter was interested in running for president, at least not in the foreseeable future. He was so young, and he only had experience with state and city politics, which was more than fine with him. He never talked about running for national office, and when people told him to run for Congress, he always said no way. Our district was gerrymandered, so the campaign would have been rough, if not impossible, but more importantly, Peter liked the work of local and state politics, where you got to see the effects of your work on the community. If you got it right, it really had an impact on people. As a congressperson, your time is filled with fundraising and fighting to keep your own seat. Running for governor of Indiana didn't make sense for him, either. He was always saying, "It's not about me, it's about what I can do differently," and he didn't feel he was the right choice.

Besides, almost as soon as Trump won, there were tons of Democratic names floating around about who would challenge him in 2020. (And, as we know, pretty much every single one of those people ended up running.) It just wasn't thinkable that Peter would run for anything other than mayor any time soon. Which, to be honest, I was grateful for: we'd been together for a little over a year and I felt like we were just settling into our life together.

Then, suddenly, at the end of 2016, he decided to run for DNC chair. I hadn't seen that coming, but as soon as we talked about it, I was super-pumped about the idea. It just made sense. The conversation in

Washington was so polarized and so far removed from the lives of everyday Americans; having a former mayor as chair would allow the DNC to shift its priorities to regular people, local leaders, and local electeds.

The campaign was scrappy, and we worked out of our house. Although I was still in graduate school at the time, I traveled with Peter for events and ran all the digital platforms myself. I never knew I had a knack for social media—I had accounts, but I never thought much about what I posted on them—but we were very successful getting his name out there. This was my first real experience with campaigning on a national scale. We were crisscrossing the country, and I was watching Peter take on national issues and debates with ease and grace. I was impressed with how he could stand next to other people onstage and calmly and clearly state his positions and opinions without making the fighting seem to be the central focus of his campaign. He had a knack for taking complex issues and making them seem understandable and solvable. As the race sped forward, we built an impressive base of volunteers who traveled to DNC debates and forums to support Peter and his take on the future of the Democratic Party. The conversations in Washington were far removed from the actual, real-lived experiences of people on the ground in places like South Bend, and we thought his experience as a mayor could help change that.

What I remember most was how fast everything went—two months from decision to concession. It was like running for president and high school senate combined: you were crisscrossing the country and all over national media to convince everyone that you were the right person to lead the party, but you were actually trying to convince about four hundred members of the DNC. The American people weren't the ones voting here.

Peter was a long-shot candidate, and he dropped out as soon as he knew he wasn't going to get the numbers. But the overall experience had been positive, the response to him was very encouraging, and he was happy to get back home, where he had more than enough on his plate as mayor. I had just proposed, and we were very happy.

During the DNC race, I was flying across the country with Peter and then making my way back to Chicago a few nights a week to attend graduate school classes. For the first time in my academic career, I really felt like I was cooking with gas. I looked forward to my classes, I dedicated myself to my readings, and I felt more driven than I ever had before. Once we were back in South Bend, my substitute teaching picked back up. By this time I had purchased a car, so I could teach full-time in South Bend while also making the two-hour drive into Chicago after school three days a week. I'd take an evening class and drive back to South Bend afterward. If there wasn't traffic, I could be home by midnight. I got by on iced coffee and books on tape.

I was devouring the work, and I loved being surrounded by other teachers and folks like me, who were choosing to pursue education as a profession. I spent hours speaking with my advisor, who encouraged me to write my thesis on the importance of teacher education work in the classroom. During my classroom observations in Chicago Public Schools, I was getting hands-on training from seasoned educators. I was excited that I was gaining the tools for a job I was really good at and motivated to wake up for.

I finished my master of education in the spring of 2017, and I wept when I received the news that I was graduating with honors. My undergraduate career wasn't easy, and for a long time, I looked down on myself because of it. Peter threw me a lovely graduation celebration, and even though I knew he was very proud of me, what really made me grateful in those days was just how proud I was of myself. For once, I was giving myself permission to feel and accept that pride.

Now, I needed a teaching job. There was (and still is) a severe lack of teachers in South Bend, but after doing a few interviews, I never got a call back. I think principals were worried about the increased scrutiny or conflicts of interest; everyone knew I was the mayor's boyfriend. A teacher I'd gotten to know during one of my interviews sent me a message to tell me that some teachers had asked why their open role wasn't being filled, and the principal had told the department, "We just don't need someone like him around here."

It was frustrating, but I understood their concerns. Even though the mayor's office is a separate entity from the school board in South Bend, for a while I contemplated not taking a job in South Bend while Peter was mayor. But then a small Montessori school just outside South Bend called to ask if I'd be interested in interviewing for a position overseeing their junior high program—they were also hoping I could start a drama program. I went in. I was very nervous about the prospect of teaching in a private school. I'd always wanted to be a public school teacher, and I also didn't want to make a political statement about private schools, which had been in the news a lot because of the Trump administration. I didn't want to offend anyone or reflect poorly on Peter. But the idea of having full autonomy over my own drama program— and of being a little out of the way, outside South Bend and Peter's domain— was really appealing, and I knew it was the right choice for me at the time. I took the job, which required another two years of certification, so by later that summer I began my extensive Montessori training.

I was every bit as excited and nervous as my middle schoolers on the first day of school. Everything they say about your first year of teaching is true. I was overwhelmed and exhausted, but I was so happy. I taught a combined classroom—seventh- and eighth-grade English, social studies, seminar, and drama. I worked hard to implement many of the elements of the pedagogies and practices I had studied in graduate school: social–emotional learning, peace curriculum, project-based learning, and arts integration. Both in school and out in the field, we spent a great deal of time on community building and care for the planet and environment. On Wednesdays we'd visit the South Bend Center for the Homeless, stocking their pantries, preparing meals, learning from the center's employees, and working with the children in their classrooms as part of our "service with" not "service for" others philosophy. I was up to my ears in parent emails and papers to grade, but I was finally feeling like I had something of my own, something I was getting pretty good at. I learned so much in the short time I was there, both from my additional training in Montessori education and from the precocious and independent students who pushed me hard every day.

Because it wasn't just the curriculum that excited me—it was the active, hard work of making space for students to feel safe and supported. I had one student with learning difficulties who had been shuffled through multiple area schools, struggling to find a place where they could learn and feel comfortable. In their first week in my classroom, they ran out the door, jumped in their mom's car, and rolled up the window while screaming, "Fuck you!" in my face. I wished them a pleasant evening. "I can't wait to see you tomorrow!" After I left for the campaign trail, they wrote me a letter to say how much they missed me. Another student struggled socially, wondering where they fit in and when to use their voice. I spent hours with them, before and after school, sometimes during lunch breaks, talking about how teenagers are complex creatures and how others' words don't always mean what they sound like in the hallway. "Other kids can be mean, yes, but other kids are also hurting and growing, too," I'd say. "Sometimes in ways they don't understand." I wasn't always sure I was breaking through to them, until one day, on the campaign trail, I received an email from them:

"Mr. B! I miss having you as my teacher so much! You were my favorite part about school. You made me and every kid feel that we were safe, loved, and unique. I miss you and think of you often, especially on my difficult days when I feel so lost."

Among everything I hoped to accomplish with my students, it was knowing I'd successfully created a safe space, the kind I never had as a middle schooler, that made me feel like I was doing the right work.

It wasn't until around August of 2018, after we got married, that running for president started to seem like it could be a possibility. I remember where I was when Peter first brought it up: he came into our bedroom, where I was folding laundry. "Do you want to sit down and talk?" he asked. "Nah," I said, "I'll keep folding." I should have sat down. When he said it, that some of his friends and advisors thought he should seriously consider running for president, I laughed. Not *at* him, of course. At the turn of events. Everything about our relationship had been so fast—now suddenly he was going to run for president. *How did I get here?* I wondered. *How did I fall in love with this person who's thinking about running for president?*

We started talking to our families about it around the beginning of September, mainly asking them to be careful with their social media and stop posting photos of me with bedhead on Christmas four years ago, Mom. (She didn't stop posting those photos.) Although it wasn't anything serious yet, the conversations started to make it seem real, especially because of the looks on my parents' faces. "What is our baby getting himself into?" they seemed to say.

Thanksgiving was the gut check . . . and both of our families were very encouraging. It's easy to be encouraging when you have no idea what you're getting yourself into, but Peter and I knew we wanted to do this together, with the full support of our loved ones, so their response was important. It wasn't ever really a question about if I'd come along for the ride: I would be with him full-time, supporting him and the campaign however I could. He never told me I should or had to leave my job; I just wanted to do it. Nevertheless, when I told him that of course I'd leave the classroom, I remember he looked so relieved. Neither of us had any idea what the experience would entail, and I think he was nervous about what this would do to our relationship and our plans to start a family. We also worried about what it would do to our income; even though I wasn't making an impressive amount of money as a teacher, I was making *some* money. But Peter did some spreadsheet magic and figured we could make it work, as long as we were very conservative.

So it was decided: we were doing it. Now what?

12

The Great Humanizer

By Christmas, steps were in place to launch the exploratory committee. We were just settling into married life, I had no idea what to expect from presidential politics, and I was worried Peter would feel like he was flying solo. Early that fall, Peter's father, Joe, had been diagnosed with an advanced and inoperable lung cancer, and he was in and out of the hospital. Soon after, his mother suffered a minor heart attack and had to have major heart surgery. There were many unknowns, so I decided to leave the classroom.

Without a doubt, this was a very difficult thing to do, but the shape of the campaign was so uncertain there was no way I could stay on in good faith. I'd warned the school that this might happen, so they weren't blindsided by the news, but when I told them we were going through with it, I said I could work until they found a replacement. They hired someone right away. I came back after the holiday break to say goodbye and tie up some loose ends.

I was really thriving as a full-time teacher, with a regular classroom and students with whom I was building lasting relationships. I felt really good about my work, and I knew I was helping my students. Right when I quit, my students had just started to open up. I didn't want to disrupt their year and all the progress they'd made. We'd built a really strong community, and it hadn't been easy. I was reluctant to leave, but I knew I needed to be on the trail with my husband and my family. I know I did a lot of good in the classroom, but it was still hard to look my students in the eye on my way out.

When I decided to leave, I had no idea when I'd be able to come back to another teaching job. I'd worked so hard to finish college, and then get my master's, and I was finally starting to feel like I was where I was supposed to be in my life. But so much was uncertain at the time, and I knew Peter would do a great job. I loved him, and I wanted to share him with the country.

Everyone knew Peter's campaign would be an extreme long shot, and even once we'd hired a few staff, found some volunteers (four of them, to be precise), and filmed a little low-budget video for the announcement, no one could really say what it all meant or what it would entail. Once it was official, he held a press conference, where most reporters couldn't even pronounce his name. The first several weeks were demoralizing: few people were taking him seriously, and I remember one TV news host even laughed at him during an interview. But not everyone was so dismissive, and watching some people immediately take to him and his message was gratifying. I was so proud and in awe of everything he was capable of doing, and how smoothly and respectfully he did it.

While Peter was very busy, the feeling of "OK, now what?" lingered for me—for a very brief period of time. I had no idea what my life was about to look like, and apparently neither did Peter. At first I thought I could spend a lot of time at home in South Bend before I would be asked to perform full-time political spouse duties. (What were those? Again, at the time, I had no idea. Smiling, waving, posting on Instagram?) Faced with a daunting amount of alone time, I took a part-time job as the curriculum director at the South Bend Civic Theatre, which was growing and had designs on totally revamping their education department. I pitched them for a month to let me come on, and getting the job felt like a huge win for me after the disappointment of having to leave teaching. They knew I might not last long, but between visits to the campaign office and supporting Peter at home or at his events, I was wondering if I'd left the classroom a bit prematurely.

This seemed like a great compromise: I could support my husband when he needed me, but when I was home, I could focus on things that brought me joy and contribute to the community as well. The theater outfitted my workspace, and I was ready to get going.

A month later, it was clear that this situation was not going to be tenable. We thought I could get by for a few months on a part-time basis, but the exploratory committee took off like a rocket. Peter's team never made direct asks of me, but I was always at their disposal, and I found myself asking them to let me go out there and do work on behalf of Peter. There was a lot of interest in his potential candidacy, and little groups of supporters around the country would often try to contact me—assuming the main event was too important—to see if I would come speak to them. Soon I had to quit the Civic Theatre job, too.

In South Bend, I thought I'd been the most active political spouse possible. I was super-accessible, available, and willing to chat with any constituent who wasn't actively insulting me, even if I had somewhere else to be. I always attended Mayor's Night Out, and I showed up at any event if it was appropriate for me to attend. I was never saying, "You have fun, sweetie—I'll be at home watching *The Bachelor*." Though at times I really wanted to.

I thought being a presidential candidate's spouse would be like that, just more so. When we started talking about running, we promised each other that we would make it as fun as possible and that we, under no circumstances, would pretend to be anyone we're not. Who the hell knew what it was actually like to run for president? When Peter asked, "Are you sure you wanna do this?" I didn't hesitate. "Yeah! I mean, I have no idea what *this* means. But yes."

....

In January the campaign began to set up shop in an old psychiatrist's office in downtown South Bend. It had yellow walls—not dissimilar from the confusing neon that once graced our own kitchen—and carpet that looked like it had been installed during the Eisenhower administration. But it overlooked the courthouse, and its shabby appearance really made you feel like you were part of an upstart grassroots operation. Every other day it seemed that there was a new staffer or two, with more and more people crowding the office, bustling past one another, talking into iPhones, resting their laptops on boxes of Peter's books or newly delivered office supplies. The proportion of usable chairs to people was comical. Notre Dame students could be found sitting on the floor or leaning against the wall. Everyone wore a look of excited terror.

There were three distinct rooms, and Peter's door was always closed. If he wasn't speaking to voters or the press, or reading something for approval, then chances are he was on the phone. Every time I stopped by, that was exactly what Peter was doing. I'd show up to drop off Chipotle, and though the closed door would indicate "phone time," I'd tap gently, slowly open the door, and immediately be faced with a surprised sea of staffers crammed into his tiny office, giving me the "he's on the phone, what the **** are you doing?!" face.

Peter would hang up a few minutes later and say something like, "Senator So-and-So says hi."

"Oh. Great," I'd reply, bewildered. "Well, here's dinner."

The campaign quickly grew, he started coming home later and later, and every free moment transformed into phone time.

I wasn't sure what was needed from me. In order to feel helpful, I'd swing by to say hello and see if I could do anything or run any errands, but mostly I'd see the offices couldn't hold another body and I was in the way. I'd peek into Peter's office, and the look in his eyes always said something like "I wish I could spend time with you, but . . ." I'd assure him it was OK—of course it was. Besides, if he became the president, he'd have to deal with much more demanding things than a husband who wanted to go see a movie.

I boosted office morale with intermediate deliveries of cookies or other treats and did my best to stay out of the way. On evening office visits, I'd get some updates on our upcoming travel and the press and book strategy. Rather than bombard Peter with questions while he was brushing his teeth and getting ready for bed, I found it easier to ask staffers what was going on. Usually my questions were quite simple, like "So, what the hell is going on?" Mike Schmul, our soft-spoken campaign manager, was famous for saying, "Yeah man, we'll see," with a look of excitement and bewilderment at just how fast life was changing for all of us.

When we had been assembling the exploratory committee for a few weeks, Joe's cancer took a turn for the worse. For a brief period, the doctors were hopeful, but Joe's lungs couldn't keep up. Peter and I sat by his bedside and held his hands, watching as Joe would dip in and out of sleep, occasionally opening his eyes to look up at Peter with such tenderness. Joe was an enthusiastic supporter of the idea that Peter run, and leading up to the holidays, he was eager to hear every update. When the time came to make a decision about whether we would fly to DC and announce the exploratory, I knew Peter was torn, but Joe insisted he go. When we returned to the hospital in South Bend, the nurses said Joe had stared at the television all day. Any time someone came into his room, he'd point to the screen and smile. When Peter and I rounded the corner into his room the next day, his father's face lit up. "Well, Dad," Peter said, as he leaned over to hug his father in bed. Joe placed his hand on the side of Peter's face as he took a seat next to the bed. Joe couldn't speak, but his face was beaming with pride. A few days later, he was gone.

....

My first sense that we weren't in Indiana anymore came during Peter's book tour for his memoir, *Shortest Way Home*, in February 2019, just a few weeks after he announced the exploratory committee. Showing up to the famous DC bookstore Politics and Prose, I was shocked to see a line around the block waiting to get in. It hadn't really dawned on me that people would come. Don't get me wrong, the book is incredible, and Peter had been making waves on national TV at that point, but the reality that people *knew of him* had yet to sink in. The bookstore staff had to set up an overflow room, and people were eventually turned away. I got a few grumpy looks from impatient fans as I tried to snake through the crowd to the front of the room, very Midwestern-like, apologizing profusely.

"Sorry, sorry, sorry. I'm his husband," I said.

"Yeah right" was the reply, though the person would begrudgingly let me through.

Besides that, the reception was warm. As he read from the book, the audience was rapt; they really wanted to hear what he had to say. Looking around, I was bursting with pride.

Afterward, he had a separate line for photos and autographs. I thought I'd be able to stand quietly off to the side, chatting with a few stray fans as I waited for him to finish. I was eager to get out of there and grab dinner. Instead, I was overwhelmed with people who wanted photos and wanted to talk . . . with *me*.

At first, this was very confusing—I hadn't written the book. I kept joking to the long line of people waiting to say hello to me that they were confused—the author was over *there*. I wasn't known as "Pete Buttigieg's Instagram-famous husband" at the time, and I didn't understand why people would be so interested in talking with me when the author, who might become the next president, was on the other side of the room. They insisted I sign his book—even after I assured them that I didn't write any of it—and then I'd pose for selfies and group pictures with eager college students. Folks were lingering around me much longer than they were allowed to hang out around Peter's table. Maybe it was the Midwestern Catholic guilt—I never want to disappoint—but I must have had a way of disarming people and inviting them into a conversation. As I looked around the bookstore, the lines didn't seem to be diminishing. Peter caught my eye from across the room, and flashed me a smile. "How about *this*?"

Watching people be starstruck by your husband is funny and weird. To me, he's just Peter. He's so down to earth, and he'll geek out on just about any subject. But students from George Washington would ask him something about civic innovation or sewer-system management (which is a real thing people are interested in), he would answer, and they'd giggle and walk away, looking like they'd just met James Dean or a Jonas brother.

To sign the books, I settled on variations of "I didn't write this book, but I love the man who did!" The dilemma of having to come up with a way to sign Peter's memoir was a representation of what the entire campaign would be like. I didn't feel super-comfortable being a person with an autograph. I also didn't want to make it seem like I was taking credit for my husband's work, or riding his coattails, but I also didn't want to disappoint these voters, who had spent time and money to hear him speak. At that point, I didn't even have an autograph; I'd never thought about what my signature looked like. But standing in that hot, crowded bookstore, surrounded by hundreds of people interested in my husband, I understood that, just by virtue of my relationship, I had become a public figure. That no matter what I said or did in my private life, there was always going to be some version of me out there shaped by and beholden to the expectations, biases, and hopes of complete strangers.

How *many* complete strangers? Again, I had no way to know. I thought, well, a few thousand. Not many politics junkies bother to learn much about political spouses—I figured I was going to be known by a subset of a subset of die-hards. I didn't have many Twitter and Instagram followers yet. I assumed the DC event was so popular because it was in DC—where politics are made (and destroyed).

But lo and behold, Peter's campaign started selling out events across the country, too. This was great for the campaign, because we had no money and had to focus on fundraising, but the response still baffled me. (In a good way!) When I was teaching part-time and working at Starbucks, I would have never paid $25 to go to a presidential campaign event, especially one I didn't know anything about. And I don't think I would have stuck around to get a selfie with the candidate's husband. Then again, politics was never an arena I thought I belonged in. These voters' passion was as inspiring as it was daunting.

It seemed like every day I was having a new epiphany about how my life was changing, and I didn't know if I liked it. All the stresses of being the mayor's husband had suddenly multiplied by fifty. On top of that, I had just quit the job I'd worked so hard to get, and it was as if I had no identity of my own—I was *only* the candidate's husband, which itself was a vague, undefined role. First openly gay presidential candidate's spouse: an objectively cool thing to be, but not one that came with a checklist. In those first months, I struggled to maintain a sense of myself, my priorities, and my history; I felt like half my personality was replaced with stress. There were so many things I could mess up—and I had no idea what they were! When I spoke to friends, they'd ask how I was, and I was only able to say, "I don't know."

In the meantime, we quickly grew out of the psychiatrist's office and had to move to a bigger office down the block, into a larger space above Chicory Cafe. Since this was where Peter and I would grab coffee before knocking on doors during his reelection campaign, the move had a nice symmetry to it.

As days turned into weeks, I felt more and more as if I were being carried along. I wanted to contribute, but the shoestring staff didn't always have the capacity to brief me on what was expected of me. Often, the campaign staff, and sometimes reporters, forgot that I was there, even as the press started to publish articles about the historic nature of my partnership. At one event, a journalist in a pack of reporters asked Peter, "So will your husband play a role in the campaign?" Peter replied, "Yes. I believe he's standing right behind you." The gaggle quickly turned around, found me leaning against a wall, snapped dozens of photos, and just as quickly pivoted back to the presidential wannabe. *Gee*, I thought. *Not my best angle.*

I was lucky that it seemed no one expected me to be a first lady–esque figure, filling a traditional, stifling gender role, but I knew there were still many lines I couldn't cross. If I seemed too gay, too masculine, too feminine, too serious, too casual, too present, or too mysterious, the press would say we were out of touch with the American people, or that I was threatening or a "liability"—one of the punditry's favorite words. The tweets would pour in, the media cycle would regurgitate them onto the chyrons, and the campaign would be toast.

But as a newcomer, Peter had to let people get to know him, so he essentially gave the press an all-access pass, which included opening up our home to television crews. My only objection was that we had very little time to set-dress. Who really cared if there were fresh flowers on the mantel, or if the books on the coffee table were appropriate? Well, I did, but there was no time or money. I really despise the floral futon in practically all of our living-room shots, but a new couch wasn't in the budget, and there was no time for the minor detail. I wanted to invite the American people into our living room. I wanted to invite them into our home, and I knew the important thing was seeing our love and affection, not our throw pillows. (Eventually, leading up to the Iowa caucuses, Peter would give the press all-day access on a bus tour, like on John McCain's "Straight Talk Express" in 2000. The press would cover events and then move to the bus for hours of on-the-record conversations between stops. With cameras on board, and the tape recorder always on, it was a minefield, and Peter made it look so easy. He was always extremely comfortable sitting in the hot seat and can talk at length about what seems like any given topic.)

Besides having to spruce up the house, though, there weren't too many live events for me to participate in, so my existing Twitter and Instagram accounts were getting more attention from me than usual. You know how it is—you're standing around waiting for something, so you scroll through your feeds, and then inspiration for the perfect photo caption strikes. I figured that if I wasn't speaking or prepping, I could pull back the curtain for my followers, which had naturally grown a bit since Peter was in the news all the time.

I could never have predicted what happened next. I'd had some conversations with the campaign about how to clean up my social media accounts, focusing on the sort of things right-wingers and Democratic opponents would try to manipulate and use against us, but they never asked me to go all in on the memes or anything like that. I'm a performer at heart, and performance involves some craft and strategy, but becoming "Pete Buttigieg's husband, Twitter celebrity" was not one prong of a grand election strategy designed to usher in the app-enabled era of millennial world domination. As a teacher, I knew my students could find my accounts if they wanted, so I was always careful about what I posted online; I started being a little more careful, but I wouldn't call it filtering myself. There are things it makes sense to post on Instagram and Twitter and things best kept to yourself; this is true for everybody, or should be at least. But I also didn't want to pretend to be more polished and reserved than I really am, like Jackie Kennedy with an iPhone camera. If I had, I would have failed. Besides, I do not think I would look good in a pillbox hat.

I was just who I am, gently making fun of politics and even myself at times. Sometimes this involved teasing my husband for his weird snack preferences. In the past, these sorts of things would have been strictly off limits for anyone working on a campaign—even jokes emphasizing negative qualities are a no-no. However, times had really changed: voters had grown accustomed to a certain level of access from public figures, and that was not always a bad thing. I wanted people to know that Peter and I were middle-class millennials going through some of the same shit as everyone else. Most people think politics takes place in serious, reverential spaces, but campaigning is exhausting, low-budget, and chaotic. Things can take a turn for the hilarious. I wanted to show people that.

Of course, I'm not the first millennial political figure to use the internet like the digital native I am, with reaction GIFs and AMAs. Alexandria Ocasio-Cortez cooking mac 'n' cheese while she answered questions on Instagram Live is a classic of the genre. Nevertheless, many people were unused to seeing someone on the national political stage who wasn't interested in talking to them like a politician, and I think they found my social media persona refreshing. Unlike political spouses of the past, I wasn't just discussing issues I care about—LGBTQ inclusion and justice, education, and the arts—or cheerleading my husband. I was also talking about life as I lived it and showing followers something pretty "normal." While Peter and his team had to focus on messaging and "the show," with my social media accounts, I wanted to make sure that our audience saw themselves in us. Yes, we walked the dogs and folded the laundry and worried about our student loan payments and the hole in the roof, but yes, we goof around, too. I'd felt misunderstood and unseen throughout my life, and I wanted to make sure people got to see us so they could feel like we saw them, too.

In March, articles started appearing about my Twitter account (and about the Twitter account that belongs to our rescue dogs, Buddy and Truman, @firstdogsSB, where they are able to address the public in their own words). I went from a thousand Twitter followers to three hundred thousand within a couple of weeks. I never thought people would find my musings about waiting for Uber Eats, or bathing the dogs, or the awkwardness of watching your husband prepare to be on national television, of interest. One evening, Peter and I were spending a rare night at home, puttering around, and I took a break from cooking dinner to check my phone, where I saw that I had a new Twitter follower. And not just any new follower. I yelled in excitement and began pacing the kitchen. I made enough of a ruckus that Peter came running up the stairs from the basement, where he was doing laundry, shouting my name and asking if I was OK. I suspect he anticipated seeing one of my index fingers rolling around on the counter, or at the very least some blood, so you can imagine the look on his face when he entered the kitchen and saw that I was not sobbing at the loss of a thumb but jumping up and down and laughing: Lin-Manuel Miranda had followed me! Lin-Manuel Miranda followed me! Peter suffers—or maybe benefits—from celebrity-blindness, so while I understand that deep down he didn't get why I was expressing levels of joy on par with those I displayed at our wedding, he was very happy for me. "How cool," he said. He went back to the laundry, and I went back to stirring pasta sauce while belting "Helpless" from *Hamilton*.

. . . .

Pundits started saying I "humanized" Peter, a word I immediately questioned. This has always been the traditional role of the spouse: to demonstrate that "politicians—they're just like us!" Spouses provide the personality when the campaign-trail routine inevitably goes a little stale. But talking about politicians in terms of "humanizing" them ignores the realities of what being a politician does to humans. It's a really hard job: you have to be light and charismatic yet deeply knowledgeable, inoffensive yet compelling, powerful yet respectful, all while figuring out something incredibly "human"—people's everyday lives! (This is why few working politicians actually manage it.) You have to do all this while answering the same ten questions over and over again, and giving the same speech over and over again. It's the most human thing in the world to fail to pull it off 100 percent of the time.

One of the hardest things about running for president is connecting with people and helping them understand that you understand. Day in and day out, Peter would have to look people in the eye and listen to their biggest hopes and worst fears. I'd go to events and watch Peter have these absolutely gut-wrenching exchanges: There was the young boy who couldn't stand to watch his parents struggle to afford his insulin. There was the black trans woman who was pushed out of her home and worried about finding a job, because local employers were violent and transphobic. How would he end that cycle of hate and inequality? In Iowa, he spoke to farmers frustrated with the Trump administration, nervous that they were about to lose the farm that had been in their families for generations. And there was always a veteran, no matter where we went, practically in tears because he had lost a friend who had been let down by the system and had fallen through the cracks.

Some of these moments made it into the news, but leading up to the caucuses, it started to feel that the need for drama, retweets, and clicks far outweighed what was actually happening on the ground with potential voters. Sometimes I'd be standing in the back of a gymnasium while Peter was talking with a voter, holding their hand, and comforting them through their painful story (i.e., being a human). And then I'd look over to the press riser and see many reporters on phones and laptops. I'd scroll through my feed and see some news item or controversy that only existed on Twitter, and then I'd know: that was what they were going to ask him about the moment he wrapped the event and went to the gaggle. "Mayor Buttigieg! Mayor Buttigieg! So-and-so said this thing today that, taken out of context, may or may not have anything to do with you. How do you respond?"

It's very hard to show that a candidate is "human" if we fail to show the kind of intimate and personal moments like the ones I witnessed every day. I would sit for interviews or Q and A sessions where people would allude to my "robotic" husband, or hear commentary about his inability to connect with voters; these commenters never got to see these deeply personal moments I became accustomed to on the trail. So my job became harder. Whether I loathed the term or not, "humanizing" him became a necessity; I had to talk about Pete Buttigieg in ways others couldn't. Nobody knows the candidate better than the spouse, and I was happy to share. Besides, as Connie Schultz, the wife of Ohio Senator Sherrod Brown, once joked, "It's not like we married turtles or something."

While on the trail, I looked to figures like Michelle Obama, who contributed meaningfully to her husband's work while carving out her own public identity and duties from the very beginning of his first campaign for president. She stood on her own two feet, and I admired how she paved her own path. It wouldn't have been strange to see Michelle disagree with her husband on an issue—something it's hard to say about many other political spouses—and I was beginning to understand that such autonomy was impressively hard-won. And I really looked up to Schultz, a Pulitzer Prize–winning journalist who had to quit working for the *Cleveland Plain Dealer*, where she'd been a columnist for nearly two decades, to avoid a conflict of interest while her husband was running. Her book . . . *and His Lovely Wife: A Memoir from the Woman Beside the Man* was a huge inspiration for me. I wasn't going to sit in the background and golf-clap when Peter said something decent.

As the first wave of press about me pointed out, it was cool that I might be the first man to pick out the White House china. But in many of these stories about how well I was taking to my historic position, I couldn't help but sense a desire to place me in the kind of traditional, feminine role that the incredible women who have held that position worked so hard to abandon. Once as I was sitting for an on-camera interview, a journalist brought up my family without warning me first. This was unusual; journalists will usually give you a heads-up about what they're planning to ask you if it's something sensitive and personal, and you're not being accused of a crime. When I demurred, she pivoted. "You've mentioned your history with sexual assault. Do you wanna talk about that?" My muscles tensed and my mind started racing. *Don't look shocked.* I felt frozen in place, but I knew the camera was still rolling. If I sat still for too long, I'd throw the interview. *Act natural. Don't nervous-smile. Don't laugh. Stay calm. Breathe, Chasten. Just breathe. How long has it been? Shit. Say something.* I could feel a bead of sweat dripping down my back. I had to keep going.

The more I made myself available for conversations, both on and off the record, the more I found myself fielding questions I was unprepared for: *If you're going to be dads, how will you conceive a child? What's your backup plan? Did you know that in some places it's illegal for gay men to adopt? Will you use your DNA or Peter's? You mentioned your student debt—can you even afford a child?*

I felt enormous pressure to be visible and, therefore, stylish. "Who are you wearing?" was a question I was completely unprepared for on more than one occasion. (I'm pretty sure I once answered by saying, "Oh, this is mine.") I had just left my job—I couldn't justify a *Sex and the City* shopping montage. Actually, when I was still working as a teacher, I couldn't have afforded one, either. Spouses are, of course, not legally permitted to be paid by the campaign, though participating in it is typically required. Ethics codes dictated that I should cover most of my own expenses while I was on the road—and out of an immense sense of caution, I paid for everything besides my food until the campaign lawyers made it abundantly clear that it was OK for the campaign to cover most of my airfare. Before that, Peter and I paid for my flights, just to be on the safe side.

I could see how some in the media were discussing me as Peter's "not-so-secret weapon," as one headline had it. As another article put it, I was not only a historical figure as the first same-sex husband of a presidential candidate for a major political party, but I was also "a surprisingly traditional one." The article would go on to quote a scholar stating that I was "not bound by any particular rules about how to behave," which meant I could just "be myself." For me, this was more disorienting than liberating: there are plenty of rules and assumed stereotypes placed on queer Americans, and I was navigating uncharted territory as an openly gay man on the national stage consistently being inundated with feedback on what that should look like. Some articles seemed to want to downplay that fact, or failed to mention it altogether. In some ways that was progress, but there were moments when an acknowledgment of my unprecedented position would have been helpful. Certain media outlets in New York and DC were also treating our campaign as if we had come out of New York and DC, glossing over the unspoken realities that queer people face between the coasts, especially in places like Mike Pence's Indiana. Remember that "gays can't have our pizza at their wedding" story? Yeah, that restaurant is in our county.

Very quickly, I felt I needed to take control of the narrative that was forming around me. I just didn't really know how.

13

A Rollout of Chasten

In April, it was time for me to give my first big speech as a campaign surrogate. The Human Rights Campaign had invited Peter to speak at their gala in Houston, and although he couldn't attend, they agreed to have me in his place, and I had to be ready in a matter of days. Although I had experience performing in front of very scrupulous audiences—the local theater patrons of the college theater department in northern Wisconsin—I had no idea what to expect in terms of speaking in front of a large political audience. I worked with our team to come up with a speech that felt personal and inviting while still landing some important campaign points. I showed up early to practice reading off the teleprompter, something I had never done before. Peter assured me it would all be fine: "Just be yourself." The teleprompter was easier to master than I had worried (the entire flight to Texas) about. On the flight I rewrote the speech until I felt comfortable with the text, and when we landed we had to send it over to the venue. I had performed in plays, yes, but standing and delivering a political speech was *real*. There was no pretending here.

Peter was in New Hampshire, so this was the first of many times I'd have to go it alone. I always understood the reasons for this, of course, and throughout the entire campaign he managed to text me frequently when we were apart to say he was thinking of me or hoping I was enjoying my day. (We took to texting the word *squeeze* back and forth.) The dissonance was strange: in order to support my partner, I had to be publicly identified as one member of a couple, but that often required being alone, in situations when I would have most appreciated him being there.

I walked onstage to Tina Turner's "The Best," and in a way, it felt like coming out all over again. My thoughts were racing and my palms were sweating. *Oh my God, there are so many people. Are my jokes going to land? Who am I supposed to thank who isn't written into the speech? There are so many cameras. That one guy in the front row isn't standing or clapping like the rest of the room. Why is he giving me that face? Don't trip, Chasten. Is my fly up? Holy hell, it's* hot. Before I could calm my nerves, I was at the podium.

Standing in front of the room, being my husband's proxy, I felt almost like I was outside myself—yet the speech breezed by. Most importantly, *I didn't fuck up.* I added personal anecdotes to the speech, and I didn't turn bright red when the audience laughed at my jokes. When it was over, I returned to my table and dove into my dinner. I was starving—I'd been so nervous that I couldn't eat anything before the speech. *Wow*, I thought. *I can do this.* Maybe I could even be really good at it.

Meanwhile, I had acquired my own staff. It was a staff of one, but still, it was mine. Having a staffer was not and is not a natural experience for me. I'm used to being in charge of teenagers, not another adult. I was technically their boss, but I often felt like an inconvenience based on the nature of the job. They controlled every minute of my life, so even though they technically reported to me, in reality I reported to them. I was always saying things like, "Oh, please, I can get my own coffee!" only to be sternly told, "No, you can't get your own coffee. I will get your coffee. You need to spend the next ten minutes approving the copy of this email before we send it tonight." As the campaign went on, and my team grew,

I found it even weirder to admit that I needed them—my responsibilities were growing to be too much for me to manage on my own. Eventually, Emily, my body woman, would start asking me things like, "Have you drunk water today?" Sometimes the answer was, *"Oh no, I forgot!"*

Around the same time of the official launch of the campaign in April, the team began to schedule me a "rollout." Yes, a rollout of Chasten. As in, people got together and decided a timeline for when and how the country should get to know me on a large scale. I'd had no idea that this was how public figures became known by the public—I'd always thought it just happened, and then the public figures dealt with it. But it turned out there was an entire team of people back at HQ discussing when and how it was best for me to tweet a *Washington Post* profile. Which had also just become a thing, by the way.

Four days after we launched the campaign, I found myself at a small bakery on the Upper West Side of Manhattan for my first interview as the spouse of a presidential candidate. As I sat down, I jokingly asked Ellen McCarthy, the journalist writing the piece for the style section of the *Washington Post*, if she was going to write about what I ordered. She wrote about what I ordered. I cautiously tiptoed around my coming-out story, doing my best to make sure the appropriate details were revealed and withheld. Frustratingly, the article made it sound like my parents had kicked me out, which caused a little unnecessary drama we'll get to later, but all in all, it was a nice piece. On a trip to Boston we did a photo shoot for the story. I showed up to the shoot, which took place in a hallway off my hotel lobby, more nervous than I should have been, and I was completely in my head and unable to focus until my staffer at the time, Ali, blasted Madonna's "Vogue" from her iPhone, which made me burst out laughing, clinching the perfect carefree shot. It wasn't until the piece was published that I noticed I had forgotten to shave that morning. Oh well—it's only on the internet forever. But I was happy to let the public continue to "peek behind the curtain."

The profile was a hit. So much so that people I didn't really remember from high school were coming out of the woodwork to post effusive updates about me on Facebook. "It's just so great to see my close friend Chasten on the national stage," said Molly I Met One Time When We Took Intermediate German Together Sophomore Year, I Think. People were sending me messages that ranged from genuine expressions of support and pride to requests for favors. "Omg, my dad really loves Pete," Tim From Junior Year Chemistry or Maybe It Was Gym messaged. "Will you send me a signed copy of his book?"

People used to just wave at me in the grocery store and then kind of move on, but now I was starting to feel like my presence was A Thing. Older people were stopping me on the street to tell me about their gay nephew in Idaho who was in the marching band. People were mailing me literature informing me I was going to burn in hell, or tweeting heinous, homophobic things at me simply for . . . existing, I guess. And some others even liked me!

In June, I attended a series of Pride events across the country, including one in Traverse City. We had never had a Pride parade in Traverse City when I was growing up—the first one took place in 2014 and I was not in attendance. So when I went home and saw the thousands of people who had gathered in my hometown to celebrate queer lives, I was overwhelmed. There were drag queens walking down Front Street. "Mom! There are drag queens on *Front Street*," I said as we held hands and marched in the procession. It was extremely powerful to see that in my hometown. There were no corporate brands, no floats, no marching bands—just thousands of people, marching down the busiest street in Traverse City, occasionally stopping traffic to say, "We're here." Just before the march, the current mayor, an openly gay man, introduced me on a stage set up in a park as I greeted a crowd of thousands. "It's so good to be home," I said, fighting back tears. I couldn't believe I was lucky enough to have my family and my closest friends—who had flown in from all over the country to surprise me for my birthday (wearing those "Team Husband" shirts)—all marching at my side.

It was a joyous, beautiful day. I was so happy to be back home after having spent the previous few months learning just how grueling the trail could be, and I was so happy that home was welcoming me with open arms. But I couldn't help but feel a little regret that I hadn't gotten to experience that kind of celebratory acceptance when I was growing up. What if diversity had been a priority for my community back then? What if more of my teachers had made it safe for me to confide in them? What if my family hadn't been taught that being gay was something bad? I imagined that if I could have come home from Germany comfortable with who I was and excited for my future, I would have had a much easier time of things. My life could have gotten started so much sooner.

But I am who I am today because of those experiences, and I'm grateful that I now get to draw on them to help kids going through something similar. During Pride season, I also went to Las Vegas to help open up a new campaign field office, and a young queer kid approached me during the parade there. They were about thirteen or fourteen, and they were crying and shaking so much that they could barely get any words out. Then they said, "I'm so grateful for you and your husband" and immediately went in for a hug. I didn't know what to say, so while returning the hug I told them I couldn't wait to get to Washington and help make it better. The next day, they showed up to the office wearing a Mayor Pete T-shirt. Through tears, they said they wanted to thank me again, because Peter and I help them feel more confident about being themselves.

More and more young people were coming to my events and confiding in me. After a roundtable with local LGBTQ youth in Florida, a young person nervously whispered in my ear in the photo line that they hadn't come out yet, but I made them feel like it was going to be OK when they did. Another young person at the same event approached me and said they weren't ready to come out—but when they were, they had no idea how to do it. Could I tell them what they were supposed to do? Usually these conversations involved a lot of tears. Young people would approach me, shaking, not just because they were meeting a sort of famous person, but also because they couldn't see their place in the world they were living in, and they were terrified. I saw their desperation, and I knew it so profoundly. It was always difficult for me to find the right words. At a talk on a college campus, a student came up to tell me they appreciated my addressing sexual assault and sharing a personal experience with it. Others asked about mental health—how did they hang on to hope when the world seemed to be closing in on them? How could they know that everything would turn out OK? Everyone says, "It gets better," but to a lot of young people, that just sounds like bullshit when they're living in a constant state of fear. At another talk, a teenager asked if I'd ever felt suicidal—because they had just come out and didn't know how to hang on.

Standing there, in front of a lecture hall of students, I had to be honest about those feelings as well. So I told them yes, I had felt like that. When I was young, I knew where my dad kept the guns. There were days it felt so bleak I'd stare at the gun safe and get lost in my thoughts. But the thing that helped me get through, I said, was my friends, who were always willing to remind me that they loved and admired me, and that they were there for me. They made the good outweigh the bad. Even if it was incremental, it always kept me grounded. I ended up telling the student who asked me about coming out to never forget that they get to write their own story at their own pace. That they don't owe anyone anything. They owe themselves the respect to do it on their own terms. "Hey," I said, as they looked up, "you don't owe anyone a damn thing." They laughed, and wiped away some tears. Once again, my training as a middle-school teacher came in handy. If you really need to make a point to the class, don't be afraid of the rare, but wildly effective, curse word.

I don't want to understate how difficult it is, even now, to respond to young people (and adults) who are overcome with emotion, who want to thank me for simply being me. It's absolutely heartrending. I feel such a huge sense of responsibility, and I worry I'll disappoint them when I mess up. I don't want to be too self-deprecating here, but I'm not a saint. Sometimes I get the urge to correct them: I'm not the right person to be a role model! Don't look up to me! But people aren't looking for perfection in their role models. They're looking for something they can recognize. At the end of the roller coaster that led me to Peter, I got to be the person I wished I would have had when I was growing up. And on top of that, I now had something to offer.

It was very strange to start telling my personal stories to the public. I've always been pretty forthcoming in my personal life, but that's very different from talking about my darkest moments in front of a crowd of thousands of strangers. In many ways, part of me is still that scared teenager. What's different now is the redeeming realization that all those things I was scared or ashamed of may be helpful for others to hear. In politics, you're not supposed to let your guard down, and if you do let your guard down, you have to follow a clinical formula for it. You're supposed to have prepared lines and readymade pivots away from difficult questions. You're a symbol, not a person with trauma or feelings. You're supposed to have your well-crafted, refined narrative: This happened to me and I learned this. I had this experience and it changed me this way. In conclusion, no further questions.

I'm grateful Peter encouraged me to be myself in every sense. When I was in front of an audience, I felt I had to talk about it all. To put it all out on the table: this is who I am, this is who we are. Pretense never felt like an option. If you're going to tear me apart, at least know who you're talking about first. And at the end of the day, if you like me, then like me for me. Running for president was not my dream—it was my husband's. But I wasn't going to sit out such an important opportunity. I decided I was going to make the most of the situation in which I found myself.

....

To say these emotional experiences changed me would be an understatement. They buoyed me when I had no idea what I was doing. When I would stare out a car window, exhausted from the feedback loop and the wear and tear of the campaign, I would think of the people who were putting so much faith not only in Peter, but in me as well. They made every single day worth it.

Unfortunately, they seemed to exist in a parallel universe to the campaign sometimes depicted in the media. In the first few months of 2019, before the campaign really got intense and took off, media narratives consistently focused more on how the media narratives were going to change than on the issues, or even on any of the candidates' skills as a politician. This was extremely frustrating. Commentators were always projecting, worrying that voters would turn out to be less accepting than they were. When Peter and I kissed onstage at the official campaign launch, some commentators tried to make it into a controversy. For progressives, it was a nice, symbolic moment, to see the first openly gay candidate for president kiss his husband in public. For others, especially on the right, it was apparently scandalous that we were "flaunting" our homosexuality. Or, as some conservatives love to say, "shoving it down our throats." (Some more information on this kiss: it was a hug, a peck on the cheek, and a wave.) It's still homophobic to say it's "OK" for gay couples to be affectionate in private but that it's unseemly in public. Even the best-intentioned commentary and assumptions can still be driven by homophobia. One common example was an innocent reporter or commentator saying something like "Of course, I don't mind if they kiss in public . . ."—(clutches pearls)—but then going on to say that they knew "real Americans" elsewhere wouldn't stand for it. It was frustrating to see folks participating in this homophobic framework: "I don't have a problem with it—look at my gay friend! We do brunch!—but I know other people will."

These kinds of discussions were so prevalent that I was often surprised, visiting pockets of "real America" outside New York, at how little my being gay seemed to matter to voters. At the beginning of the campaign, members of the "coastal elite" wondered, pointedly, "Is the country ready for a gay president?" "Let them vote and find out!" I'd scream (in my head, of course). I remember one early interview during which the journalist was so dismissive of Peter that I assumed he'd be painted as a single-issue candidate (the single issue being that he was gay) and no one would take him seriously. Even in one of my final interviews on the trail, a journalist tried to surprise me with some arbitrary polling numbers about whether the country was "ready or not." The possibility that all these stories would have an effect was really hard to think about—the prospect of the campaign tanking not because America hated gay people, but because Americans assumed that most other Americans hated gay people.

Then I would go to a campaign event in Iowa or New Hampshire, and it would be packed. There would be Never Trumpers hoping Peter was the best way forward out of the mess we were in, as well as people who'd voted for Trump in 2016, who regretted their choice, and who were looking for an alternative they could believe in. There were moderates. There were social conservatives worried about affording healthcare. There were progressives, there were young people, queer people, people of faith, immigrants, DACA recipients, veterans, teachers, Moms Demand members, people who had never felt welcome in the political process before. The events went by fast, and it was often the case that, in those forty minutes, no one asked about

Peter's sexuality at all; many of the voters in attendance didn't even realize Peter was gay. (I know this because, for the entire fourteen months of the campaign, I continued to be mistaken for a staffer, and he continued to be asked where his wife was.) I'd emerge afterward to shake hands and welcome the crowd, and find a receptive and welcoming room, from whom I usually fielded questions about the dogs, not our romantic life.

For the most part, it seems the answer to "Is the country ready for a gay president?" is "Obviously." While there are unfortunately some people who still think we're sinners bringing shame and misfortune on this country, I don't think they make up as significant a portion of the electorate as I'd been led to believe. From veterans in beat-up, often very cool, leather jackets to farmers in overalls, the people Peter and I talked to while touring states like Iowa, Nebraska, Utah, and, of course, Michigan didn't seem to care too much about our private lives. They were more interested in Peter's thoughts on soy bean tariffs, the lack of support for public schools, and getting funding for rural hospitals and the VA. Just a few months after all these news stories had reached their peak, we were drawing huge crowds in rural America. Eventually, the headlines would catch up. Pete Buttigeig was drawing the largest crowds in [insert rural town].

That's not to say we experienced no homophobia on the trail. The sudden introduction of security into my life was a rough adjustment. I'm really not the type of person to leave my suitcase on the curb and accept help opening my car door, but it no longer mattered what type of person I was. I had to let other people carry my bags because I had transformed into a security "concern" and had to get in the car as fast as possible.

Peter and I used to get random mail from strangers all the time, but before he was running for president, the letters were usually innocuous: invitations to chicken dinners, graduation ceremonies, and the occasional letter from a fan of his work as mayor. Once people everywhere learned his name, that changed completely. We started getting a postcard or letter with no return address every other day, and it would always contain more or less the same message: renounce your sinful ways, God hates fags, burn in hell.

I was surprised that actual hate mail was still a thing. It's so retro to send snail mail—why not tweet your opinion at me so I can see it instantaneously? But I suppose I appreciate these people taking the time to write on a piece of actual paper and send it to us. Rather than recycle the letters, I would occasionally take them upstairs to the office and shred them, which was kind of fun.

At one point, I asked the team who was responsible for scanning packages and opening the mail at the office if there were really death threats in there. Their blank stares at one another told me exactly what I needed to know. That hidden in the mountain of beautiful letters from families and kids around the country, there were people spending their time writing us letters about how they wished we were dead. I had been beaten up and harassed in school, and I had gotten some very hateful replies on Twitter, but I had never been mailed a death threat before. I asked the security team: Are the death threats like the ones you see in movies? With individual letters cut out of magazines and pasted into an ominous message?

No. They're just typed up on regular old printer paper, probably with a couple of spelling or grammar errors, but nothing too embarrassing.

It wasn't the first time I was forced to think about being killed while on the campaign trail. It was a hard thought to get used to, that somewhere, someone like the people who mailed us those letters, might hate me or my husband so much that they felt motivated to do something about it. The type of vitriol coming from Trump's White House didn't help. People felt emboldened and encouraged by our president to be openly hateful toward others. I would march in parades with Peter, running up and down the sidewalks, shaking hands with hundreds of supporters, and the thought would appear. *What if someone, in any of these buildings surrounding us, opened a window and fired a gun?*

It's not as if I think Americans have put bigotry behind them. Not at all. And it seemed equally ludicrous to me that, while all this was going on behind the scenes and journalists were wondering if America was "ready" for a gay president, I also had reporters asking me things like "Do you think people will only vote for your husband because he's gay?" "Honey," I wished I could reply, "I think people will vote *against* my husband because he's gay." There were just *so many concerns* about Peter's sexuality: if it wasn't that rural Americans would refuse to vote for a gay man, it was that urban Americans would feel obligated to do so.

Regardless of their backgrounds, I was always stunned and grateful that supporters would show up to events, even driving hours to get there, all because they felt a personal connection to the campaign. Sometimes that was because we were gay men, and yes, having a gay American in presidential politics should help the gay community. I don't want to downplay the significance of that milestone, especially having grown up in the closet in a conservative part of Northern Michigan, never imagining a future for myself or my country like the one I lived on the trail. Peter and I knew we stood on the shoulders of giants. We knew how incredible and important it was for voters who'd lost their loved ones to AIDS to be able to come to our events and tell us how it felt. The thought of two men standing on a stage, running for president, in their lifetimes, had been unfathomable. We knew that our presence, for them, could be enough.

Sometimes, these tensions could get me down. When one of the other candidates wore a slightly flamboyant outfit to Pride, I naturally got a little jealous—if I had done that, I would have been pilloried in the right-wing press. And probably by some on left-wing Twitter, too, for being a stereotype, or, even worse, a panderer. But I always kept my cool because I know that voting is private. In a race with approximately seventy-five other options, no one was going to vote for the gay man because of a sense of duty alone. We got a lot of support from the gay community, of course, but I trusted the gay community to vote for the candidate they felt would do the best job, not just whose identity most closely matched theirs. As a gay man myself, I'd be annoyed if someone thought they were entitled to my vote just because of that identity. I wished some of these reporters could have seen the roundtables I did with vulnerable queer youth; the idea that some people would only vote for Peter because he was gay seemed a lot less relevant when I was meeting teenagers who were swimming in violence, homophobia, and transphobia every day.

It was as if everyone was operating under the assumption that bigotry was to be expected and therefore not worth examining, and it was hard as hell to watch some straight people have their homophobia go unchecked. Straight people who suddenly come around on gay rights are rarely pressed about it. Even those who hold very visible positions in American media have been allowed to leave their explicit and visible homophobic pasts practically unquestioned. It is not just conservatives who need to do the work here. There are still many people who claim to be allies online while consistently proving that they're not elsewhere. The campaign trail revealed to me just how much work still needs to be done in this arena.

While out on the trail, I personally wanted to do more to beckon people to the right side of history, rather than spend any time policing others' belonging in the community. I spent a great deal of time touring and speaking with members of local LGBTQ centers across the country, as well as at local needle exchanges and health clinics. I also felt it was important to make space for people who needed to be shown there was a healthy way toward allyship, which required a certain level of vulnerability when campaigning in deep red places where I knew some may not have always supported gay rights. I advocated strongly on the campaign trail that there is more to be celebrated in doing the work that helps others feel like they truly belong in this country than shunning them and pushing them into the arms of hateful people like Donald Trump. While making no excuses for hatred in any form, if we want change, then it's on us to help make space for that change as well.

....

In June, the campaign sent me to Merced, California, to tour the UC campus there and have dinner with a few DACA students whose parents were field workers in the community. In the mornings, some of the students worked on farms themselves before heading off to their classes. At a different event in Austin, teachers described the anger and anxiety they felt on behalf of their students whose parents were learning English as they were being deported from the country. These were intimate, raw events that showed me so much about what it means to "do politics," and they proved to me that the campaign couldn't just be about Peter's and my identity as gay men. By running for president, Peter and I were making a commitment to help as many people as we could. People who are struggling need to be able to tell their stories to those in power. They need to be reminded that there are others committed to fighting and caring for them. It wasn't just about the visibility or the historic nature of the campaign—it was also about good policy. A candidate's identity shouldn't obscure his politics. It's policy that shapes the realities of people's everyday lives.

I know this firsthand. My transition from "Republican" 4-H'er to sensitive Obama voter wasn't just about coming into my truth as a gay man. During my senior year of high school, my mom had to have some cancerous spots on her skin treated. At the time, it wasn't seen as too big of a deal. Many folks may find a spot or two, go to their doctor, have the spot removed, and that's it. At the time, that's what we expected to happen. The word *cancer* is never easy for a family to hear, but when Mom only had a few spots, we felt blessed it was treatable with what we assumed would be a simple fix.

Then, in the spring of 2007, almost a year later, she learned it was going to be more serious than getting a few moles removed. I was in Germany at the time, bouncing around from host family to host family. I'd already considered going home, and her worsening illness made me more certain I should. Mom had always been pretty good at hiding her pain and downplaying her treatments. But even as she insisted over the phone that I should finish the year in Germany, I could tell the pain was worse, and that she would prefer her son to come home to be with her. She had begun extensive, complex treatments for a rapidly spreading and rare form of squamous cell carcinoma. I felt guilty for being far away. But I didn't really know what her diagnosis meant for her life.

As you know, I ended up completing the term abroad and made sure to make it home for high school graduation. For the next two years, Mom's cancer remained at a steady level, and she'd go in for random treatments here and there.

Then they started to happen more frequently. Once I left home, "When's your next treatment?" became a regular part of our check-in calls.

The cancer kept coming back. After a few years of topical treatments and some minor surgeries to remove the deepest tumors, our questions proliferated. The doctors were even more confused. The cancer kept spreading, getting worse, and getting deeper. Eventually, surgeons would have to use skin grafts to repair some of her spots. While most people with squamous cell carcinoma end up getting one or two spots that can easily be taken care of with treatment, my mother began to show hundreds all over her body. They had started appearing on her arms and legs; now they were everywhere, including her head, too deep for outpatient surgery. The doctors feared that the cancer could easily spread to her brain, her blood, or her major organs. They still had no idea why this was happening—why the cancer regenerated so quickly and appeared so randomly.

Today, my mother is still doing OK, even if every visit to the oncologist has the family on the edge of our seats, to say nothing of the anxiety that must descend on her. But the stress was never entirely medical or existential. On top of the horrible fear that it might get too bad, and on top of the pain, she worried constantly about paying for treatment.

When she was first diagnosed, in 2006, President Obama hadn't even seemed like a viable candidate for the next election; he was being discussed as a dynamic junior senator with potential. Obamacare was a glimmer in his eye. And even though the Affordable Care Act passed in 2010, most provisions of the law didn't go into effect until four years later.

So when I was living at home, going to community college, I watched as my mother tried to make her insurance do what the company claimed was impossible: cover the exorbitant costs of her medical treatments. Before the ACA, she and my dad purchased insurance as owners of a small business, and the coverage was fickle and arbitrary. I'd been raised to understand that with a reasonable amount of responsibility and attention, everything would turn out all right. My mom's cancer proved that that was not true. Stability was conditional, and while you could control some conditions, others were out of your hands.

Now the ACA has helped to curb some of the rampant extortion by both providers and insurance companies that the previous system encouraged; the onus is less on the patient to cover treatments that can cost tens or hundreds of thousands of dollars. But you still have to be vigilant, and to know your policy well, because the insurance companies still try to get out of paying however they can. Often, they succeed.

By the time Peter and I started dating, my mom had started using an aggressive form of topical chemotherapy creams, which involved donning latex gloves and systematically rubbing a toothpaste-like cream all over her body, quadrant by quadrant. The purpose of this treatment, essentially, is for the cream to reach any cancer in the dermis, but like the more common intravenous chemotherapy treatments, it's inexact and extremely painful—it burns through all her skin, while she remains bedridden for days, covered in ice packs, hoping that it's worth it.

It's a strange reality of the United States that this horrible and necessary experience is considered a luxury. Obamacare helped my family afford those treatments. Before the ACA took effect, we couldn't afford every topical chemo the doctor prescribed, and my mom could never approach treatment as rigorously as doctors encouraged. Doctors suggested trips to the Mayo Clinic, the University of Michigan, and other larger hospitals with specialists, but we couldn't always afford the deductibles. One trip to the University of Michigan was about as useful as a Google search. "Dunno" was essentially the answer she often received, but it cost a lot of money.

Once the cancer appeared, it started to feel as if there were always a dark cloud hanging over my mom, or else approaching in the distance. It isn't as if having one health crisis prevents others; when it rains, it pours. Around the same time Mom's cancer appeared, she had a work injury in her shoulder. Then, a few years ago, a freak accident crushed her hand; she was walking into the school gymnasium for a high school basketball game on a particularly windy day when the double doors, which were installed improperly, swung together as she reached for the handle. The handle sliced open her hand and crushed it. She still has limited movement in the thumb, which had to be rebuilt, and she sustained a nerve injury that meant she struggled to move her shoulder or neck for years. At times she had to be in a specialist's office multiple times a week.

I remember watching her doing payroll and invoices for the company, and she'd become so exasperated that she'd throw the bill in the air and pound the table. Sometimes she'd show up for a critical appointment only to learn she'd been cut off from insurance—she was denied service because the company would claim they'd already paid more than it was their responsibility to pay. Sometimes this would be negotiable; other times not. Sometimes she'd go to the pharmacy to pick up a prescription, and the pharmacist would inform her, guiltily and quietly, that this random tube of cream cost $2,000. She would have to leave the pharmacy empty-handed, tell the doctor she couldn't afford what he'd prescribed her, and then they'd have to try something else. If cost wasn't presented up front, news of an expensive oversight could always come in the form of a surprise bill, meaning uncertainty loomed over both the beginning and end of her treatments. Because she never knew what treatment was going to look like—for some procedures and drugs, it's possible to cut corners, though not ideal—she couldn't prepare herself for them, and afterward she could find little comfort in knowing the treatment was over. It took a huge toll on her mental health. She was completely disempowered by the impossibility of paying for everything she needed, which meant that surviving the devastation of a life-threatening disease somehow became a secondary concern. More often, she would talk about how this was going to bankrupt them. "What's the point of being alive if you can't afford to stay alive?"

For so long, we didn't know what to expect at all—would she go to the doctor and find out the cancer had progressed to her blood? Or would she go to the doctor and find out she would be unable to pay for the tests that would tell us if the cancer had progressed to her blood? From the beginning, she'd accepted this was something we couldn't manage, and that one day we'd find out it had spread to her brain and that would be that. The way she talked about it was so defeating—this was going to be the thing that killed her. I don't know how much of the financial burden contributed to that sad sense of futility. I just know how heartbreaking it was to watch. My mother has always made sure I had everything I needed to live a full, happy life, and I couldn't do anything for her but help her to the chair, rub her hand, and tell her I loved her. She's the caretaker in the family. She cared for both of my grandfathers, my great aunt, my grandma, and her own friends while they were sick and dying, and she also took care of all the financial and administrative elements of the family business while maintaining other part-time jobs. She ran our home and made sure we were all fed, clothed, clean, and enjoying ourselves. But when it comes to her own health, it's never a matter of what would be best, always a matter of fact. It's a matter of what we can afford to do, and what we can't.

As I said, Obamacare has ameliorated this struggle somewhat. But it is by no means easy, and my experience in Germany, as well as my more recent crash course in politics, has made it clear to me that healthcare does not have to produce the constant anxiety and limitation that it currently does for everyone but the wealthy. Before my mom was diagnosed and I began to see just how difficult the process of paying for treatment was, I had never felt like politics had touched my life in any visceral way. Besides feeling like Washington didn't *like* me, I never felt it pierce my daily life. As a kid, I was kept happily ignorant of the costs of healthcare. Realizing I was gay and coming out definitely made me feel more connected to the wider political landscape, but it felt so personal and fraught that I didn't understand it as a political issue at the time; I just thought it was the way things were, and the fact that they should or could be different didn't necessarily occur to me. Hearing Obama talk about healthcare and specifically address the fact that families like ours were struggling to keep their heads above water because of medical bills made the issue click. Being on the hook for $3,000 for one month of medical treatment was simply not something that people could afford, which meant that anyone who wasn't wealthy and who was suffering from chronic or severe health issues had to choose between treating themselves and maybe going bankrupt, or forgoing treatment and maybe dying.

You really aren't free if you live in fear of the envelope from the hospital, wondering if today is the day you'll get the bill that pushes you over the edge. Having to decide which you value more, your health or your finances, is technically a choice. But a forced choice isn't freedom, as Peter would go on to outline on the campaign trail. How do you attempt to go on with your life, to retain some sense of normalcy and possibility, when you're afraid that any minute, the nurse is going to begin a sentence with "We're so sorry . . ." and tell you that the insurance company you rely on has determined that the cost of sustaining your life is more than you're worth?

After watching Mom juggle insurance companies, treatments, specialists, and diagnosis after diagnosis, I knew I was on the campaign trail for the right reasons when I saw her story resonate with others as I described the importance of reforming the American healthcare system. Politics is deeply personal to people, and the more I shared stories like Mom's, the more I could sense just how important it was for me to continue sharing them.

14

This Is Nuts. Eat the Nuts.

As the campaign progressed, figuring out just what my role was became harder and harder to do. (After all, there is no playbook.) Even as I was (or, my social media was) being praised in the media, and I was expected to give 150 percent on everything, I was sometimes made to feel as if I were expendable—an accessory. One evening, Peter and I attended a dinner on the sidelines of a conference. Within five minutes of sitting down, a well-known political commentator looked me up and down as I scanned the menu and flatly declared, "You know, you really should lose some weight." So often I found myself fielding criticisms—of me, my husband, our appearance, our politics, our strategy, our team, and our biographies, in ways that would never have been presented to Peter. Sometimes, I knew the critic would never want what they'd said repeated to Peter. If I could offer a lesson to aspiring politicos here, it's never to forget that spouses remember *everything*.

What was surprising was that the comments I'd get from seasoned political operatives on the trail were no different from the kinds of comments I'd get at functions I attended as the mayor's partner. "Oh, I heard you're a teacher—that's so *nice*." Sometimes it was sincere, sometimes it was condescending. All of the spouses were introduced at events as something of a marvel or a curiosity—"the candidates' spouses!" As if most of them weren't wildly successful in their own right. Jill Biden is a successful professor and former second lady of the United States. Douglas Emhoff is a lawyer. John Bessler and Bruce Mann are both professors. We all have individual identities distinct from our spouses!

Meanwhile, I was busy with something pretty much every day. When I returned to South Bend, I often had to don my first gentleman hat to step in for Peter while he was on the trail: showing up at programs, parks, and festivals, attending graduations, and boosting morale at both offices. My profile was bigger at home than it was anywhere else; I couldn't go any-where without stopping to chat with people about the campaign.

This was most noticeable when I least expected it. I laugh whenever I think back to riding around Traverse with my dad, how he was con-stantly stopping to talk with everyone in town and how I used to find it so irritating: karma! Wherever I went, I had to be on. There was no more throwing on jeans and a T-shirt (or—gasp!—going out in workout clothes). I always had to be prepared to take selfies, or to appear in the photos of someone pretending to take a selfie so they could snap a picture with an unsuspecting me in the background.

Everyone was so proud of us—alongside all the difficulties of the cam-paign were so many people who seemed to genuinely care about us, two strangers, and our well-being. One family in particular could be counted on to visit me every time I was in New Hampshire. They'd drive up every weekend to knock on doors or make phone calls. Even if I could only say hello for a few minutes, I always tried my best to catch up with their son, who was going through typical middle-school issues. Over the year, I cherished our conversations more and more. My team would place bets on which stop we'd see this family at. They were always there, familiar faces and a big family hug. It felt like coming home, in a way.

And there was Kathy in Keene, New Hampshire, whose daughter, Colleen, was a local field organizer. Kathy brought me local apples and homemade ice cream every time I came through town. There were the voters who, because we were so young, treated us like their own children: "Are you getting enough sleep?" they'd ask in the photo line. "Are you taking your vitamins?" One woman brought me a care package of daily vitamins and fruit. Another a bag of bubble bath and a face mask. "I hope you're getting time to relax!" was always the message.

It was very sweet. But no, I was not getting much time to relax. It took a lot of schedule jiggling, but I was able to take a weekend off to attend a friend's wedding in Milwaukee. It was such a relief to be around my old friends and not have to think about optimizing my performance for a crowd of potential voters. (Even though, of course, that crowd was all potential voters, too, I suppose.) The wedding was wonderful, but it was not as relaxing as I thought it would be, with my anxiety about getting caught doing less than first-gentlemanly things. I jumped into a late-night polka with some college friends, and we laughed as we clumsily shuffled around the dance floor. At a certain point in the song, dancers would stop to do a call-and-respond: "Alice? Who the fuck is Alice?!" (Don't ask questions. This is Wisconsin.) While hopping around, I noticed a rather intoxicated family member laughing along in the middle of the dance floor and pointing her camera directly at us. Then I froze. Right in the middle of the polka, surely stepping on my friend Kathy's feet, I thought, *Oh, shit.* What happens if a video of me scream-asking, "Who the fuck is Alice?!" goes viral on Twitter tonight?

Thankfully, it didn't, and I was spared the humiliation. It was good to dance and forget about the complexities of the campaign for a bit, but it bothered me that there was always that reminder lurking in the back of my mind: You are an ambassador of your husband's campaign. Everything you do reflects on him.

I came to think of my role as being everything and nothing. If I messed up, I was everything, the center of attention; if I did a good job, I was nothing, just doing my job of being Peter's husband. "There is only one star," one campaign operative would tell me. Doing a good job, being perfect, *is* the job. You don't get praise for not fucking up. That's the job. Sometimes I'd work eighteen-hour days, traveling to three or four states, and it would hit me: I'm doing all this for my husband. It made me feel great to be a supportive partner, and I'm lucky that I got to focus on and learn about the issues that matter the most to me. But to be honest, I got tired of talking about my husband all the time. Especially because I couldn't even see him.

Luckily, I was changing time zones so frequently that I stopped getting jet lag; I simply felt like it was 5 a.m. all the time. Sometimes Peter and I would get to travel together, but more often we would only get to see each other because we were flying into the same city from different locations. We'd end up reconvening at an event, or in a hotel room at 11 p.m. The next morning we would wake up and leave for the airport so we could get on two different 6 a.m. flights. During the later stages of the campaign, Peter spent most of his time in Iowa, which he had to win in order to stay viable for the remainder of the primaries. The rest of his surrogates, me included, were standing in for him everywhere else. I would check my phone to see if I could figure out where he was at any given time.

I'll be honest: this wasn't how I had envisioned newlywed life. We were literally two planes passing in the night. At one point Peter was flying from New York to San Francisco and I was leaving Los Angeles for New Hampshire, and we waved at each other somewhere over Nebraska. Not seeing each other often was a strain, and our stolen moments had a bittersweet quality. Throughout the campaign, my good cheer flagged, and it was hard to give him a sense of what was going on with me. This had nothing to do with how he behaved toward me; he is amazingly re-silient, and I was often shocked at how buoyant and unbothered he could seem after I knew he couldn't have slept more than four hours and he'd just finished a grueling series of interviews about a ridiculously conflated controversy for which he was being criticized. My issues were minor in comparison to his, so I didn't want to add to his (silent) concerns by complaining, and I didn't want to waste the one hour we had together by whining about how I didn't feel respected by some of the campaign staff. This was our special time to be like "Hey, did you see this YouTube video?" Then we'd compare our schedules for the upcoming week, watch *Family Guy* or catch up on *Saturday Night Live* videos, and go to sleep.

I also really missed working with kids, being in charge of my classroom, and, above all, having my own thing. I missed my friends, my family, my dogs, and normalcy—I don't think I realized when the campaign started that I would care so much about not having a routine. My staff was extremely help-ful, but I never fully got used to our blurry relationship. I was their boss, but it felt more like they were mine: they were always telling me where to go, what I could and couldn't say. I'd run almost everything by them first. Tess, my chief of staff, would have to run a million things up the flagpole every day, even if I mentioned wanting to go to the hotel for fifteen minutes before an event. Security, the advance team, Peter's staff, cars—everything had to be adjusted if I wanted to put on some fresh deodorant and press a shirt.

When it came to actually getting a meal on the trail, Peter would eat anything. If it's announced that we have to skip lunch, that's fine—he reaches for a Clif Bar like it's no different from a sandwich. This is where he and I really part ways. I don't want to be dramatic here, but I will not eat a Clif Bar. Clif Bars are candy that taste awful. Just be-cause something tastes bad doesn't mean it's healthy. They are just as unhealthy as candy. They make my stomach turn just thinking about them. But in those first few months of the campaign, when meals were being skipped almost every day, I ate enough Clif Bars to last a lifetime. If lunch is canceled and we have to eat candy instead, then please, by all means, give me real candy. Kind bars taste better, which makes sense: they're covered in chocolate. Which is why they don't count as a meal, and Clif Bars unfortunately do.

So if a Clif Bar is my only option, I will skip lunch. This happened regularly during the campaign. When we were on the ground in states, the team would often build in time to eat at local spots, but some days I'd wake up for a 6 a.m. flight, Emily would hand me my coffee in the car on the way to the airport (thank you, thank you, thank you, Emily), and by 10 p.m. I'd realize, "Huh, I don't think I ate today!" I would usually supplement this lack of diet with yet more coffee, which was great for my anxiety.

Eventually, Saralena, Peter's body woman, knew to not even offer me a Clif Bar; Emily would make eyes with volunteers when they offered a selection of Clif Bars while we waited. (Why were Clif Bars everyone else's go-to choice?!) But first, something unthinkable had to happen. A staffer tattled on me to Peter that I didn't eat the Clif Bars when they gave them to me, and they were starting to get worried. I knew that it was bad when the staff had to mention to Peter that I wasn't eating. So my husband sat me down in front of our principal opps team and gave me a stern, but loving talking-to: "If they offer you nuts, Chasten, then eat the fucking nuts. You don't know when you'll get an opportunity to eat again." "Eat the fucking nuts" became a joking refrain on the trail. I didn't get too upset about this—I knew Peter was genuinely concerned for my health. Peter had already noticed I was losing weight quickly, and over the course of the campaign, I lost over thirty-five pounds. I wasn't drinking alcohol, I stopped eating meat, and I was pretty conscious of what I ate (when I actually ate) in terms of what was going to give me energy, because I couldn't afford to crash. Over time, I started eating more nuts.

I began to feel that I was losing control over everything—from my friendships to my diet. But even as I sometimes felt like a helpless child, I did have control over the shape of many other people's lives, and that pressure was hard to bear, too. If I overreacted, I could cause a crisis; if I underreacted, I could cause a different kind of crisis. One day I went to get the mail and found a bent tube wrapped in layers and layers of tape; it was addressed to me. I didn't like the look of it, so I left it on the porch and went back inside. I asked the campaign to let the security guys know about it. Following protocol, the campaign sent someone from the security detail over to inspect. Our security team inspected and didn't like the look of it, either. So they called the city police. The city police came over. They didn't like the look of it, either. So they called the state police. The state police didn't like the look of it, either. So they called in the K9 unit to check it out. All I did was go get the mail, and within thirty minutes there were several cop cars outside our house and a dog on the scene. The neighbors were worried. Once they finally removed the package—the news crews had sensed drama and showed up, too. So I had to call the campaign again and tell them a local news crew, surely eager to get a story picked up on national news, was now filming in our front yard.

I did the right thing, but the whole episode unsettled me, and not just for the obvious reason that it's weird and scary to receive suspicious packages at your home. It was also disturbing because I saw how, with just one phone call, I could disrupt an entire team of people's days. If I *really* messed up, I could even change the course of my husband's career. (I never found out what was in the package.)

By the fall the pressure had started to get to me. Luckily, in April, I'd had the foresight to place a hold on the first week in August to take a trip with friends. "Just make it to August" I'd tell myself as I'd collapse into the springy bed at the airport Courtyard Marriott. By the time August rolled around, I felt so guilty leaving the trail, and Peter, for an entire week. Nevertheless, and with Peter's encouragement, I took a week off, and spent it on vacation with friends.

I was thankful for the time away, but in some ways it revealed just how consuming the campaign had been. By now my phone had become another appendage, and it was hard for me to look away from the news. I'd find myself lying awake at night just worrying about Peter, letting my mind race and thinking the worst. Every time I stopped to take stock of my feelings, I would notice just how tense my shoulders and jaw were and how uneven my breath was. I was holding on to a lot.

15

Did You Ever Imagine?

I was burning out repeatedly. There's not much time for gathering your energies on a campaign, and I was extremely lucky to have escaped for a week. The trip was great, albeit far too short. Spending a week with a dear friend who reminded me exactly why I got into this relationship and this campaign in the first place was exactly what I needed in that moment. But then I was right back in it, and it felt like I had never left. By the time I made it home, a full-blown head cold had set in. I was scheduled to be in California the next day for an event with the DNC, where I was expected to fill in for Peter. I spent all day in bed, but the team urged me to just make it to San Francisco if it was at all possible. They *really* needed me this time. So I got on the plane, made it to California with a fever, delivered a speech I don't fully remember, and went right back to bed. I spent the next day flying back home to Indiana, and when I finally crawled into my own bed, I felt just as exhausted as I had when I left for vacation.

In the early fall, I knew I had to make a concerted effort to refocus. I had to give myself permission to be where I was. Feeling like an imposter because I knew very little about politics did little to change the fact that I was in politics, learning about what I didn't know firsthand. I'd never felt like I was allowed to participate in political debates before, so when people started asking me my opinions on them, I panicked. When reporters would ask me questions like "Did you ever imagine this is where you'd end up?" and "What prepared you for this?" part of me felt like they were saying, "People like you don't really belong here. So what makes you think you do?"

But I started to realize that I did belong there. Not only that: it's vitally important for people like me to be involved in politics. Not because I was handed a list of talking points, but because none of it was hypothetical for me. Everything I talked about on the campaign was deeply personal and real, and those are just some of the stories we should bring to Washington. Peter's campaign was a historic first. And whether I realized it at the start or not, my role was a historic first, too.

I believed so strongly in my husband and our marriage that I got to the point where I was forced to start believing in myself, too. After all, I'd gone from being a suicidal teenager sleeping in the back of my car to being a person who Rush Limbaugh found important enough to attack. Even better, my authentic response to that criticism was *Who cares what Rush Limbaugh thinks? That sort of homophobia isn't new for me. Think of how his words affect queer kids.* My priority was no longer bad camera angles; it was being myself no matter what photo of me was running on a news story. And you know what? People continued to take photos. Awful angles emerged on front pages. But my chins are what they are. I quit spending so much time wondering if I was being misinterpreted, or if my stump speech was perfect. I stopped getting sidetracked when someone heckled me; I stopped worrying about whether someone on the street was secretly recording me walking my dog so they could make me look bad online. Instead I started to focus on the good that comes from rolling up your sleeves and *doing the work*. Hanging out with kids meant just that. Hanging out. Making eye contact, getting on their level, and getting absorbed in their stories, not focusing on the twenty adults with cameras gleefully hovering over us. The work was simple if I broke it down to what I could control. Sometimes it was just working a line and saying hello to hundreds of people waiting outside a venue instead of focusing on the cable news embed chasing me, asking me about my husband, and reminding me of some piece of drama they'd read online. I started focusing on why these people in line were there in the first place: for connection, to feel like they belong. The more time I spent with them, investing in the presence and excitement, the more I realized I was pretty good at this.

I went from "How did I get here?" to "This is my life now." I started training with our comms team to gain confidence fielding questions and handling myself in interviews. Eventually, if someone raised their hand and asked, "Does being gay even matter?" it would just roll off my back. They taught me how to field really hard, sharply worded questions. I'd head into HQ and spend a couple of hours getting grilled with rude, difficult comments so I could feel it in my system. I also trained on sore spots on the campaign. That was the most difficult aspect: I always want to come at harsh criticism with the cold hard facts, but I could never be seen arguing with supporters or the kid with the iPhone at my car door. Instead, the response went like this:

First, I would acknowledge the statement or question, and tell the voter that it's a really important issue and something we value.

Then, I would recite a few talking points from the respective plan. After three, people stop listening, so keeping it brief is as important as keeping it on topic.

Finally, I would thank them for bringing up that important issue, and remind them that they could read the full policy plan on our website.

I believe in these things anyway, so I never felt like I was trying to sell a junk product. But sometimes it was grueling. The sharply worded questions could be *very* sharp. If someone was asking me a question I couldn't really answer, I tried to say, "We're building a campaign that not only can win, but deserves to win. We've put forward the most comprehensive policy on this issue; please go to the website to learn more." Sometimes folks would say, "Pete's never said anything about [insert topic] before! Why doesn't he support [insert position]?" Never mind that he had spoken about it, in detail, in multiple interviews or in detailed policy proposals that were published on the campaign website.

I understood how frustrating it must be to have a politician's spouse respond to your legitimate anger with a thesis statement and a website referral. But I often found that the sharply worded question with an iPhone in your face wasn't really a search for an answer—it was an opportunity to make a statement. As a teacher I can tell the difference between when someone genuinely wants to talk and when someone is just worked up beyond conversation. In the classroom, we had the "volcano" gauge: everyone's volcano is resting at a different level each day. Sometimes it's still and quiet, and sometimes it's seconds from eruption. And when the volcano blows, nothing good usually comes until it can cool down again. Most often, on the trail, the protester wasn't there for dialogue. If someone was up for a conversation, I'd invite them to meet with me afterward. I'd give them their time to offer their criticism or worries. I could respond without an audience, and we could go our separate ways, hopefully with both of us feeling a bit better, whether they were going to vote for my husband or not. I knew some people came to events in bad faith, but most were there for reasons that deserved respect. Sometimes I found the dialogue really rewarding and appreciated when both parties felt better after talking with each other, realizing that, in many ways, we were on the same team.

Fielding criticism from voters was hard enough, but it took longer for me to get used to people I admired saying negative things about my husband, especially when it sometimes seemed like they were just doing it for sport. I follow a lot of reporters and news outlets on Twitter, which means

I was inundated with feedback about the person I love. I had to learn that when a candidate or surrogate was criticizing Peter, it was often never about Peter himself. It was about an attempt to seize and expand on a particular moment in the media cycle. Politicians were personal brands before "personal brands" were a thing; their personas have always been divorced from who they really are. But it's still hard to watch the criticisms without replying, "First of all how *dare* you come after my man!" with that GIF of Kelly from *The Office*. After all, this is what a rapid response team is for.

This feeling reached its peak whenever a debate rolled around. Before the debates, Peter would spend some time prepping, and then we'd attempt to unwind by getting a pizza, going for a walk, watching some television, or playing a video game—anything to take our minds off the hamster wheel for a few before the big show. And it was a big show. I quickly learned that presidential debates are a lot like reality TV—they have all these planned, made-for-TV moments that everyone pretends are spontaneous. Everyone is waiting for their opportunity to steal the spotlight in an effort to produce the most viral clip. Each debate would be preceded by days of speculation in the media about who would perform well and who would tank, and whichever candidate was polling highest would always have to prepare for the "fight of their life." Sitting at a gate in an airport watching networks air the same ad promoting a primary debate was like watching a promo for a Vegas boxing match. The dramatic music, the fast cutaways, the deep voice. It's all there for a reason: everyone wants a bloodbath, because a bloodbath is good television.

I was happy that I got to use my experience watching *Survivor* to analyze presidential debates, but Peter hated this element of the experience. He likes debating policy and talking about real people's lives, not waiting for the moment he can deploy a canned line. Throughout the day, I would try to get him to practice zingers or prep for incoming attacks, but mostly he just needed me to remind him of all his strengths. My training as an actor came in handy: I was always reminding him to be aware of his body language and facial expressions while he was thinking or prepping a response. Audiences will read into your expressions, even if you're not speaking. Are you looking the person who is criticizing you in the eye? That suggests confidence. If your eyes dart around while someone is saying you were a terrible mayor, you might look like you're cowering. Where you're looking and how you look as you're taking criticism will be analyzed by everyone. It says a lot about the candidate if they can't look you in the eye.

When the time came to head to the debate, I'd go with him to the venue and sit with him during hair and makeup. Just before the network would come to seat me, I'd ask the team to leave the room and I'd give my pep talk. With a kiss on the forehead and a slap on the back, I'd promise, no matter how tough, I'd be right there in the front row. Then I'd go take my seat and wait.

I said I never wanted to be defined by my husband's job, but as soon as I walked into the debate arena and saw all the other spouses, I transformed into a stage parent. I always joke that if you want to see the real drama of the debate, you should watch the family section. In the pre-debate mingling period, it wasn't rare for someone to plant minefields of playful passive aggression: "How is he feeling tonight? Is he ready?" Obviously, they were secretly hoping he'd flounder. "Come on!" I'd say. "It's Pete Buttigieg. He's unflappable!" When one of the candidates would go after Peter onstage, and I'd be sitting two people down from their spouse, it would take all my willpower not to turn to the person and raise a skeptical eyebrow. I was an ambassador of that human on the stage, and I didn't like that nonsense! But for spouses, "grin and bear it" was the name of the game.

This sense of righteousness always evaporated, leaving behind only awkward discomfort, as soon as the concluding remarks were made. Everyone would put on their cheerful, supportive faces and congratulate one another on a good game. Although after one particularly intense sparring between Peter and another candidate, the other candidate's spouse went in for a hug, and I instinctively pivoted to a handshake.

Eventually, watching Peter get aggressive with the other candidates was sort of fun for me. I'd never seen him get aggressive before, and I knew he hated it—he always wants to focus on policy and strategy, not character. But that's not always possible. It was great to watch him throw some elbows occasionally—even if I knew he quietly couldn't stand that this was the television he was being prodded for. What was amazing to watch was how true to himself he remained throughout the campaign. I never saw him say something that made me feel disappointed in him, or that made me think, *Oh, that's not like you.* I had some moments of vertigo as his profile was growing, but they were never rooted in anything he did. Sometimes I said something like "Hey . . . so . . . this is a reflection of me, too, so please don't mess this up . . . for me. And for the country!" But this was more a reflection of my nerves and insecurities than anything he did. I never doubted he'd rise to the occasion of campaigning.

I know that this is just how politics is. At the end of the day, we're all on the same team, so it's healthier not to take attacks or criticisms too personally. Of course, that's easier said than done, and nobody was perfect when it came to civility all the time. Occasionally I felt like a cartoon character with steam coming out of my ears. But the more time I spent in the arena, the more I thought about the bigger picture and who we were there to serve. Our campaign was about belonging, and I thought of Michelle Obama's "When they go low . . ." mantra at least five hundred times a day.

. . . .

When folks would ask, "Just what prepared you for this?" I'd always joke that teaching middle school was the perfect preparation for a life in politics. Emotions are high; compromise is a crucial aspect of daily life. The biggest hurdle is trying to separate yourself from the drama in front of you in order to see the big picture. Scraps of hard-won progress, day in and day out, lead to bigger achievements over time. When you're helping a student navigate an emotional breakdown, you have to remember that their behavior has nothing to do with you—it's about something going on beneath the surface. Adults should know better, but they often don't.

As our profiles rose, we started dealing with backlash of the kind I couldn't have expected. In the beginning, many journalists tried to turn on the charm for some inside access, and I had to learn quickly that reporters are not my friends. Lis Smith, our senior communications advisor, was always there to reinforce that statement for me. I'd get word that a reporter had called a family member or friend; they'd even find people I went to high school with on Facebook to try to get a quote. It didn't necessarily matter how close the person was or was not to me; their perspective could be taken as fact.

Politics was never my family's regular topic of conversation. There could be awkward moments in the house between my brothers and me, especially when it came to the usage of the terms *fag* or *gay*, and I never really felt like I could push back on language like that, lest I be outed as what they seemed to hate. But other than injustices when it came to the household vernacular, political issues stayed off the table. Before the 2008 presidential election, I remember getting an Obama T-shirt and feeling like this guy made more sense for people like us than McCain. I didn't talk to my brothers about the election much, but I remember standing in line at Blair Township Hall with my mom on Election Day, telling her I thought she should vote for Obama but not feeling comfortable trying to persuade or pressure her. Other than brief chats like this, politics went untouched.

So after my *Washington Post* profile was published, and I saw my oldest brother, Rhyan, on Fox News, attempting to convince Laura Ingraham he had the authority to speak on my family's behalf, I was shocked. The year before, I had invited my brother to our wedding out of a sense of obligation. As a born-again Christian, he declined, saying he wouldn't condone something he didn't believe in or celebrate something against God's will. We hadn't spoken much in the years leading up to our wedding, and we haven't spoken since our brief encounter burying my grandmother a few months after Peter and I were married.

I sat for that profile because I'd wanted to help voters get to know me and Peter. I did it because I thought my story was important to tell; it helps others who may be going through something similar know they're not alone, and it helps people who will never experience anything similar know that life is not easy for working-class gay kids, especially those growing up in conservative places, like I did. I guess seeing me talk about this must have triggered Rhyan, because soon enough friends and family were calling to say my brother had gone on Fox News to denounce me and call me a liar, saying I had misrepresented my experience growing up while still finding time to add "Trump 2020." I don't watch Fox News, and no one ever reached out to me for comment, so I had to watch the clip after it aired. I never want to be seen giving Laura Ingraham an ounce of credit, but I'm pretty sure she could smell right through Rhyan's bullshit, too.

All of a sudden, strangers were accusing me of being a liar because someone who hasn't spoken to my family in years had convinced them I was. It was one thing for me to learn to let this roll off my shoulders, but when you run for president you're asking your friends and your family to bear that burden as well. I was so upset that my mother and father, two people who worked so hard to give us everything, had to have their names end up in the fray as well.

I felt guilty, and so did Peter. I felt bad because I had complicated his campaign; he felt bad because he felt like his choice to run for president had opened up the opportunity for me and my family to get hurt in a very public way. And not just by anyone, but by a family member. Breitbart and Fox followed up the interview with all kinds of profiles and editorials. It got to the point that even my Trump-supporting family members were calling to express their disappointment that Rhyan had pretended to speak for a family he didn't want anything to do with.

It was painful, and I wished it hadn't happened. I'd been dealing with people who hated me for my whole life; I just wish that my family hadn't had to be subjected to that type of ugliness.

16

Out on the Trail

The feedback loop can be vicious, and it serves up some wild and peculiar hot takes. Of all the things I'd been accused of throughout my life, not being gay enough was never one I saw coming.

My initial reaction was disbelief. I'd been getting death threats. Was having to install a special security system on my house so I didn't get murdered in the night by people who hated me simply because of my marriage *not gay enough*? Could someone send me the checklist? Was there a meeting I missed out on? Surely, I thought, at least I'd get some points for, you know, being married to a man.

Peter, thank goodness, has such thick skin; nothing riles him up. In our five years together I've heard him raise his voice a handful of times, and every time it was because Truman tore into the trash and spread coffee grounds around the house. Peter has been doing this forever and just moves on. He is also not one to return shittiness with shittiness—something I admire and envy him for. He's also well-versed in leftist ideology because he reads everything—he was familiar with the kinds of theoretical critiques being thrown at us. But this was very new for me. I've been profoundly shaped by my past. Living in my car, as one of those

suicidal gay teenagers everyone loves to talk about protecting, is the experience that has most impacted my perspective and my image of my hard-
won queerness. But for some, because I wore chinos and a button-down
on the cover of *Time*, and hold similar but not identical opinions to some
people on social media, this trauma is not sufficient.

This, of course, made me want to scream in frustration. Why were we
doing this to one another? Even in an article where the author claimed
she was against homophobia, and "didn't know anything about" Peter,
she still found a way to measure queerness so that two men in chinos
would never fit. It started to seem almost bizarre. At one point we were
described as "straight men without women." A prominent national outlet had to pull an article making references to our genitalia. Thankfully,
there had been an outcry on our behalf; people started tweeting that they
were canceling their subscriptions. The editor was finally forced to call
and apologize to Peter. All while people were sending letters to my home
informing me of how I was sufficiently gay to be damned to a life in the
fiery pits of hell, or worse, the beneficiary of their death wish.

Of course, I could understand some of the legitimate policy arguments
being made against Peter. The idea is less that we aren't gay enough to earn
their support, and more that we aren't progressive enough, because government's failures to protect the vulnerable disproportionately impact queer people. I want many of the changes folks to the left of our campaign want, too.
Campaigning as a Democrat in the United States is like living in two different
worlds at the same time: even if you're just trying to appeal to your own party,
and fight for progressive causes, you have to keep an eye on how the Republicans will see you, too, and that means figuring out a way to actually *get stuff
done*. Republican and conservative media filters into liberal and mainstream
media. Conservatives also vote. The differences between Peter's approach and
that of those to the left of him are mostly differences of style, not content. You
can't change anything in politics if you don't win, and Peter presented a dif-

ferent path to forming a movement so that we could get to Washington and *make those changes* all while bringing people together. Had he been elected, Peter would have been the most progressive president in modern American history, and a part of me understood many of those kids holding those Sharp-ied signs protesting my events hadn't even read the policy page to see just how alike they were. If only they'd spent that time canvassing or phone-banking for their candidate, maybe they would have won. I had many friends who supported other candidates, and none of them felt the need to mock me, pro-test my events, or tell me my marriage was a disgrace to the movement. We stayed friends throughout the campaign, comparing notes, learning from one another. Because that's what friends do.

I was continuously reminded of just how invisible many queer people's stories and realities are, especially when I was visiting orga-nizations in rural America. On a trip to Oklahoma, I visited Tulsa's Equality Center, which is run by a local LGBTQ organization that's been around since 1980, to learn about their work. Oklahoma is not the easiest place to be gay; early on, OkEq's landlord didn't allow the organization to identify themselves with signage or flags out of fear of vandalism. The Center is located in a former torpedo assembly plant because it was the only real estate the city would let them acquire. It's a tremendous resource to the community—it has a wellness center, a black box theater, community spaces, and a lending library, and it's one of the largest LGBTQ centers in the region. Seated around a table with local electeds and members or friends of the Center, I listened to the story of a young man who'd walked miles barefoot into downtown Tulsa because his parents had kicked him out of the house in the middle of the night. Most of the time, the Center is left to do their own thing, while, of course, some portions of the population silently disdain them. They've had their fair share of vandalism and threats over the years. But during tornado season, everyone wants to shelter there. Which means

LGBTQ people end up literally producing a safe space for people who made it hard for them to secure a space in the first place.

That gay experience in Tulsa is just as gay and valid as other, more visible experiences in the media, and attempting to police anyone's gayness sets a dangerous precedent. It equates identity with presentation and prioritizes lifestyle over the conditions of someone's life. It places even more needless pressure on a population that is already struggling. It says to that young person walking away from his only home, barefoot in the middle of the night, that there is a right and wrong way to exist when he may be contemplating if he even wants to at all.

I've been dealing with homophobia my entire life—the only difference is that now it's public and it's magnified. I don't mean to suggest that I was a victim of how mean people were to me; I'm very lucky, and I can handle it. But it was strange at first to see people who I thought would be on "my side" hang me out to dry.

You're only setting yourself up for failure and sadness if you expect everyone to like you. Some people are always going to hate you. This is true for almost anyone, not just public figures. (But actually, how does Tom Hanks do it?) What's important is, in the last few months of the campaign, I started getting asked about queer leftist pushback to our candidacy a lot, and I was proud to be able to respond, "I, Chasten, myself, have visited more than one hundred LGBTQ youth and homeless centers since this campaign began. If you think Peter or I take this community for granted, then you are mistaken." My work spoke for itself. I'm not just going out there to say, "Hey y'all, just a reminder that I'm gay, so I get it." I'm committed to the cause.

I understand that my privilege as a cisgender white man is what allows me to have this platform in the first place. That's why I made it a priority to use my time and platform to talk with people who have it worse than I do. I went out into shelters to look kids in the eye who were dealt a shittier hand than mine when I ran away from home. I made a consistent effort to listen to trans women of color share their experiences with housing, employment, and criminal justice. My team knew to continuously seek opportunities to show up and listen to the community, no matter what city or state I was in. I wanted to make sure we were reaching and listening to as many corners of our community as possible. I spent time at New York's SAGE, a center designed for older LGBTQ adults. I met with leaders at Equality Utah in Salt Lake City, learning how they convinced conservative Mormon Republicans to vote for pro-LGBTQ legislation. I toured the newly constructed Gloria Casarez Residence in Philadelphia, part of Project HOME, which provides thirty beds to LGBTQ young people aging out of the foster care system. While I was there, their first tenant gave me a tour of her unit and told me her story as we celebrated that she had her very own place to herself. In New Orleans, I met with runaway queer youth at Covenant House. In Iowa, I became a guest camp counselor for a day at Pride Camp in Des Moines, where I met with transgender teenagers whose parents drove them for hours just to find a safe space to sit on a lawn surrounded by other kids like them. Back in New York, I cooked lunch at the Ali Forney Center, where a kid made me promise I wouldn't forget him if I made it to the White House. I still haven't forgotten. I attended the National LGBTQ health conference in Georgia, held roundtables on queer issues facing citizens in rural Michigan and the desert communities surrounding Las Vegas. In California, I toured the Central Valley Pride Center in Modesto, where half the attendees were shocked I actually came; they were used to being overlooked. And then, in Florida, I visited the memorial of the Pulse shooting in Orlando with survivor Brandon Wolf, listening to his harrowing story of the night a gunman walked into the nightclub and opened fire, killing forty-nine people and wounding fifty-three others. I laid flowers at the site and read the names of each of the victims, looking at their pictures and reading messages loved ones had left on the walls surrounding the site. I struggled to find any words in the hours after I left.

Part of the politician's job is to make sure we show up and listen to people's stories so we can bring those stories to Washington. As Peter kept pushing through early states, I kept traveling the country, listening, and bringing back the stories to our team as a constant reminder of who we were fighting for: the people whose lives had gone ignored by those in positions of power.

....

Campaigning requires carrying others' pain and grief. Sometimes I would end the day with a feeling I could only describe as vulnerability fatigue. There was just nothing left to give. After touring Pulse, I met with a survivor of the Parkland school shooting, and after that meeting, I was needed at a few other scheduled campaign events. It was hard, sometimes, to carry all those stories and experiences and keep a clear head, and to make sure that I was showing up emotionally for everyone I met or stood in front of. At times, it was all too overwhelming, and I'd start to forget to care for myself as well.

A lot of campaigning is waking up every single day knowing that the only thing you can be certain about is that you're going to get your ass handed to you in a million different ways. There were many times on the trail that I wondered why anyone wanted the job in the first place. There were days I selfishly wanted to take Peter home because I'd had enough, and I felt like the country didn't deserve him, or I didn't have anything left to give. It was like I shined my shoes every morning knowing that by the time I got to the hotel that night they'd be covered in shit. But we kept going.

It helped that the worst was never what I experienced on the trail—the worst was in my phone. It's not like I was a Luddite before. In fact, I liked social media. I liked posting pictures of my dogs and travels on Instagram; I liked following comedians and journalists on Twitter. I liked being able to keep up with friends and family who were far away. I liked finding the perfect reaction GIF (you can always count on *The Devil Wears Prada*) and responding in real time to the premieres of TV shows. When the campaign began, I was briefed about how I'd have to be more careful, and I scrubbed my accounts of anything that might cause controversy, not that there was much to begin with. (Just Jimmy Buffett concerts.) I figured I would retweet the campaign a lot, promote my events, and get some new followers, but otherwise things on social media would stay pretty much the same for me.

Once again, I have to laugh at myself. Oh, to be so young!

When my accounts started getting really popular, the campaign sat me down for a series of tone-of-voice meetings. Essentially, the team creates two lists of adjectives: one with words you'd use to describe yourself on social media, and one with words you wouldn't use to describe yourself on social media. Then, they have a bunch of other people do the same exercise. At the end, they combine both lists and determine how you're seen by others so they can emphasize your best qualities and minimize your worst ones. It's sort of like astrology without the mascots.

The experience was kind of cool (though if I'd learned that people thought I was boring, vindictive, and unintelligent, I would probably think it was less cool). A lot of people who participated in this exercise thought I was funny, kind, happy, and inspirational; they said I was never mean-spirited or aggressive. People got the impression that I talked a lot about teachers and rarely attacked others. Generally, everyone agreed my social media presence was very positive. The team, therefore, recommended I lean into this, which was fine with me.

I didn't think I was censoring myself, or that my tone had changed all that dramatically. I was still the goofy husband I was in January. The campaign was chaotic, but I always managed to make light of it in some way.

But then at some point, I started getting a comment that disturbed me. "You know," a friend or acquaintance would say, "you used to be really funny on Twitter." It even started happening with strangers in photo lines. *Used to be?!* Laughing a little to disguise my disappointment at the crushing blow they'd just dealt me, I'd reply that I didn't think I'd changed at all— what did they mean? And they would just say, "Oh, I don't know. You used to be funny, and now you're . . ."

What? Now I'm what?! Yes, I'd been sharing a lot of Peter's posts, and articles about the need for immediate action on common-sense gun laws and the importance of paying teachers a living wage. And maybe I'd gotten more in my own head, turning every potential post over and over, wondering: *Do I really want to tweet this?* I'd started spending time drafting my posts and then never tweeting them. Many thoughts and musings are just not worth the headache that would come after publishing them. (This applies to people who aren't involved in politics just as much as it applies to me. Just draft it first!) I didn't need Breitbart to publish another piece about me. I didn't want to be defined by disagreements or negativity. I had other more practical policies, too: I shouldn't send direct messages because they can always be interpreted the wrong way; even if a reporter asks me for comment over DM, I can't respond. Similarly, I can never unfollow anyone—there are bots that track that and publicize it. (And sometimes individuals will notice on their own and take it very personally.) No posting photos of myself drinking alcohol. No posting commentary on any individuals involved in any campaign. Basically, if you can't say anything nice, don't say anything at all, and actually, just don't say anything at all anyway. I'm lucky that the campaign didn't take my passwords or forbid me from tweeting without their permission. (Or maybe I'm unlucky, depending on your perspective.) They trusted me to think things through. Ultimately, I learned that every time you tweet, it's a press release.

But to a certain extent, this careful policy of mine didn't really matter, because the internet has a mind of its own. There's a saying commonly attributed to Mark Twain: "A lie makes it halfway around the world before the truth puts its shoes on." That seemed to play out a lot on social media. Our research and rapid response departments spent so much time fighting disinformation and bad faith attacks that it seemed some people were after likes—or the dopamine rush of a thumbs-up emoji—not the truth. The rapid response team would reply to any false information, and the account that posted it would apologize, but that didn't matter much. The original tweet had already been retweeted and liked hundreds or thousands of times. Unless the original lie or slander was deleted, people were more likely to see the false accusation or doctored video rather than the apology or corrected response. And slowly, lies became others' truth.

The internet creates and perpetuates its own drama, regardless of what's happening offline. Once, a friend forwarded me an article claiming I was worth millions (accompanied by at least twenty laughing-with-tears emojis). The language of social media made its way into headlines so that the headlines would perform well on social media. Even if I was making a factual comment, within a couple of hours there would be fifteen articles about my imaginary Twitter beef, and Breitbart and Fox News would be running stories, too. I was always said to be "clapping back" or "shredding" other politicians, even if all I was doing was gently correcting or disagreeing. Unfortunately, social media is often not used for dialogue. Folks are usually just talking past one another.

There were people who seemed more interested in winning Twitter than the election. The "fandoms" that form around politicians are similar to those that follow pop stars; stans will go on the attack if they find someone criticizing their "king" or "queen." It's funny to refer to a pop star or your awesome friend who got a promotion at work as royalty, but it's kind of weird to refer to a democratically elected official that way. The entire point of them is that they are *not* kings and queens.

To sum it all up, it's a total mess; everyone comes out looking dirty. No one will ever win Twitter. Twitter wins Twitter by making it so that it seems like everyone on Twitter already hates everyone else, which makes it feel as if you *need* to spend all your time there. Nuance is lost, context is lost, and if you say the wrong thing, the immediate response is "You are canceled. You can't sit with us." It's an illusion that you can win anyone over on the platform. In my stump speech, I always joked that I'd never seen anyone on social media respond to another user's post saying, "Wow, Carol! I totally see it from your perspective now! Thank you for the education. I will go out and vote for your candidate!" You can't talk at voters—you have to talk with them. But social media doesn't allow for much genuine exchange. No one is going to see a post from me ranking my favorite nineties movies and decide "Oh, I'm definitely voting for Pete Buttigieg now."

The chicken sandwich saga demonstrates how this can get taken way too far. What is the chicken sandwich saga? Well, first, a little backstory: The first time Peter went on the popular radio show *The Breakfast Club*, he and the host, Charlamagne Tha God, had talked about, among his campaign policy proposals and responses to the weekly news, how Peter didn't like Chick-fil-A's anti-LGBTQ politics, but he did like their chicken. Peter had joked that maybe he could "broker a peace deal" between the gay community and Chick-fil-A. It was a long, substantive interview that included a bit of lighthearted riffing—no big deal, except that the lighthearted riffing was what made headlines, not any of the detailed policies they'd discussed.

Then, a few months later, just after the Popeyes chicken sandwich went viral, Peter went on the show again. As a callback to their previous, chicken-related interview, Charlamagne asked him if he'd tried it.

(If you're wondering: How does a chicken sandwich go viral? It's very simple. In August 2019 the fried-chicken chain Popeyes introduced a chicken sandwich across the country. Popeyes is known for being really delicious anyway, and the chicken sandwich was no exception. Everyone loved the sandwich, and they made all kinds of memes about it. People were talking about the sandwich online for days.) Peter was confused; he'd been out campaigning nonstop, so he hadn't heard about how the new sandwich had become a meme. When Charlamagne explained it to him, Peter made a joke: "Why wasn't I briefed on this?" Someone off mic could be heard saying, "Someone's getting fired today." (Another joke.)

Once again, most of the interview had dealt with policies and issues, specifically the Douglass Plan, a comprehensive agenda the campaign had put forward to address systemic racism and the need for, among other things, a dramatic increase in funding for HBCUs, housing, entrepreneurship, and criminal justice reform. The chicken-sandwich bit was just a little entertaining commentary at the end of the segment. (Peter doesn't get credit for being funny, but he's pretty funny. Not as funny as I am, of course, but pretty funny.) Yet once again, the only thing that made headlines was the chicken sandwich. Everyone wanted to joke about the chicken sandwich, as if the sandwich were the only thing he'd talked about.

I don't mean to suggest that our team was uniquely mischaracterized. This happened to every candidate. But it was still so discouraging. At times it was very difficult to remind myself that this feedback loop wasn't representative of the entire country. When I looked online, it seemed like the only people who liked us were the people who loved us, and everyone else hated us. Of course, that wasn't true. Even if they didn't like us, most people had nothing bad to say about us. They just favored another candidate. Many of these online spaces are unrepresentative of the huge swath of voters who don't participate in online political discussions. Even if they decided to vote for another candidate, they wouldn't consider us scum. But I still found myself looking at my phone far too often. I felt like I needed to know about any news as soon as possible.

So I decided to take control of my input as well. I made a list of people whose opinions I trusted—a mix of staffers and journalists who reported on issues that I cared about. The staff also circulated emails with highlights from Peter's interviews as well as select tweets from supporters, which helped me get over my tendency to check the app constantly.

Promoting a positive message about the campaign could sometimes feel like an uphill battle, and that was without all the nonsense that was thrown at us from both ends of the political spectrum. (There were some people who claimed Peter and I weren't actually married, or even gay. And Peter had somehow single-handedly fixed Canadian bread prices at the age of twenty-six as an entry-level associate at a consulting firm. Oh, and he was also a secret CIA operative waiting for his turn to overtake the Democratic Party, while cleverly disguised as an intelligence officer in the Navy, while also serving as . . . the mayor of South Bend, Indiana?) Being a public figure today means that anyone, anywhere, can make up anything they want about you and promote it as if it's true, as if they have some secret knowledge. And the nature of the beast is that there are a lot of people who desperately want to believe things that aren't true.

....

Early on I did my first "Chasten as the main event" fundraiser in Philadelphia, and overall it was a very supportive room. Even without Peter present it turned out I could still bring in a helpful amount of money, and I was excited, yet nervous, that people were eager to hear me speak. It was flattering and intimidating. Some of these donors were doing a lot to make the campaign possible, and there were also people who were spending their disposable income on an hour to listen to Chasten talk about life and politics. I didn't want to let anyone down.

But they weren't all easy. I'd begin each evening nicely enough, by asking people to introduce themselves to the people sitting around them. (Just like church!) Break the ice with a little humor, and then I'd give my speech, starting with a call for belonging. "I stand before you, the husband of the first openly gay major presidential candidate, not because I was asked to be, but because I feel I need to be. We are at a moment of crisis in this country, and we've got one shot to get this right. One shot to defeat the worst president in American history. And we won't win by promising the American people a way 'back to normal,' just as we won't win saying, 'It's my way or the highway.' As a young gay kid growing up in Northern Michigan, politics wasn't the thing I was interested in as a hobby—it was just the thing that *happened* to me. That's just it. Politics is deeply personal, and for many it's just the thing that *happens* to them. It's in our living rooms, our classrooms, our communities, and yes, even our marriages."— *flashes wedding band*—"It's the thing that determines whether people's lives are easier or harder."

I was only in the room for an hour, but I wanted to make sure everyone in the room felt like they were part of something bigger. And then it would come time for the question-and-answer period. Most of these were tame—*What's Pete like at home?*—but often some folks cared very deeply or were involved in certain causes, so they would occasionally show up with something highly specific they wanted to know—or just grill the candidate on—via their spouse.

Unfortunately, I often couldn't answer those questions. Though, as time went by, the more I studied our policies and read up on the issues, the more I could take a stab at answering the questions. But sometimes it wasn't a question; it was just an insult framed as a question. I'd immediately get sweaty and hot, especially because I knew at least twenty people would be holding up their phones to record my response. Besides wondering to myself why they'd paid money to be here, I'd stammer through something apologetic like "I never want to speak for my husband on an issue he hasn't publicly discussed," and then tell them to check out peteforamerica.com. Silently, I would be thinking, *I just told you I'm a middle-school drama teacher, and you're asking me to clarify specific statements my husband has made on Israel. You know I'm not a policy wonk or the one running for president!*

That's not to say I knew nothing about Peter's policy proposals or his record as mayor. I studied all that intensely. One of the scariest responsibilities came when I was asked to represent the campaign in Europe during a swing of events with American Democrats Abroad—and answer very specific questions on policy. There was a lot happening with Brexit at the time (which I realize could describe any point of the previous three years), and I was nervous I was going to be asked about things I wasn't qualified to speak on. What initially sounded like a glamorous jaunt across the pond, like the kind of thing I'd fantasized about as a teenager aching to escape, quickly transformed into the thing I was watching inch closer on my calendar with anxiety. I just knew I was unqualified to go overseas and speak about heavy issues. I took multiple meetings with Sonal Shah, our policy director, to learn more about our policies and issues at large, and as the trip to Europe drew near, Sonal was drafting memos on specific expat policies I should be well versed in. The issues facing Americans living abroad were very specific—confusing taxation codes, access to vote-by-mail, policies in the EU, and, of course, Brexit.

The trip was exhausting. It was a three-day feat of physical and mental agility. After an entire day campaigning in Las Vegas, I joined Peter for a day of events in New York, and then late that evening took an overnight flight to London. By the time we landed, it was straight into events all over the city. First was a room full of eager American college students studying abroad, who were very, very excited to ask me about the many things I was nervous about. Our national investment chair, Swati Mylavarapu, who had studied abroad in

England herself, had flown over to join me on the trip, and halfway through the talk she motioned for me to drink the coffee in front of me. We hopped a train to Paris the next morning, met with American students studying in France, and held our usual evening event—a room full of academics and expats excited to press me on the latest developments in international news. I looked around the room and thought, *Ten months ago I was teaching middle school. How am I now in Paris convincing American professors that my husband has what it takes to be the leader of the free world?* There was no time to adjust for jet lag. The sun was coming up. In the car on the way to the train station, while I was reading the daily brief, we passed the Eiffel Tower and I realized I had completely forgotten we were in France. By the time we reached Switzerland, time was irrelevant. My body was finished. My eyes were half-open, and eyedrops and coffee weren't cutting it. I tried every trick to stay awake. Each day was full of impatient Americans who wanted to know everything about my husband, our policies, our campaign, and our plans for Europe. Seventy-two hours after we landed in London, we were back on a plane to the States. I had never worked that hard to both stay awake and to represent the campaign. The Americans in Europe were a tough but loving crowd. Before falling asleep on the plane heading to meet Peter in New Hampshire, I wondered if this was what being first gentleman would feel like. If it was, I was starting to have reservations.

I had quickly become the surrogate of choice for the campaign. The appearances and fundraisers continued to build up, stretching my days earlier and ending them much later. I was worried that I wasn't spending enough time talking with people who would have really gotten a lot out of talking to me. Our system isn't structured for campaigning like that (not if you're an upstart campaign like ours with no money in the bank, no independent wealth, and no leftover millions from your congressional race to transfer to your presidential). It takes a lot of money to stay competitive and to win. A lot. You have to hold fundraisers. Our campaign started with nothing and quickly became a fundraising powerhouse, and it took a lot of work that we're proud of. But I hated that I had no idea elections worked this way until I had to participate in one.

I struck an agreement with the scheduling and investment teams. I wanted to spend 80 percent of my time meeting with teachers, touring children's theaters, going to homeless shelters, visiting LGBTQ centers, and hosting roundtables on the arts and education. They could figure out how to fill in the fundraisers wherever I was.

In order for the fundraisers to work, I stopped obsessing about being perfect, meeting everyone's criteria, or passing every purity test. Although some of these people were paying $2,800 to hear me speak, I tried to make sure there was always a $15 student/young professional ticket, and then $25 tickets, so it would be somewhat accessible, but it bothered me that not everyone would get to hear what I had to say. We often gave out free tickets to the organizations I'd spoken at earlier in the day—though a double dose of Chasten was probably not their idea of a rollicking good time, there was at least free finger food.

"And by the way," I'd add at the beginning of my question-and-answer session, "I won't be able to answer these questions as knowledgeably as Pete can. He's the candidate, I'm the teacher. So, if I can't answer your question tonight, I hope you'll visit ask.peteforamerica.com where you can search any keyword and find our policies, and watch interviews where Pete answers a question about that topic. The search engine works great! It will even take you to the exact point in the video where he answers that question!" And the crowd would collectively go, "Oooh. Neat!"

It was nice to set the tone and talk about why I love Peter and why I think the country deserves a president like him. No matter my preamble, people would still ask me extremely political questions, but I became firmer in my responses: That's a great question for the website. Watch Peter's interview on that subject—hear his answer from his mouth.

As time went on, there was one awkward question I could answer very confidently, even if I wasn't allowed to do so publicly. "Why aren't you polling well outside Iowa?" "Well," I'd reply, "because we're spending a lot of time in Iowa." "Why is Peter spending so much time in Iowa?" Nobody was allowed to say, "Well, because Iowa is our path to the nomination." If you did, the story would be "You're turning your back on the rest of the country!" But that simply wasn't true. It was just that Iowa was where Obama had made history as well. It was why voters had given him a second look. Peter was a long shot, too, with even less name recognition than Obama had, and he needed to dominate Iowa to prove he could win.

And then he did. Sort of.

17

Landing the Plane

The primaries are too long. Everyone knows this, but you don't really know it until you live it. You campaign for a year to prepare for four months of voting that require you to crisscross the country multiple times a week. And the ideal outcome is that you get to campaign some more. I liked being on the ground campaigning, talking to voters, and learning about issues I didn't really understand before. I've always liked performing, so there's a part of me that enjoyed that aspect, too. I felt real pride when I nailed a speech, when everyone laughed at one of my jokes. I liked it when reporters would say I was an asset for the campaign. I even liked it when people complimented the kind and positive nature of my Twitter account. But at the end of the day, this was not my chosen work—I chose to do it, but I wouldn't have been doing it if it weren't for my husband. That's what a marriage vow is: a promise to make sacrifices for your partner sometimes. A promise that though things might not always be easy, or go exactly the way you want them to, you'll do your best to support your partner, even if that means putting your own wants aside for a time.

Beyond having to quit my job, and the uncertainty about when I'd be able to go back, the hardest thing to deal with was putting our family on hold. I've never had extreme professional ambitions; that's part of the reason I vacillated so much about what to study in college and what to do afterward. I always knew I needed to do something, and I wanted to be able to make a difference in my work, but the thing I've always wanted most in my life was to have a family. Once I realized that this was a possibility for me in my life as a gay man, I was excited to start. But part of Peter's decision to run meant having to put the family on hold—to stop pursuing adoptions, which we'd been doing before he decided to run, because it would have been impossible to get to know our new child in that environment. The general understanding was that, if the campaign didn't work out—i.e., if Peter didn't win—then we would get to start our family.

I never thought it was impossible. I just knew it was a long shot. He was up against really high-profile people, including the former vice president of the United States and senators who had decades of name recognition and millions of dollars in the bank. There was rarely time to think about what was happening more than one day in advance anyway; the campaign was focused on breaking out of the pack and gaining momentum. Every time the campaign scored a major win, I'd celebrate; every time something went wrong, I felt terrible. But the presidency remained abstract. I was trapped in the present. Anxious to know whether I'd get to see Peter, or whether I'd get to eat, I checked my Google Calendar a hundred times a day. It was organized down to the minute. (I'm so glad the team archived my schedules and email—I barely remember anything!) If you'd asked me at the start or middle of the campaign how I felt about the possibility of making it to the White House, I probably would have made some astute observation like "Well, yeah, the White House would be an amazing thing." From the outside looking in, it looked glamorous and important.

As the campaign dragged on, though, I began to have conflicting feelings about it. Being the first gentleman of the United States—even the *first*

first gentleman of the United States—was never the end goal for me, of course. I doubt that any political spouse wants to be that. I don't want to speak for others, but I think it's fair to say that we want our partners to succeed, and we think that our partners would be good for the country. But I also think it's fair to say that being identified as your partner's spouse for the rest of your public life isn't the most appealing proposition. (Having a public life may not be an appealing proposition, either!) Your relationship has to take a backseat: you may run out of things to talk about because you're deeply entrenched in a single purpose, and it's the only thing on either of your minds. You do give up something in exchange for the opportunity to do this vitally important work. It's not for the faint of heart.

Maybe because Peter and I are so young for a political couple, I always felt as if there needed to be something beyond being the president. I know that sounds silly: being the president is the #1 job. There's nothing above it! But I'm not talking about advancement; I'm just talking about after. At some point, I realized that I was holding on to the possibility of a "normal" life once the campaign was over, but that had gone away.

I could live with that. But what was going to take its place? Once again, I had no idea. The size and scope of the race were unprecedented, and the twenty-four-hour news cycle emphasized that point all the time. The endless possibilities created by having so many candidates in the race made trying to game things out in my head tempting, but trying to predict what was going to happen was impossible. "OK . . . let's say Bernie's down next week and Elizabeth Warren's up, and Biden's holding steady, that means . . ." What if someone polling in the single digits suddenly turns it around and wins Iowa? What if someone says something stupid on MSNBC and their numbers drop? Wait a minute—there's another candidate entering the race two months before the Iowa caucuses?!?! There were too many variables. I think it would have been exciting to follow along if I hadn't been involved—watching the media roller coaster from the comfort of my own living room, being able to switch over to Netflix whenever I got tired of the drama, might have been fun.

After months and months of campaigning, things started to really heat up in November. A poll came out of Iowa that had Peter in the lead, and it shook the campaign. No one had anticipated him doing that well that early. But there he was, on the front page of the *Des Moines Register*, standing on top of a bale of hay. He was declared the front-runner.

Of course, polls are polls, and a clear front-runner can end up in fourth place in a matter of weeks. But going into the holidays it was a whole different campaign. Christmas was bursting with energy and confusion and nerves and what-ifs. All of our focus shifted to the Iowa caucuses, which the campaign saw as the make-or-break moment. Peter spent a lot of time on the phone, and I spent a lot of time in my pajamas, eating Christmas cookies, watching Hallmark movies, and wondering what the hell was happening to my life.

As the caucuses approached, the stakes became even clearer. Pete Buttigieg just might pull this off. It was all chips on Iowa. We were investing so much time and energy there, but we were running out of money, and we needed to pull out a big win. Peter's team was adding more and more Iowa days on his schedule, so they sent me everywhere else, especially to New Hampshire and Nevada. In the back of my mind I kept thinking about how strange it was that the fate of the rest of the campaign hinged on how a few states voted. But I couldn't think too much about that—the pressure was on. Hoping we'd be coming to New Hampshire victorious, I spent those weeks leading up to Iowa rallying the troops to prepare for a historical victory.

Caucus day was a blur. We spent a majority of it with our families. There were a few events around Des Moines to rally the troops, but the majority of our time was spent trying not to feel the day drag on. That evening, as the results started to trickle in, it was clear we were having a good night.

I couldn't sit still. Nobody could. Mom, Dad, and Anne were sitting on the couch watching the excitement and the commotion around them. There was a big spread of food, but no one was eating—we were all too nervous. Peter was tossing a ball around the room with his friends, trying to keep his mind off the television and the talking heads. The team was shouting news from around the room as everyone repeatedly refreshed polling sites and Twitter. A few minutes of nothing and then an eruption of cheers and celebration as data came in showing positive returns from counties we knew we needed to win. The internal data the team was receiving was more than encouraging. Peter and I kept looking at each other from across the room with a nervous enthusiasm. We just might pull this off.

And then we won.

But that's not how it was reported. It wasn't reported at all. The night went on, and there were no official results. Our campaign had done its unofficial tally and found Peter in the lead, and we desperately wanted the confirmation. But no confirmation came. Instead, we were hearing about problems with . . . the app.

There was an app the Iowa Democratic Party was using to report results, and it wasn't working. The party's backup phone reporting system couldn't handle all the calls it was getting. Meanwhile, news was coming out of different precincts that the results contained errors, some that suggested precincts hadn't reported their data properly. The complicated caucus system only made all this more confusing. As many Americans living outside Iowa were learning for the first time, a caucus is not the same as going into the voting booth, filling out your form, and getting a little sticker that says "I Voted!" No winner was officially declared that night. Other candidates were trying to spin the evening as a win. Both our campaign and Bernie's campaign eventually requested (multiple) recounts.

Everyone had to move on; there was no time to wait around for the official winner. Peter made his speech and we jumped on a late flight to New Hampshire. Once it was clear we'd had a good, if not great, night, the comms team approached me. "We need to get you on TV this week," they said. "Would you be OK with that?" This was such a huge message of confidence in me. I'd been asking to go on TV for a year.

As Peter and I settled into our hotel bed in Manchester at around 4 a.m., I couldn't help but think how unbelievable it was that I had some- how married the first openly gay presidential candidate to win the Iowa caucuses, and perhaps (I kept shaking my head and chuckling in dis- belief) the next president of the United States. I just hoped the official results were out there when we woke up in three hours.

They weren't.

This uncertainty was followed by a highlight of my career as a political spouse: I got to represent the campaign on TV. But during the week after the caucuses, the anticlimax really bothered me. I couldn't believe it. The organizers and staff had worked impossibly hard for over a year trying to set up this moment. It needed to be a moment, too—the spark for the rocket. President Obama had gotten his momentum in 2008 by winning the state. Had Peter single-handedly won, even if he'd only beaten Bernie by the tiniest margin, it would have been the story, and that story would have been historic. I kept thinking about how thirteen-year-old Chasten would have felt, watching the news as a gay man and his husband gave a victory speech in the first state of the American Democratic primaries. How it would have looked on the chyrons. I felt robbed, not only as Peter's partner, but also as a gay man.

The days went by, and there was still no news about who'd won. The media cycle eventually had to move on to something else; the story became more about the myriad failures of the evening than about who won it. Even as the New Hampshire primary was approaching, the party still hadn't released results, and the campaigns were going back and forth debating numbers. It was so deflating. By the time the party certified the results and declared Peter the official winner, three and a half weeks later, a couple of days before the South Carolina primary, no one cared. It was barely in the news.

Had we won Iowa definitively and gotten the news cycle that would have come with it, we might have done better in New Hampshire, and who knows what would have happened from there. Obama got his second look after Iowa, and no candidate had won both Iowa and New Hampshire and not won the candidacy. But New Hampshire was Bernie's to lose, and that race coincided with Senator Klobuchar's surge, which ultimately took away from Peter's numbers. That primary was frustrating, too—I remember watching the returns in our suite at the Courtyard Marriott, seeing the margin between Peter and Bernie getting slimmer and slimmer. The staff started pacing the room as the numbers were getting promising and tempting. Could he pull it off? There was an immense sense of hope heading into the night, but as the remaining precincts trickled in, it was clear that the one to two points we needed weren't coming. Bernie had won New Hampshire by 22 points in 2016. This time around he beat Peter by about 1.3 points, tying for national delegates. A muddy return, and still no reported victory in Iowa with a less-than-exciting return in New Hampshire, meant storm clouds.

Although we did much better than most expected, the race quickly began to seem predictable. Without a solid win in Iowa or New Hampshire, not many were giving Pete Buttigieg a second look. Our hope had been that strong wins in both those early states would convince the following states that Peter was the candidate to beat and the candidate who could win, but Bernie crushed Nevada, as he was expected to. The campaign knew that if South Carolina didn't offer a result that could be interpreted optimistically, we would have to start thinking about getting out.

From there, everything happened very fast. The South Carolina primary took place on a Saturday. Biden dominated even more than he was expected to. Everything else fell into place as it did.

We had made our way to Plains, Georgia, late that night for a break-fast with President and Mrs. Carter the following morning. Sitting in the Americus, Georgia, Hampton Inn, Peter asked me: "What do you think we should do?" But he already knew, and so did I. I got up from the bed, walked across the room to where he was sitting at the desk, hugged him, and said, "Let's go home, love."

I felt incredibly guilty, but I knew what was coming, and I couldn't help but be a little bit happy for the life we were getting to return to.

I don't know how I would have handled the campaign if I hadn't be-lieved he could win. If I thought he was just running to build a profile, or if I thought the presidency was a pipe dream, a vanity project. Peter always had a really good chance of winning, and I think the country de-served the opportunity to see an alternative way for the Democratic Party to move forward. We deserve a different kind of politics. We deserve to have a government that takes care of us, and we also deserve a president we feel good about. An intelligent, service-driven leader who believes in science and the Constitution, who values our educators and fights for our families. Our country is hurting and has been for a long time. A lot of people feel mad, left out, and misunderstood. I love so many things about Peter, and one of them is how naturally he made me feel the opposite: safe, appreciated, and a part of something bigger than myself. I wanted the country to feel that way, too. To look to Washington and take a deep breath, knowing that the president, the first gentleman, and an entire administration were there because they cared about the American people.

But the numbers just weren't there. If anyone had a case to stay in the race, to try to represent the space between Bernie and Biden, it was Peter, but that wasn't what the country needed. It would have been unfair to the American people for him to continue, and it was necessary to begin to move our party forward, rather than fracture it further.

I felt guilty saying all this to him, though of course he knew better than I did how the situation stacked up. For once, the right thing to do was crystal-clear. In that moment, my role was obvious: husband. He didn't need any advice on the numbers or the spin, he just needed me. "You're so young," I kept saying. "You could wait thirty years and run again. Or never run again. Your, *our*, entire lives are ahead of us. Let's go home."

"Let's sleep on it," he said, and we turned out the lights and stared at the ceiling. Having a life again seemed like a good consolation prize. Who knows what the next thirty years will look like? Or even the next five?

We woke up the next morning, and the answer was clear. Peter knew it was time to suspend the campaign. But you don't just send an all-staff email and wash your hands of it. There was a specific process to follow. We had to tell certain people first, and we were also still on the trail, with an entire day full of events across three states.

First, we made our way into Plains to have breakfast with Jimmy and Rosalynn Carter in a dining room full of memorabilia from their administration, followed by a joint appearance at a local café. I kept looking at the photos of Rosalynn and thinking of what could've been for me. Next, we flew to Alabama and walked the Edmund Pettus Bridge with the other candidates to commemorate the Selma-to-Montgomery march. I felt so grateful that we stayed in long enough that I got to experience that. Surrounded by scores of unfathomably courageous activists and thinkers, I was reminded of how small I am, and how politics is so much bigger than one tough campaign, tensions with others, and the noise.

Afterward, we got on the plane. I watched as Peter announced to the press traveling with us that the plane wasn't going to head to Texas, as it had planned; instead we'd be flying north to South Bend, where Peter would be making an announcement. Our race was ending, the press knew it, but nothing could be said beyond, "Stay tuned."

I don't know how best to describe what I was feeling. I was really sad for my husband. I don't know if I've ever felt more *for* someone in my life. He'd worked so hard, and I was so proud of him and how he poured everything into the last year. I thought of the team and how this dream was ending for them, too. And then I thought about how *I'd* worked so hard, and I was proud of myself, too. Ever since we'd started polling well in Iowa, there'd been the hope that maybe it would happen—maybe we were going to pull it off. I was disappointed that we didn't do it. But I also couldn't wait to go home.

The plane ride was mostly silent. I sat across from Peter and poked him periodically. He'd look up, I'd smile, he'd smile back, and we'd both go back to looking out the window. As the plane began its descent into South Bend, I exhaled, and my shoulders dropped in a way I hadn't felt in over a year, knowing the trail was now behind me. I wiped away my tears so the press wouldn't see my face as we deplaned. But they knew. Maybe things wouldn't go back to normal, but they would be manageable. Stepping off the plane felt like coming home for the first time in over a year.

Then, about ten minutes before the event was to start, a staffer in the SUV asked, "Hey, Chasten. Do you wanna introduce him?"

I could see why they were so casual about it. The event had been planned in less than twenty-four hours, and it was a suspension speech: there wasn't a campaign left to mess up. By now I was a pro at speeches on the fly, and I'd introduced Peter many times before.

Yet I was a wreck. We arrived at the Century Center, where some of our staff members and our parents were there to greet us. Emily was there, and we joked that we'd talk to each other some other time, as we wiped tears and laughed. Mom and Dad hugged me, and hearing them say how proud they were of me only made me cry harder. I watched as Anne embraced Peter and her face beamed with pride (and maybe relief)—her son was home and safe. Knowing her husband, Joe, wasn't there to welcome him home, to celebrate what his son had accomplished, hurt all the more.

It was like the end of a TV show when the gang all gets together again, which is always moving to me. But that doesn't explain why I couldn't seem to stop shaking. Something about having to introduce Peter in that moment made my brain short-circuit. It's not just that I was sad—I was sad, but I was also every other emotion. I was so overwhelmed. It was like it was my responsibility to send him off, to convey the weight of what we'd done together. And I had to go do it *now*.

I turned to a staffer and asked them to smack me in the face. They refused. I was outside myself, and I could see that I needed to get a grip because I had a job to do, but I couldn't make my body listen. So I smacked myself in the face. That didn't work, but it elicited a few laughs from the team. I tried my best to compose myself, and finally I walked onstage. The roar of the room brought me home, and the familiar faces in the crowd were just as moved as I was.

I stood at the podium and looked out into the room full of supporters, scanning the faces of the hundreds of staffers I had come to admire, all the way back to the press riser and the bright lights erected to illuminate the stage. "Hello, South Bend," I said. "It's good to be home." The crowd cheered as I gripped the edges of the podium tightly, hoping it would give me the grounding I needed in order to find the right words to describe the gratitude I felt. "About a year and a half ago my husband came home from work and told me—well, he asked me, 'What do you think about running for president?' And I laughed. Not *at* him but at life. Because . . ." I was already starting to get misty. The room continued to cheer with encouragement.

"Life gave me some interesting experiences on my way to find Pete. After falling in love with Pete, Pete got me to believe in myself again. And I told Pete to run, because I knew there were other kids, sitting out there in this country, who needed to believe in themselves, too."

"You saved lives!" one man shouted.

"Yes, we did, together. We did." I looked over at my team and couldn't believe our time together was coming to an end. All of the people we had met. The things we had seen. The hope we were filled with. The change that we had made, together.

"This campaign was built on an idea of hope. An idea of inclusion. An idea of addition, rather than subtraction. An idea about bringing people together. An idea of looking your neighbor in the eye and saying, 'Maybe we don't agree on everything, but let's agree on this. We've got one shot.'" I saw Anne standing alongside my parents, and the look of pride on their faces made it even harder to continue speaking.

"That's what we did. We went out there with that one shot and gave it everything we had, because it is time for every single person in this country to look to the White House and know that institution stands for them. That they belong in this country." I felt this mixture of anger and passion and sadness and hope burning in my stomach, the mix of mistakes and repression and sadness that had been burning there for thirty years. It had all led me to this moment. This unbelievable moment in life. We were so close. So, so close. I was heartbroken it wasn't going to be Peter, but I had never felt more hopeful.

"It has been an honor and a privilege to share my husband with the rest of this country. And I am so proud that the same person you saw on the debate stage, the same person you saw at a town hall, is the same person who comes home to me every night." I knew I had arrived at the closing, and I could feel my breath come back to me again. I had made it to the end.

After I walked offstage, I couldn't believe the lightness. Anne and my parents hugged me. I fist-bumped my team. For the first time in months and months, I had nothing to worry about, and I had nothing to be ashamed of. I hadn't messed up. I never misspoke. I never stepped out of line. I dealt with all the bullshit that came my way, and I didn't cause a single problem in the process. I was so proud of all the things I stood for and had accomplished. I met kids who told me their lives were saved by just the image of our campaign. That their worlds had been changed because of what seeing Peter and me on the television had meant to them. I met thousands of supporters, worked with hundreds of teachers, and toured countless centers, theaters, shelters, and clinics, sharing my story with as many people as I could because I believed in what Peter and I could do for the country. I also found a belief in myself, and my story, that I had never known before.

What's more, our marriage didn't fall apart. In fact, I'm pretty sure we love each other a lot more than when we started.

When Peter and I finally made it back to the house, a few staffers and family poured in, and then everyone started calling. I mean everyone. Just as our campaign came to a close, someone had leaked Peter's personal cell phone number, so he was getting endless calls and texts. Some were unkind, from followers of another campaign, but others were heartfelt messages of gratitude and encouragement. The team gave out my phone number to a few other teams in the meantime. (A few days later, Senator Kamala Harris, who must've gotten my number from a staffer, would wake me up just calling to check in. Yes, I allowed myself to sleep in late.)

Our families sat in the living room as Peter and I paced the house on our phones. Happy to have us home, Buddy and Truman were trailing our every move. Just like campaigning, it felt like being in the middle of a blender. Everything was swirling around me, but for the first time, I felt like I was standing still in the middle, just watching.

Finally, we kissed our parents goodbye and climbed the stairs; neither of us had the energy to carry the suitcases up. We brushed our teeth, gave Buddy and Truman some pats on the head, and crawled into bed. Instinctively, I quickly turned over to check my calendar one more time before putting the phone away. Tomorrow's column was empty. *Oh. Duh*, I thought, as I chuckled to myself. It was over.

At the same time, Peter and I turned to face each other and, with a grin, looked one another in the eye. We were finally home.

Epilogue: Is This Thing Still On?

It's wonderful to be in a position to be asked "What's next?" but the truth is, I don't know. For most of my life, things didn't feel like they added up, and the bright side seemed closed off to me. When Peter told me he was thinking of running for president, I wasn't sure I belonged in national politics, and I feared I would just end up tagging along for the photo ops and cheering him on from the sidelines. I wanted to help, but I didn't know if I could. I wasn't sure if people "like me" belonged in the most visible, cut-throat political game in America there is—running for president.

But the more time I spent out on the campaign trail, the more I realized my experiences and qualifications were not lacking or strange or shameful—they were fitting. Somehow campaigning for president—with all the in-built dysfunction, stress, drama, and hope—made it all make sense. Folks used to say I was "just a teacher," but it turns out a farm-raised, theater-geek, middle-school teacher can be really good at politics. A "not-so-secret weapon," even! I've never worked so hard in my life, and although the race was never about me, I was surprised to find that the harder I worked, the better I felt about being out on the trail. I wanted to visit more states, meet more people, and learn more about how it all works and how I could contribute, should my husband become the forty-sixth president of the United States.

In the beginning, I worried a lot about saying the wrong thing or revealing too much, but as time went on I saw how those fears were misguided—I connected with people the most when I was willing to be uncomfortable and vulnerable. Sometimes that required standing in front of a packed room, taking a deep breath, looking voters in the eye, and sharing stories I thought I'd keep locked up forever. I grew up thinking people in politics didn't understand me or care about me. Out on the trail, I saw that feeling reflected in the eyes of my fellow Americans; I saw just how hurt, scared, and forgotten some feel. It's our job to go out there and convince them that it's going to be OK. One way we can contribute to making others feel like they belong is to share our stories, too. The world is changing so fast, and there is so much at stake. I may not have grown up thinking this was where life would lead me, nor did I ask to be in the position I'm in, but that doesn't change the fact that I'm in it, and I want to do my best to keep contributing to a kinder, more welcoming America.

In the meantime, things have calmed down dramatically since we landed back here in South Bend and Peter and I waved goodbye to the campaign. As soon as Peter stepped off the stage, life seemed to go from one hundred miles an hour to zero. I've been able to spend my time doing things I missed. I've been able to do some home-improvement projects, continuing work on the house that we had to pause while we campaigned. (I think I've finally got that squirrel out of our roof for good.) I've spent time with family and friends, finally being able to invest more time in the question "So what's up with you?" I love being able to hang out with my dogs and my husband, making pancakes and reading the morning paper, or taking walks along the river (talking about anything other than running for president). I've even treated myself to a few nights of Netflix and a pint of Ben & Jerry's. And I liked writing this book, even though it scared me and required going down a lot of dark roads. My hope was that some good could come from it. And maybe a few laughs.

I'm realizing that some things will never go back to normal, though, and while that can be uncomfortable, it's also exciting. Just the other day I was grabbing some dog food at the pet store when a neighbor spotted me. "Chasten!" she said. Instinctively looking around for the camera and a journalist, I chuckled when I realized it was just a friendly face from the neighborhood. "My goodness. What a year you've had, huh? What was that like?" For a brief moment, I had forgotten that people still know who I am. And it turns out they're still interested in what I have to say.

Acknowledgments

While touring the Castro during one of my many campaign stops in California, I made a quick visit to the GLBT History Museum in San Francisco. I remember the last display in the museum quite vividly. Through a window were several buttons, placards, and other pieces of campaign memorabilia from Harvey Milk's 1977 race for a seat on the city's Board of Supervisors. And then, in the center, dimly illuminated, were the rumpled, bloodstained jacket and shirt Milk was wearing when he was assassinated. Overhead, a recording of Harvey played. He'd made it shortly after he was elected, understanding full well the fatal repercussions the office might entail. The weight and significance of Peter's race came flooding in, and I stood frozen before the display case as I thought of every person who had fought for me. Of the trans women and drag queens and other queer protesters at Stonewall who stood up and said *Enough*. Of those who showed up and put in the work, who protested police brutality and bigotry and fought hatred head on in the streets and in the courts, marching for justice and demanding equality. And of those like Harvey, who suffered the ultimate consequence for living an open and truthful life, who took a bullet simply for demanding to be treated and seen as an equal.

I owe so much to the generations of brave individuals who came before me and made it easier to stand on the platform I have now. I know I wouldn't be who I am today if it weren't for the courage of people like Marsha P. Johnson, Sylvia Rivera, Harvey Milk, and countless other LGBTQ activists and organizations who fought for my right to exist freely and openly. I'm grateful to the many champions of the movement, like Edie Windsor and Jim Obergefell, whose determination and efforts for our right to wear these wedding bands I cherish with my whole heart. I'm also grateful to the actors and comedians I used to watch on television with admiration—especially Ellen DeGeneres and Sean Hayes, who both made me feel better about being myself before I could even muster the courage to say it out loud—for bravely stepping forward and giving a voice to gay Americans. To everyone who fought for me, and believed in me, whether I know your name or not, my gratitude is boundless.

I never imagined growing up to become a person worthy of writing a memoir. At least, I hope my story and experiences are worthy of that. I spent most of my life believing I'd keep these stories locked up forever, often feeling that they would be what prevented me from being anything other than broken. My agent, Alia Habib, believed in me from the beginning and encouraged me to share those truths, from the absurd to the scary, with the rest of the world, even when I wasn't sure I was ready. My hilarious and witty editor, Rakesh Satyal, encouraged me to put my stories and experiences on the page in an honest, vulnerable, and authentic way that was ultimately profoundly freeing. Alongside Rakesh, the lovely folks at Atria and Simon & Schuster made the process a little less scary, and I am grateful for their dedication to this project, as well as their patience with my endless emails, edits, and frantic voicemails.

I called on a lot of people to help me write this book. My team—Ali, Jess, Tess, Emily, and Deion—saw me through the most grueling fourteen months I have ever faced. Your tenderness and resolve carried me through it all, and I thank you for the endless coffees, confidence, expertly crafted memos, and many laughs along the way. The incredible staff and volunteers on Pete for America built a game-changing and historic campaign that left it all on the field. Senior leadership patiently took time to help me grow as a surrogate and trusted me to shape the role into something new and make it my own: Mike Schmuhl, Lis Smith, Brandon Neal, Jess O'Connell, Hari Sevugan, Michael Halle, Nina Smith, Chris Meagher, Sonal Shah, Abbey Watson, Laura O'Sullivan, Marcus Switzer, Anthony Mercurio, Larry Grisolano, Katie Connolly, and many others who saw me through this adventure. A special thank-you goes to Peter's body woman, Saralena, for looking after him, especially when I couldn't. Together, we made history, and I am grateful for everything you all contributed to our pursuit of a kinder, more inclusive America.

To "Team Husband," who took my late-night calls and helped me remember stories, anecdotes, and embarrassing mishaps from the campaign trail, college, and, yes, even high school for the book: each one of you has buoyed me throughout this journey, and life, in endless, generous ways. You've housed me, fed me, let me cry on your shoulder, and made space for me to share with you my fears and my dreams. Hannah, Erin, Kathy, Eddie, Caroline, Trevor, Aubrey: I cannot thank you enough for your friendship over the years. Your patience, never-ending encouragement, and belief in me are gifts I cherish dearly. My grandmother used to tell me that if you could count on more than one hand the truly good friends you had, you were a lucky man. Indeed, I am beyond lucky to have you all in my corner.

If I were to list every member of my ever-growing family who has encouraged, tormented, and shaped me into the man I am today, we would need more pages than my editors will allow. You know who you are, and I love you to the moon.

To my mother and father, Sherri and Terry, my staunchest allies and fiercest supporters: your love of me, this family, and the world are unmatched. I am so proud to be your son. Thank you for loving me.

And to Peter: sharing you with the country wasn't always easy, but I would do it again in a heartbeat. I am so grateful for your gentle spirit, your tenderness when the world seems upside down, your encouragement to write this book and find strength in my story, and what seems like limitless patience, especially with my tendency to ask a million questions or failure to fold the laundry. You promised me it would always be an adventure, so with you by my side, my love, I can't wait to see what's next.

About the Author

Chasten Glezman Buttigieg was born and raised in Traverse City, Michigan. A thespian, two-time 4-H blue-ribboner, and decorated member of the high school bowling team, he received his bachelor's degree in theater and global studies from the University of Wisconsin–Eau Claire and his master's in education from DePaul University. He has worked as a busboy, dog walker, nursing assistant, waiter, cashier, bartender, and, most recently, a middle-school drama and humanities teacher. He lives in South Bend, Indiana, with his husband, Peter, and their two rescue dogs. This is his first book.

Twitter: @Chasten
Instagram: @Chasten.Buttigieg